1

Logic and Contemporary Rhetoric

Second Edition

The Use of Reason in Everyday Life

Howard Kahane

Bernard Baruch College
City University of New York

Wadsworth Publishing Company, Inc.
Belmont, California

For Bonny sweet Robin . . .

Ignorance is preferable to error; and he is less remote from the truth who believes nothing, than he who believes what is wrong.

Thomas Jefferson

It ain't so much the things we don't know that get us in trouble. It's the things we know that ain't so.

Artemus Ward

Philosophy Editor: Kenneth King
Manuscript Editor: Kathie Head
Production Editor: Mary Arbogast
Designer: Gary A. Head

ISBN 0-534-00449-0

L.C. Cat. Card No. 75-32922

Printed in the United States of America

2 3 4 5 6 7 8 9 10—80 79 78 77 76

Preface

*We are responsible, not just our
leaders, since we elect them, and we
choose to follow them.*

Harold Gordon

The preface to the first edition of this book stated that this book "was written . . . in an attempt to raise the level of political argument and reasoning by acquainting students with the devices and ploys which drag that level down." The second edition was written, quite simply, to do a better job in that attempt.

The second edition contains four major improvements:

1. The exercises have been expanded and greatly improved: overly difficult items have been eliminated, new more manageable ones added, and the items in each exercise set ordered more closely from fairly easy to more difficult. This is particularly true of the key exercises in the first four chapters.

2. A chapter on language has been added, featuring material on the emotive overtones of language and how they are used to con, and on sexism in language.

3. The chapter on advertising now deals with advertising in general, considering political advertising just as an interesting example and not the focus of the chapter.

4. The order of material in the first three chapters has been changed to reflect better pedagogical order.

In addition, many minor improvements have been made in every chapter. For instance, the section on television in the chapter Managing the News has been greatly expanded and improved. And several plain old errors have been corrected. For example, the fallacies of *false dilemma, straw man,* and *begging the question* are now dealt with in the theoretically correct category *fallacious even if valid,* and the misleading category *false charge of inconsistency* has been replaced by the broader category *false charge of fallacy.*

The focus of the second edition, as of the first, is the avoidance of false belief, and in particular *fallacy,* because today as always most public rhetoric deceives by means of fallacious argument. So the first four chapters are devoted to fallacious reasoning. Almost all of the examples are taken from recent political speeches, newspapers, or magazines, and concern social or political topics of current interest.

Chapter Five is an entirely new chapter, dealing with the emotive side of language and how opinions are swayed by emotional or deliberately unemotional language.

A section on doublespeak explains how that sort of language is used to con. And a section on sexism in language illustrates how sexist attitudes have become embedded in the English language.

Spotting fallacies is only part of the process of critical analysis. Chapter Six deals with the analysis of lengthier passages: editorials, political columns, and a presidential speech. And Chapter Seven deals with advertising, including political advertising.

Good thinking does not occur in a vacuum. Successful critical analysis cannot be done with an empty head, or worse, a head stuffed with falsehoods. Chapter Eight is concerned with the ways in which the standard mass media (newspapers, mass circulation magazines, television) manage the news; it tries to explain why and how the mass media present a distorted image of the current state of the world.

Newspapers, magazines, and TV are not the only villains by any means. After TV, public school textbooks constitute perhaps the most important part of the mass media, and they too are guilty of the errors of omission and distortion just mentioned. Chapter Nine discusses examples of this distortion, how it arises and what we can do to guard against it. Again, the problem is vitally related to cogent reasoning about political issues, because the ill-informed reasoner (no matter how intelligent) is much more easily taken in by a clever fallacious argument.

Finally, exercises have been included at the end of each chapter (but *no busy work!*). Only a few of these exercises are of the standard clearcut-answer variety. We all like exercises with definite unarguable answers, but examples from daily life seldom fit that mold. So most of the exercises in this text are of the messy variety over which reasonable men may differ. With respect to these, the way in which a student defends his conclusion often will be more important than his conclusion itself. (An appendix contains answers to selected exercise questions, to be used by students as a guide. Needless to say, these answers are *not* presented as the revealed truth; reasonable men are likely to differ over them.)

Textbooks must be objective. But what sort of objectivity is required? In a sense, all true statements must in some way be considered within the bounds of objectivity. However, for our purposes, a different kind of objectivity is required, although it is not clear exactly what it consists in. The man who luckily utters the truth on the basis of outrageous prejudice has not achieved this kind of objectivity. Nor has someone failed to achieve it who unluckily utters falsehoods based on intense research and cogent reasoning. Roughly, we want assertions based on *sufficient evidence* (and cogent reasoning) to count as objective in this sense, whether or not they later turn out to be true.

But many arguments, particularly political, religious, or moral ones, concern problems for which sufficient evidence rarely is at hand, one of the main reasons these topics are so controversial. We therefore must settle for *good* rather than sufficient evidence, although it is not always clear what constitutes good evidence in specific cases.

So good evidence (plus cogent reasoning) is the criterion of objectivity used in this text. For instance, the text takes it to be an objective fact that Blacks in the United States never have received and still do not receive the treatment they are entitled to by law and by the Declaration of Independence. The text assumes it to be an objective fact that *in general* there is a tremendous gap in the United States between ideals, standards, and the law, on the one hand, and day-to-day actual practice, on the other. This assumption is made on the basis of what the author takes to be good (although certainly not conclusive) evidence.

The opinion is widespread that objectivity requires the omission from textbooks of all value judgments, moral or otherwise, because such judgments are subjective. But has there ever been a satisfactory textbook in the humanities, or even in certain areas of the social sciences, completely devoid of value terms and value judgments?[1]

Nor, in my opinion, is such a strict admonition against value judgments proper. In the first place, it begs philosophical questions about the objectivity or subjectivity of value judgments; the view that value judgments *can* be objective is a time-honored one, including among its adherents Plato, Aristotle, Aquinas, Spinoza, Kant, and Hegel, to name only a few.

Then why should we require textbooks dealing with topics such as *practical* reasoning, reasoning about political and social problems, to be divorced from the value realm? The vast majority of moral, rational men believe that murder, slavery, rape, racial discrimination, and grand theft are morally wrong. Why then object to textbooks' stating that slavery and the racial discrimination which followed it in the United States were, and are, morally wrong? Why object to their stating the moral evil of the white man's grand theft of the North American continent from its prior owners, the American Indians?

But this textbook definitely is not a partisan political or moral effort. Opinions about anything other than logic intrude only when necessary to make a point of *logic,* or to illustrate devices used to con the public. Issues are never discussed merely for their own sake; nor are value judgments gratuitously introduced. Republicans and Democrats both take it on the chin quite frequently, for instance, although Democrats on the whole come in for less criticism, because Republican administrations have been in power since 1968, before this text was written. But they are attacked only by way of illustrating fallacies or points of logic.

This book was written with one and only one idea in mind; it is an attempt to raise the level of political argument and reasoning by acquainting students with the devices and ploys which drag that level down. The intent is not to move students to the left or right on the political spectrum, but rather to move them *up* on the scale of cogent reasoning about political issues.

The level of most political argument in this country has always been extremely low. Yet if representative government is to function as it should, we must have

---

[1]Imagine a psychology text that tried to do without value terms such as *healthy, normal,* or *sane.* A whole discipline within psychology—abnormal psychology—is defined in terms of values; merely odd behavior, remember, is not thereby abnormal.

an electorate sufficiently sophisticated to demand a high level of political argument. If this book helps even in a small way to produce such an electorate, it will have served its purpose.

Acknowledgments

In the first edition credit was given to those who help made that edition possible, namely Professors Leland Creer, Peter K. Machamer, Gerald Messner, Paul O. Ricci, and Ray Kytle, the then Philosophy Editor Michael Helm and Production Editor Robert Browning, and Carol Hubbs. In addition to those, the second edition of this text owes a great deal to Professors Frank Fair, Sam Houston State University, Robert Cogan, Edinboro State College, Martin Billing, Southwest College, Clayton Morgareidege, Lewis and Clark College, Monte Cook, University of Oklahoma at Norman, James Heffernan, University of the Pacific, Gene D'Amour, West Virginia University, Wallace Dohman, College of the Desert, Henry Byerly, University of Arizona, Vincent Barry, Bakersfield College, Don Burrill, California State University of Los Angeles, Joan Straumanis, Denison University, and Charles Di Domenico, Middlesex Community College, to the current Wadsworth Philosophy Editor Kenneth King, Manuscript Editor Kathie Head, and Production Editor Mary Arbogast, and to Professors B. Robin Kahane, Judith Lichtenberg, Carole Burns, Arlyne Landesman, Shirley Liebowitz, Susan Decker, and Judy Dente.

Finally, I ought to thank another Judy for having inspired several of the exercises in this text. But then, we don't always do what we ought to do.

Howard Kahane

January 1976

Contents

Introduction

What This Book Is About

Every day we are bombarded by language and pictures intended to persuade us in one way or another. This barrage is frequently successful, because we are all receptive to ideas favorable to what we want to believe. Part of this barrage is self-inflicted; we often want to convince ourselves to do some things and avoid doing others. But a great deal is inflicted on us by others, sometimes with malice aforethought, sometimes from the best of motives.

Unhappily, the cases in which the persuasion is successful frequently are not those in which it *ought* to be. And that is what this book is all about.

People try to persuade us about many things. We'll deal primarily with political persuasion, but other types of persuasive rhetoric (advertisements, religious tracts, and newspaper advice columns) will be considered also. We'll examine actual arguments from television, newspapers, magazines, political speeches, press conferences, and (interestingly) textbooks. Occasionally, we'll throw in examples from memory or imagination, or even from the dim past before, say, 1970.

Let's call uses of language or pictures intended to *persuade* anyone of anything an **argument.** In this sense, "Don't go near the edge; you might fall" is an argument. So is an advertisement. And so are the words "I love you" when intended to influence someone of the opposite sex.

And let's say a **fallacy** is an argument that *should not* persuade a rational person to accept its conclusion. (Whether it does or not is another matter.) We can then say a person **reasons fallaciously** if he is convinced by a fallacious argument, and **argues fallaciously** when he uses a fallacious argument in an attempt to convince someone else.[1] Anyone who argues or reasons fallaciously will be said to **commit** a fallacy.

In this book we're going to spend much more time on the avoidance of bad reasoning than we do on good reasoning. This may seem to be a somewhat negative approach, but in fact it is not. For one of the most important ways to improve

---

[1] It follows that a person who argues fallaciously does not automatically *reason* fallaciously (in the sense of that term just described). The charlatan who tries to convince others with reasoning he knows to be shoddy is an example of a person arguing fallaciously without reasoning fallaciously.

the quality of our reasoning is to avoid being taken in by incorrect reasoning or bad argument. By thus avoiding fallacies, we make sure we don't get into trouble over "the things we know that ain't so".

Some fallacious arguments are so obvious that they are hardly likely to fool anybody. Unfortunately, many others are all too apt to con even the wary. This fact has not gone unnoticed. Politicians, for instance, know that getting elected requires at least a small amount of verbal con artistry.

Since we all engage in a certain amount of self-deception, we are all verbal con artists to some extent, at least able to con ourselves when it is comforting to do so. But few of us can compare with the professionals, the people who are paid to persuade on a large scale by means of words and pictures.

Most professionals are honest. Some may be unaware of the verbal devices they employ. Some, however, are fully aware of their con artistry. But for whatever reasons, the fact is that most of the persuasion used in politics and advertising is a strange, complex mixture of cogent and fallacious argument. The job of the rational person is to sort out this conglomeration so as to fend off verbal con artistry as much as possible. Failure to do so makes rational decision making quite difficult, if not impossible. The verbal con artist, in ourselves and others, is our natural enemy.

Truth Is Booty, Booty Is Truth

"There is already an inclination to trust the Veep-designate precisely because he is rich. 'When somebody is one of the wealthiest men in the world, said Rep. John Rhodes of Arizona, the Republican leader in the house, he's got so much money there would be no point in cheating.'" (Newsweek, Sept. 2, 1974)

Does this Sorel political cartoon (*Village Voice,* September 17, 1974) illustrate a fallacious appeal to the authority of money?

Chapter One

*It would be a very good thing if every trick
could receive some short and obviously
appropriate name, so that when a man used
this or that particular trick, he could at
once be reproved for it.*

Arthur Schopenhauer

In logic textbooks, arguments, premises, and conclusions usually are neatly labeled so that there is no doubt which statements of an argument are offered in support of others—a sentence labeled "premise" clearly is intended to support one labeled "conclusion". Real life is another story.

In everyday life, few of us bother to label our remarks, for one thing because few of us bother very often to distinguish one argument from another in our own minds, much less separate premises from conclusions. But we do often give clues. The words "because", "since", "for", and the like, usually indicate that what follows is a premise, a reason given in support of some other statement. And expressions like "therefore", "hence", "consequently", "so", and "it follows that" usually signal a conclusion. Here is a simple example:

> Since the Cambodians have illegally detained a U.S. vessel, *it follows that* the President of the United States has the duty to obtain its release by any means necessary, *because* the President has the duty to defend all U.S. property and the lives of all U.S. citizens.

Put into textbook form, the argument reads:

1. The President of the United States has the duty to defend all U.S. lives and property.

2. The Cambodians have illegally detained a U.S. vessel.

3. The President of the United States has the duty to obtain its release by any necessary means.

Life is too short and talk too plentiful for us to bother separating out arguments, premises, and conclusions all the time. But it is a good idea to learn how to do so and to develop the habit of doing so when important subjects are talked about. It's surprising how much of what we hear or read consists mainly of unsupported conclusions, and it's even more surprising how persuasive such argument-less rhetoric can be. Yet, an unsupported statement should never convince us of anything we don't already know.[1]

Roughly speaking, a **valid argument** is an argument whose premises, *if true,* provide good, or sufficient, grounds for accepting its conclusion. All other arguments are said to be **invalid.**

Here is a made-up example of a valid argument:

> All Democratic politicians are honest (first premise), and Lyndon Johnson is a Democratic politician (second premise). So Lyndon Johnson is honest (conclusion).

The premises of this argument provide good grounds for accepting its conclusion, *if those premises are true.*

But we all know from sad experience that the first premise of this argument is false, a fact that makes the argument itself unsound. To be **sound,** an argument must be both valid *and* have all true premises. Nevertheless, the argument is valid, because *if* its premises were true, they would provide good grounds for acceptance of its conclusion.

Fallacious reasoning is just the opposite of what can be called **cogent** reasoning. We reason cogently when we reason (1) validly; (2) from premises well supported by evidence; and (3) using all the relevant evidence we know of. The purpose of avoiding fallacious reasoning is, of course, to increase our chances of reasoning cogently.

Let's use the notions of argument validity and argument invalidity as the basis for a division of fallacious arguments into two basic categories: (1) arguments that are **fallacious because invalid;** and (2) arguments that are **fallacious even if valid.** Chapters One and Two deal with arguments that are *fallacious because invalid* and Chapter Three with those that are *fallacious even if valid.*

But when using these basic fallacy categories, or any fallacy categories, we must remember that the arguments of everyday life frequently cannot be placed in a particular category with 100 percent certainty, because so many arguments in daily life are *vague, ambiguous,* or both.

In addition, remember that arguments in daily life don't have labels on their component statements indicating which are premises and which conclusions. It is often difficult, or even impossible, to tell one from the other. When that is the case, there is no point in undue worry over which fallacy labels apply. Fallacy categories are not built in heaven; they are, after all, just useful tools for spotting fallacies. Deciding which label applies in a given case is important only in helping us to see that the argument is fallacious and to understand *why* it is fallacious.

---

[1]The margin note method for summarizing an extended passage will be discussed in Chapter Six. It provides us with a method for analyzing written passages into arguments, premises, and conclusions.

Let's now discuss arguments that are *fallacious because invalid.* This is a vast category; almost one hundred species are distinguished in recent literature on the subject. In this chapter and the next, several of the more important species will be considered.

1. *Appeal to Authority*

No one knows everything. So we often must consult experts before making decisions. But there are good and bad ways to do this; improper appeals to experts constitute the fallacy of **appeal to authority.** For instance, the fallacy of *appeal to authority* is committed by members of Congress who respond to Defense Department budget controversies by automatically accepting the opinions of Defense Department experts, because it is precisely those opinions that others challenge. In such a situation, we should expect our elected officials to examine the *evidence* of the military and others and draw their own conclusions.

The problem is to distinguish proper from improper appeals to authority, a difficulty about which the relevant authorities (logicians and writers on rhetoric) have had relatively little to say. There are, however, a few rules of thumb which are of some practical use:

a. An authority in one field is not necessarily worth listening to in another. The opinions of famous athletes who endorse Gillette blades in television commercials are a case in point; there is no reason to suppose that athletes know any more about razor blades than anyone else. Similarly, to cite an example from politics, a man who is expert in making and selling automobiles (whether his name is Charles Wilson or Robert McNamara) is not thereby qualified to oversee the defense of the nation.

b. It is generally fallacious to accept the *opinion* of an authority (as opposed to his arguments) on topics about which experts disagree. The same is true of opinions in fields about which relatively little is known. Judges and juries often violate this principle, and thus commit the fallacy of *appeal to authority,* when they decide about a defendant's sanity or competence solely on the basis of one psychiatric opinion. Judges, of all people, ought to know how easy it is to obtain contrary expert testimony on most psychological matters.

c. When experts disagree, the rest of us must become our own experts, turning to acknowledged experts for *evidence, reasons,* and *arguments,* but not for conclusions or opinions. This is especially true with respect to political matters because of the tremendous controversies they arouse. But it applies elsewhere too. The judge who merely accepts a psychologist's opinion ought instead to ask for the reasons which led the psychologist to his opinion. Similarly American presidents need to go into the complex details which lie behind the opinions of their economic advisors, rather than confining themselves, as President Eisenhower is said to have done, to whatever could be typed onto one side of one page.

d. Finally, anyone who feels that he must appeal to an expert in a way which violates any of the above rules should at least consult the past record of that authority. Experts who have been right in the past are more likely to be reliable than those who have been wrong. It is surprising how often even this rule of last resort is violated. Think of the many members of Congress who accepted expert military opinion that the war in Vietnam would end in 1969 or 1970, even after having heard military experts testify incorrectly so often over the years about the end of that longest war in American history. Or recall President Nixon's economic advisors, who remained in favor with the President even though their predictions for 1970–74 on inflation and unemployment proved to be way off the mark. If you have to rely on expert opinion, at least choose experts with a good track record.

The danger of the fallacy of *appeal to authority* results largely from the tendency to trust in the authority of pronouncements by high officials and other famous people. Senator Joseph R. McCarthy's charges in the early 1950s that Communists infested the Department of State ("I have here in my hand the names of . . .") were taken seriously, and caused so much trouble for our country, precisely because he was a *United States Senator.*

But it is the word of the President of the United States which is held in highest respect in the United States, Richard Nixon notwithstanding. Thus, in 1974, many Americans accepted the idea that inflation was our most serious problem primarily because President Ford said so quite strongly in his first major speech after succeeding Nixon to the presidency. But those Americans who merely accepted Ford's word on the matter reasoned fallaciously. For many "experts" felt then that other problems were more serious (the international situation, overpopulation, poverty, hunger and starvation, racism, law and order), and Ford failed either to deal with their arguments or to explain *why* inflation was more serious. You commit the fallacy of *appeal to authority* in accepting the unsupported word of a politician on a controversial issue even if that politician happens to be the President of the United States.

Here is a more subtle example of *appeal to authority.* After introducing a formal impeachment resolution to the House Judiciary Committee (July 24, 1974), Representative Harold D. Donahue, Democrat from Massachusetts, argued for impeachment as a legitimate procedure by appealing to the opinions of founding fathers:

> Mr. Gouverneur Morris, a delegate to [the Constitutional Convention of 1787] . . . wanted no impeachment clause in our Constitution. But he listened intently as first Benjamin Franklin and then James Madison argued on behalf of such a clause and finally . . . announced that his opinion had been changed by the arguments presented in debate.

But Donahue failed to provide us with Franklin's and Madison's *reasons,* instead, inviting us to accept their *opinion* as authoritative. So he invited us to commit the fallacy of *appeal to authority.*

Dumb is Good

A while back, *New Times* picked the Hon. William Scott (R-Va.) as the dumbest senator of them all. Since the field was crowded, naturally a controversy arose—aided and abetted by Mr. Scott himself, who called a press conference to deny our findings.

Well, the last word on the controversy has been had by the John Birch Society, which recently ranked Scott as No. 1 in its list of the top 10 senators. Earl Landgrebe (R-Ind.), who weighed in quite high on our list of the 10 dumbest congressmen, was also hailed by the John Birchers as No. 2 on their top 10 list.

Reverse appeal to authority. The John Birch Society may be neanderthal in the eyes of left-wing publications like *New Times,* but it shouldn't follow, even for them, that the Birchers are *automatically* wrong in their judgments of members of Congress.

There are two important variations of the fallacy of *appeal to authority.* They result from the fact that the "authority" need not be a single person or even a group of persons. The first variation is **popularity.**

Everyone knows how difficult it is to speak out in a group against the general sentiment of that group. The power of human cowardice, wedded to the desire to be on the winning side, is the basis for the fallacy of *popularity,* which is simply the human tendency to go along with the crowd, to believe what others believe. (Sometimes this is called the fallacy of **democracy,** or of **numbers.**) In other words, for many people the crowd is the authority. For many, the fact that a view is widely held, and thus "representative", is sufficient to make that view respectable; the fact that a view is *not* widely held is sufficient to make it suspect.

Here is an argument that has these two assumptions as implicit premises:[2]

The freedom and flexibility afforded the broadcaster under the "fairness doctrine" to select in good faith the spokesmen for the **representative**[3] viewpoints seems the best means yet devised for insuring that the public is exposed to all **significant** points of view on important public issues.

In other words, only popular viewpoints are significant, an utterly foolish idea in light of the initial unpopularity of so many great ideas.

---

[2]A remark by Leonard H. Goldenson of ABC, reported in a newspaper column by John S. Knight, August 14, 1970.

[3]Bold face type within quotes is added for emphasis.

Here is former Vice President Spiro Agnew and another example of *appeal to authority.*[4]

> Before I came down here, one [political pundit] told me that Southern voters wouldn't listen to Republicans. Southern voters won't support Republicans, and Southerners won't vote Republican. He told me he was *never* wrong. And then he drove off in his Edsel.

And since Edsels were a big sales flop, they obviously were the wrong car to buy. A humorous example, but human beings, especially in large groups, are manipulated by such trivia.

Politicians know that it's good practice to defend themselves when attacked not by answering the charge but by attacking the person who leveled it. Florida's former Senator George Smathers used the fallacy of *appeal to authority* in his "defense" against an accusation of wrongdoing raised by the late columnist Drew Pearson. Pearson specialized in investigations of political wrongdoing and over the years enjoyed the wrath of countless political figures. Said Senator Smathers in his defense against Pearson's accusation:

> I join two Presidents, 27 Senators, and 83 Congressmen in describing Drew Pearson as an unmitigated liar.

All of which was irrelevant to the truth of Pearson's accusation.

Finally, let's consider an example from the law. In the 1970 New Haven Black Panther trial, the jury first reported to the judge that they were deadlocked. The judge then read a part of an old Connecticut charge called the "Chip Smith charge", which is used to prod the minority on a jury to go along with the majority verdict. It asks the minority to reconsider their position in view of the verdict of the majority of jury members who "have heard the same evidence with the same attention and with equal desire to arrive at the truth and under sanction of the same oath."

The legitimacy of the Chip Smith charge rests on the assumption that the majority is more likely to be right than the minority. But if a juror is convinced by the Chip Smith charge that the majority view is correct "beyond a reasonable doubt" *because* it is the majority view, then he commits the fallacy of *appeal to authority,* the majority being his authority. For he places the indirect evidence of the majority verdict ahead of the direct evidence of courtroom testimony.

The second interesting variety of *appeal to authority* is **traditional wisdom,** which trades on the psychological fact that the past and the familiar have as secure a hold on us as the opinions of others.

---

[4]Mississippi Republican Dinner, Jackson, Mississippi, October 20, 1969.

But "traditional wisdom" should not be accepted automatically. It's true that the old have more experiences to draw on than the young, so that their view of a problem often carries special weight. However, it is fallacious to suppose that the opinions of an older *generation* are based on more experience than those of the current generation. In fact, just the reverse is true; those alive today have more experiences to draw on than did past generations, for knowledge tends to be handed down from generation to generation and thus on the whole to increase. (Much that is false is handed down, too, but no one ever said thinking correctly is easy.)

Nevertheless, the fact that something has always been done a certain way seems to be a sufficient reason for many people to continue doing it that way. Here is Senator Sam Ervin, of North Carolina, telling how he replied to women who were in favor of the equality-for-women amendment to the Constitution:[5]

> I tell them, "Why ladies, any bill that lies around here for 47 years without getting any more support than this one has got in the past *obviously* shouldn't be passed at all. Why, I think *that affords most conclusive proof that it's unworthy of consideration.*"

It's hard to imagine a more clearcut case of the *traditional wisdom* variety of *appeal to authority.* But most cases of *traditional wisdom* are not so clearcut. The appeal to tradition often is concealed or halfhearted. Here is an example from an article on judicial abuse of migrant laborers in New Jersey.[6] Richard A. Walsh, deputy state public defender, in reply to the charge that migrants were being deprived of due process of law, is quoted as saying:

> It's not right, it's unjust and we know it, *but that's the way the system works down here.*

This was a halfhearted use of *traditional wisdom* because Mr. Walsh never quite said that past practice constituted an excuse, but, in the absence of any great effort to correct the admitted injustice, the last clause does function to excuse that injustice.

Another example of *traditional wisdom* is furnished by John S. Knight in a column which dealt with a complaint by Senator J. William Fulbright of Arkansas that President Nixon was getting too much television exposure. Senator Fulbright wanted Congress to get equal time. Said Mr. Knight:

> The Senator . . . must recall Franklin D. Roosevelt's famous "fireside chats" over radio which did so much to influence the nation's thinking during his years in the White House. *No one protested then that FDR was being unduly favored.* . . .

---

[5]Quoted in the *New York Times Magazine,* September 20, 1970.

[6]*New York Times,* August 17, 1970, p. 34.

Perhaps someone should have. In any event, the dispute is not settled by appeal to past practice as the authority on the matter.

2.   *Provincialism*

The fallacy of **provincialism** stems from the natural tendency to identify strongly with a particular group, and to perceive experience largely in terms of in-group versus out-group.

This tendency has some good things to be said for it, since a person's well-being often depends on that of his group. But when in-group loyalties begin to intrude on the process of determining *truth,* the result is often fallacy. The tendency toward provincialism results, for one thing, in normally enlightened people displaying shocking ignorance or prejudice. Here is an example from an American newspaper series on Japan:[7]

> The [Japanese] empire supposedly was founded about 600 B.C., but for the next 24 centuries the Japanese people lived in almost complete isolation from *the rest of the world.*

"The rest of the world", of course, meant the Western world. The writer ignored the great influence of China on Japan during much of that 24-century period.

> Henry J. Taylor was guilty of this fallacy in one of his political columns:[8]

> . . . the great Declaration [*of Independence*] begins:
>   'When in the course of human events . . .'
> and *for the first time in man's history* announced that all rights came from a sovereign, not from a government, but from God. . . .

But as every schoolboy ought to know, that idea goes back a good deal further than 1776.

Provincialism often results in a false conception of the importance and moral quality of one's own group. The "space race" between the Soviet Union and the United States furnishes a good example.

From 1957 until some time in the 1960s, the Soviet Union was ahead of the United States in space by a very small margin, chiefly due to our lack of a powerful propellant. During this time, although we were behind, American exploits received bigger headlines and greater coverage in this country than did those of the Russians. But the Russians did receive good coverage. When the United States forged ahead, coverage of American space shots greatly increased, while coverage of the Russians declined. Compare, for instance, the coverage of the *second* American

---

[7] *Lawrence* (Kan.) *Daily Journal World,* August 8, 1970.
[8] *Topeka* (Kan.) *Daily Capital,* July 1970.

manned moon flight with that of the Russians' *first* unmanned soft landing and return from the moon. (It hardly need be said that Russian coverage of the space race has been much more provincial than ours.)

Yet throughout this period, the achievements of both space efforts were very close; both accomplished important and similar tasks. The average American, however, relying on news reporting which played on the already provincial nature of its audience, received the impression that by 1968 our achievement had become far superior to that of the Russians. This helped confirm many Americans in their conviction that our system (capitalism) is superior to theirs ("atheistic social-istic communism"). Thus, it intensified our tendency to think we are the smartest, strongest, and best, and our tendency to overlook the accomplishments of the rest of the world.

In its extreme form, the fallacy of *provincialism* turns into a worse vice, the fallacy of **loyalty.** This is the fallacy of believing (or disbelieving), in the face of great contrary evidence, *because* of provincial loyalty.

The reactions of many Americans to the My Lai massacre constitute a good example.[9] On reading about My Lai, a teletype inspector in Philadelphia is reported to have said he didn't think it happened: "I can't believe our boys' hearts are that rotten." This response was typical, as was that of the person who informed the *Cleveland Plain Dealer,* which had printed photos of the massacre, "Your paper is rotten and anti-American." Surveys taken after wide circulation of news about the massacre revealed that large numbers of Americans refused to believe "American boys" had done such a thing. The myth of American moral superiority seems to have been a better source of truth for them than evidence at hand. One wonders if any amount of evidence would be sufficient to convince those people who set *loyalty* above the truth. They are like the clerics who refused to look through Galileo's telescope to see the moons of Jupiter because they *knew* Jupiter could not possibly have moons.

Let's end our discussion of *loyalty* and *provincialism* on a lighter note. The *New York Times* (September 17, 1970) carried a photo of a smiling President Nixon addressing a pleased-looking audience at Kansas State University. Underneath the photo, the *Times* reported that the President had just noted to the audience that he was wearing a tie with the K.S.U. school colors, purple and white. Having thus made the provincial appeal, the President then had a more receptive audience for serious subjects. Wearing a particular tie is so simple a matter; yet human minds are often controlled by such gestures.

3. Irrelevant Reason

Traditional textbooks on fallacies often discuss a fallacy called *non sequitur* ("it does not follow"), usually described as a fallacy in which the conclusion does

---

[9]See Seymour M. Hersh, *My Lai 4: A Report on the Massacre and Its Aftermath* (New York: Random House, 1970), pp. 151–152.

not follow from the given premises. But in this sense, any fallacy in the broad category *fallacious because invalid* can be said to be a *non sequitur.*

Other writers use *non sequitur* to describe those arguments in which the "evidence" in the premises is *totally irrelevant* to the conclusion, and not, as is sometimes the case with such fallacies as *ad hominem* and *appeal to authority,* relevant but insufficient to establish the conclusion.

Let's replace the ambiguous term *non sequitur* with the expression **irrelevant reason,** to refer to reasons or premises that are or come close to being totally irrelevant to a conclusion, provided another fallacy name (for instance, *ad hominem* argument) does not apply.

A newspaper columnist, for instance, was guilty of this fallacy when he argued that prices had gone much too high by pointing out that the average housewife spends at a rate of $20 per hour at the supermarket, while her husband earns only $2.95 per hour. The rate of speed at which a housewife spends money is completely irrelevant to the charge that prices are too high. A man may spend a third of his yearly salary when he buys a new automobile, or an entire year's salary merely as down payment on a house. But this tells us nothing whatever about whether automobile or house prices are rising too rapidly, or even rising at all.

Politicians often employ this fallacy when their arguments are weak, or too controversial. Thus, in a discussion of a particular public housing bill, a congressman went on and on about the need for more housing for the citizens of this great country, while saying nothing about the merits of the bill in question, confident that some of his listeners would fail to notice the irrelevance of his remarks to the real question at issue. For the issue was not whether we ought to have good housing for all, but whether the bill before the House was the right one to accomplish that goal.

The fallacy of *irrelevant reason* was committed on a wholesale basis by Democrats during the Johnson administration and Republicans during the Nixon administration. In reply to charges that the United States had no business in Vietnam, either morally or to satisfy our national interests, politicians during that period frequently replied that such talk only prolonged the war by making the enemy believe that America's will to fight was declining. This reply in all likelihood was true; but it was utterly irrelevant to the question of our justification for being in Vietnam.

4. Ambiguity

A term or phrase is **ambiguous** when it has more than one meaning. Most English words are ambiguous, but their ambiguity usually is fairly harmless. The English word "snow", for instance, can be used to refer to the quite harmless flaked form of H_2O or to the extremely dangerous drug heroin. But in most cases in which this word is used, it is clear from the context which meaning is intended.

However, some uses of ambiguous terms are far from harmless. When the ambiguity of a word or phrase leads to a mistaken conclusion, we have the fallacy of **ambiguity.** (A person who tries to trade on ambiguity to confuse his listeners *argues* fallaciously, but typically he doesn't *reason* fallaciously because he isn't convinced by his own argument.)

Here is an example of the fallacy of *ambiguity* from a Rowland Evans and Robert Novak column (June 30, 1970):

His [Nixon's] claim that his new Administration really intends to fulfill [William] Scranton's *evenhanded policy* between Israel and the Arab states . . .

The expression "evenhanded policy" here could mean either a policy halfway between the Arab and Israeli positions or a fair policy. By describing the Scranton policy as "evenhanded", Evans and Novak entice support for it from those who favor a "halfway" policy as well as from those who will endorse any policy they consider "fair". The columnists also mask the fact that labeling a policy "evenhanded", even if accurate in one or another sense of that term, does not provide grounds for adopting it. (In defense of Evans and Novak, it should be pointed out that the Scranton policy was widely referred to as "evenhanded". They were just passing on the ambiguous label.)

"It is he that sitteth upon the circle of the earth."
Isaiah 40:22

Ambiguity: Almost any statement can be interpreted in various ways if we have a mind to do so. The Bible is a happy hunting ground for those intent on taking advantage of the ambiguity of natural languages, because many people take what it says to be the word of the Ultimate Authority on all matters. The above passage from Isaiah once was used to prove that the earth is flat, but after Copernicus, Kepler, and Newton to prove that it is a sphere.

Finally, here is an excerpt from a May 2, 1969, speech by Spiro Agnew. Notice that the ambiguity occurs in an aside, which makes it just that much harder to detect:

Aside from the small point that our primary and secondary schools should strengthen their curricula in civics . . . so that even our youngest children learn that civil rights *are* balanced by civil responsibilities . . .

The word *are* in this passage is ambiguous. The passage can be taken to say either that (1) we should teach children the moral truth that there is a responsibility (duty) corresponding to every right, or that (2) *in fact* in the United States our civil rights are upheld and balanced by our civil responsibilities. Many minority groups (American Indians, Jews, Negroes, Puerto Ricans) would vehemently deny the second interpretation. (Construed in this way, the passage is guilty of *begging the question*—a fallacy discussed in Chapter Three.) But if attacked, Agnew just had to switch to the first meaning—that civil rights and civil responsibilities ought to balance—to win the argument.

Studied ambiguity is the perfect device for protecting yourself from legitimate attack; to defend yourself you simply shift meanings at the opportune moment.

So long as the economic system meets these demands [for more jobs, higher income, more consumer goods, and more recreation], and so long as the demands take these forms, the perennial questions about *power* and *control* need never be asked. Or, better, those whose demands are being met can be congratulated on having "power," *for what is power but the ability to have one's demands met?* (Ben Wattenberg, *The New America*, p. 49)

Ambiguity (very subtle): Do we have power if we have the ability to get *all* of our demands met, *some* met, or even *one?* Just about everyone has some power. The political question Wattenberg evaded is whether average Americans (or Wattenberg's *real majority*) have power equal to their numbers—Wattenberg's opponents don't deny the middle class has power, they just deny they have their fair share.

---

5. Slippery Slope

The fallacy of **slippery slope** consists in objecting to a particular action on the grounds that once an action is taken it will lead inevitably to a similar but less desirable action, which will lead in turn to an even less desirable action, and so on down the "slippery slope" until the horror lurking at the bottom is reached.

According to a slightly different version of *slippery slope,* whatever would justify taking the first step over the edge also would justify all the other steps. But, it is argued, the last step is not justified, so the first step is not either.

People frequently argued against Medicare in the late 1960s on the grounds that it was socialized medicine for the aged and would lead to socialized medicine for all, and then to socialized insurance of all kinds, socialized railroads, airlines, and steel mills. It was also argued that whatever justified socialized medicine for the aged justified it for everyone, and justified as well socialized railroads, and so on, "down the slope" all the way to a completely socialistic system.

The fallacy of the slippery slope is committed in this example if you accept *without further argument* the idea that, once the first step is taken, the slide all the way down is inevitable. The fact is that the first step sometimes does and sometimes does not lead to more steps. Even in Great Britain, under socialist governments, the economy has not been fully socialized. Further argument is needed to determine the facts in particular cases like that of Medicare.

A Quick About-Face

Perhaps intimidated by flak from Capitol Hill, the Social Security Advisory Council has backed away from a proposal to increase the maximum pay subject to Soc-Sec taxation from $14,100 to $24,000 to keep the plan on a pay-as-you-go basis. Instead, it has recommended shifting the cost of medicare to the general fund.

The proposal, if adopted, would begin the process of transforming Social Security into an out-and-out welfare program. Once we start in that direction, where do we stop? *(New York Daily News,* January 21, 1975)

Slippery slope, a favorite of the *New York Daily News.*

The variations on slippery slope are almost limitless. Two, the **Balkanization theory** and the **domino theory,** have been employed quite frequently in recent years.

The *Balkanization theory* was employed during the Nigeria–Biafra civil war. People argued then that we could not permit Biafra to break away from Nigeria because such a break would produce a chain reaction in which every tribal group in Africa would attempt to gain independence, thus "Balkanizing" Africa. But there was little or no evidence to support such conjecture. In the first place, an independent Biafra would have been larger in population than over half the nations in the world, so it would hardly have exemplified "Balkanization". And second, civil wars of independence gain their impetus primarily from factors internal to the nation in question, not from the success of attempts in other nations. The Biafran attempt to gain independence is itself a case in point, since it came after secessionist attempts elsewhere in Africa (as in the Congo—now known as Zaire) had failed.

The classic case of the use of the *domino theory* is, of course, Vietnam (Indo-China). Everyone seems to have used it at one time or another, starting with the French:[10]

---

[10]General Jean de Lattre de Tassigny, general in charge of French forces in the Far East, September 20, 1951. This, and several of the examples which follow, are mentioned in the book *Quotations Vietnam: 1945–1970,* compiled by William G. Effros (New York: Random House, 1970), Chapter Three.

Once Tongking [Northern Indo-China] is lost, there is really no barrier before Suez. . . .

The Americans then joined in, one of the first being John Foster Dulles:[11]

If Indo-China should be lost, there would be a chain reaction throughout the Far East and South Asia.

Here is William P. Bundy:[12]

If South Vietnam falls, the rest of Southeast Asia will be in grave danger of progressively disappearing behind the Bamboo Curtain, and other Asian countries like India and even in time Australia and your own [country—Japan] will in turn be threatened.

Even Bob Hope got into the act:[13]

Everybody I talked to there [Vietnam] wants to know why they can't go in and finish it, and don't let anybody kid you about why we're there. If we weren't, those Commies would have the whole thing, and it wouldn't be long until we'd be looking off the coast of Santa Monica [California].

All of these versions of the *domino theory* reveal the simplistic attitude that is characteristic of *slippery slope* in any of its variations, the attitude that once the first step is taken, the rest are inevitable. But sometimes that first step will lead to others, sometimes it won't. We must examine each case individually for the details that make all the difference. If we fail to do so, we reason fallaciously.

Summary of fallacies discussed in Chapter One

1. *Appeal to authority.* Improper appeal to authority.

   Example: Senator Smather's defense against Drew Pearson by appeal to the authority of two presidents, 27 senators, and 83 congressmen.

   a. *Popularity.* Appeal to the crowd as the authority.

   Example: Spiro Agnew's characterization of a man as wrong in buying an Edsel because Edsels were a sales flop.

---

[11]Secretary of State under Eisenhower, April 5, 1954.

[12]Assistant Secretary of State for Far Eastern Affairs under President Johnson, September 29, 1964, in Tokyo, Japan.

[13]Anthony J. Lukas, "This is Bob (Politician-Patriot-Publicist) Hope," *New York Times Magazine,* October 4, 1970, p. 86.

b. *Traditional wisdom.* Appealing to the past as an authority.

Example: Senator Ervin's statement that Congress's 47 year failure to act on a proposed equal-rights-for-women amendment was a conclusive reason for rejecting the amendment.

2. *Provincialism.* Assuming that the familiar, the close, or what is one's own is *therefore* the better or more important. Also, the failure to look beyond one's own group, in particular to the ideas of other cultures.

Example: The far greater coverage in the United States of American space efforts than of Russian efforts.

a. *Loyalty.* Deciding the truth of an assertion on the basis of loyalty.

Example: Refusal to believe the overwhelming evidence that U.S. soldiers had shot and killed defenseless women, children, and babies at My Lai 4 in South Vietnam.

3. *Irrelevant reason.* Use of evidence entirely irrelevant to a conclusion.

Example: Arguing that prices are too high on the grounds that the average housewife spends at a rate of $20 per hour at the supermarket.

4. *Ambiguity.* Use of ambiguous terms to mislead (or which in fact mislead).

Example: The Evans and Novak description of the Scranton Middle East policy as "evenhanded", which could mean either a fair policy or one halfway between the Arab and Israeli positions.

5. *Slippery slope.* Failure to see that the first step in a possible series of steps does not inevitably lead to the rest.

Example: Claims—unargued for—that Medicare would inevitably lead to complete socialism.

a. *Balkanization theory.* The conclusion that the break-up of one nation into parts will inevitably result in the break-up of others.

Example: The belief that if Biafra successfully broke away from Nigeria, all sorts of tribal groups in Africa would try to establish independent nations.

b. *Domino theory.* The conclusion that if *A* falls, so will *B*, then *C*, and so on.

Example: The belief that if South Vietnam goes Communist, so will Laos, Cambodia, Thailand, the rest of the Far East, and so on.

Exercise I for Chapter One

Each of the following passages contain some sort of poor reasoning or arguing. Determine which of the fallacies discussed in Chapter One occur in each item, and *explain why* you think so. (Remember that the fallacy categories may overlap, and that a given item may contain more than one fallacy. Remember also that the material is quite controversial and thus open to differing interpretations. So your *explanations* are more important than the fallacy labels you put on an argument.) (Starred items (*) are answered in an appendix at the back of the book.)

1. *Ad for Masterpiece pipe tobacco: Eva Gabor:* Darling, have you discovered Masterpiece? The most exciting men I know are smoking it!

*2. *Judy:* Well, that [*The Exorcist*] was the best picture we've seen all year.
   Judy's John: Don't be silly. *Cries and Whispers* was the best flick.
   Judy: I didn't see that. It only showed for a couple of days here—to half-empty houses. But *The Exorcist!* I waited two months before braving the long lines to see it. Just about everybody saw that film.

3. Texas Observer, *March 16, 1973 (quoting State Senator Walter Mengden):* The base cause of inflation is an unbalanced federal budget . . . "If the rate of inflation becomes too excessive, the result of this inflation is that the economy will stop . . . because the dollar will be losing value so fast people will stop exchanging goods of real value for dollars. . . . Now this isn't conjecture; this has happened before, many times, . . . If you don't control inflation, . . . you will destroy the economy, and in a few weeks there will be no food to buy, little water, no electricity and services, and there will be such panic and disaster that some hard-pants general is going to move in and say, 'I am now running the show,' and the Army or somebody like him will take over, and that's the end of the Constitutional Republic. And that's what's going to happen if we don't control inflation."

4. *John:* What's *wrong* with two single consenting adults sleeping with each other?
   Judy: Well, if that's OK, why not husbands and wives having affairs? Why not mothers sleeping with their sons? Or daughters, for that matter.

5. McGovern is right. Amnesty was granted by U.S. presidents after the Civil War, World War I, and World War II. So we ought to grant amnesty to Vietnam draft dodgers.

6. *Advertisement:* Thousands of Americans suffer from malnutrition. So make sure *your* family gets a good breakfast every day. Serve your family Snicker Snacks, in the familiar box.

*7. *Article in college newspaper:* A committee on teaching evaluation in colleges is the coming thing.

8. *John Corry in* Harper's *magazine, November 1970:* "We will have our manhood even if we have to level the face of the earth," Huey Newton told the Panther convention, and this is not so much inflammatory as it is sad, a confession that the Panthers do not have something that the other boys in town take for granted.

9. *Pierre* (translated from French): Yes, America is a rich country. More powerful, and larger; the West is very vast and majestic. But I could never live there

and be so far from the most beautiful, sexy, sophisticated women in the world. And you, who can afford to live anywhere. How can *you* live so far from such feminine class, and settle for these American women?
How: These heavenly females you're raving about, they're French, of course.
Pierre: Of course!

*10. *Judy:* O.K., it was politically unwise of Ford to pardon Nixon before he was even formally charged with a crime. But it took guts, and so we ought to support him on this issue.
John: Yeah, I suppose you're right, but it feels funny agreeing with a Republican president.

11. You're wrong to reject Tang because it's not a completely natural product. It's probably fairly nutritious. After all, NASA selected it for use by the astronauts.

12. *President Ford, August 28, 1974, soon after taking office:* The code of ethics that will be followed by those in my administration will be the example I set.

13. Lots of parents let their children have an occasional nip of wine or sip of beer. Some even give their kids a taste of harder stuff, like gin. But no *responsible* parent does this, because, well, as the old saying goes, "one drink leads to another". Once you start your child down that boozy road, they're not going to turn back. If you want your children to be alcoholics when they grow up, be "nice" to them and let them have a taste of your drinks when company comes over.

14. Hartford Courant, *December 20, 1972, in an article on the possibility of women priests in the Catholic Church:* Citing the historic exclusion of women from the priesthood, however, the study [of a committee of Roman Catholic bishops] said ". . . the constant tradition and practice, interpreted as of divine law, is of such a nature as to constitute a clear teaching of the Ordinary Magisterium [teaching authority] of the Church."

15. *Beginning of a book review:* Erich Segal's *Love Story—Romeo and Juliet* it isn't. But who cares. It's guaranteed to give you a good cry now and then. And it couldn't have gotten off to such a flying start for nothing. Everybody is going to be reading this novel, so you better go down to your nearest bookstore and pick up a copy.

16. *Judy:* Historians already are dealing too harshly with President Johnson. True, he was wrong on Vietnam, but every one of his State Department and Pentagon advisors, from MacNamara on down, were advising him he had to plunge in.
John: What about George Ball?
Judy: Well, O.K., but it was one or two against all the rest. He had to pay attention to all that high powered advice. Let's blame them, not LBJ.

*17. *Dr. Max E. Eisenring, on the occasion of his election to the Insurance Hall of Fame:* I started my insurance career as an actuary. But it needs no actuary to know that there is no insurance without statistics. Yet there are no statistics, in the sense used and necessary for insurance operations, without the recurrence of similar events. Even life insurance, in the classic form, would become obsolete if, say, some wonder drug were all of a sudden to produce a longevity of hundreds of years. While such a thing is fortunately rather unlikely to happen in the foreseeable future, the idea of perhaps revolutionary changes is by no means far-fetched in regard to the non-life (insurance) lines.

18. *Letter from a father to his college daughter:* Dear Helen, Gladys tells me that Fred has invited you out for New Year's Eve. She says you're just going out with him because you need a date for a New Year's Eve party. But if your old man means anything to you now that you're so grown up and in college, *don't* go to that party with Fred. Before you know it, you'll be going steady with the guy, and according to Gladys he's on marijuana. If you go steady with him, you're going to try the awful stuff, and God forbid end up one of those—what do you call it—speed freaks, or maybe when that wears out a dope addict. Don't go out with that boy Fred—or forget about Europe next summer.

*19. *John P. Roche, political column, October 1970:* Every society is, of course, repressive to some extent—as Sigmund Freud pointed out, repression is the price we pay for civilization.

20. *Arthur Schlesinger, Jr., supporting Senator McGovern's candidacy for President, in the New Republic:* Though a country boy, he [McGovern] has immersed himself in the problems of the cities. In New York, for example, he has the support of Democratic leaders . . . ; indeed, Prof. Richard Wade, our leading urban historian, is managing his campaign.

21. *How:* Do you realize that most of the philosophical confusion over the concepts of determinism and cause-effect is due to a failure to see that these are epistemic, not ontological, concepts?
    Judy: I'm afraid that's over my head. But tell me, what even mildly important philosopher ever thought that?
    How: None, to my knowledge.
    Judy: Think again, genius.

22. *Column by Joseph Alsop, January 4, 1971:* You can argue about the exact moment when . . . after World War I (the world passed from a postwar to prewar period)—about whether it was when Hitler reoccupied the Rhineland without resistance or when the harsh resulting challenge met with no adequate response from Britain or France or anyone else.

23. *Bertrand Russell, on entering a vain friend's yacht:* I thought your yacht was bigger than it is.
    Russell's friend: Only an idiot would think something is bigger than it is.

*24. *Nat Hentoff in the* Village Voice, *March 3, 1975:* . . . City College [of New York] is hardly unique [it censured five history professors for what Hentoff believed to be an exercise of their rights to free speech], among schools of higher education, in its ambience of ignorance of the functions of the First Amendment. It is an ignorance which leads inexorably to contempt for total free speech.

Exercise II for Chapter One

Find examples in the mass media (newspapers, TV, radio, magazines) of fallacies discussed in Chapter One, and explain why they are fallacious.

Analogy: Questionable?

Chapter Two

Fallacious Because Invalid—II

It don't even make good nonsense.

Davy Crockett, remarking on a statement by President Andrew Jackson

Let's continue our discussion of the more important fallacies in the category *fallacious because invalid.*

1. Ad Hominem Argument (Argument to the Man)

The fallacy of **ad hominem argument,** sometimes called the **genetic fallacy,** consists of an irrelevant attack on the person argued against, rather than his argument.

Senator Jenning Randolph was guilty of *ad hominem* argument in a U.S. Senate debate on a proposed constitutional amendment requiring equal protection of the law without regard to sex (August 26, 1970), when he dismissed women's liberationists, and thus their arguments, with the remark that women's liberationists constituted a "small band of bra-less bubbleheads". This may have been good for a laugh in the almost all-male Senate, but it was irrelevant to arguments the women's liberationist representatives had presented. Randolph attacked *them* (through ridicule) rather than their arguments. So he argued fallaciously.

Al Capp, the creator of Li'l Abner, is a frequent user of ridicule, and thus of *ad hominem* argument. Students leaving in protest during one of his addresses once prompted Capp to remark:[1]

Hey! Don't go! I need an animal act! You with the beard! Why don't you walk on water?

In ridiculing women's liberationists as "bra-less bubbleheads", Senator Randolph resorted to namecalling, on a rather low level. But *ad hominem* namecalling need

---

[1]Reported in the *Hartford Courant,* September 6, 1970.

not be so crude. Here is an example with a good deal of literary merit, representing then Vice President Spiro Agnew at his very best:[2]

A spirit of national masochism prevails, encouraged by an effete corps of impudent snobs who characterize themselves as intellectuals.

Agnew attacked his intellectual opponents without bothering to consider their arguments.

Mr. Rockefeller's most persistent antagonist has been Robert Byrd, of West Virginia, who was once a member of the Ku Klux Klan. *(Wall Street Journal* editorial "On Mr. Rockefeller," November 14, 1974)

True. But what did that have to do with Senator Byrd's objections to Rockefeller as vice presidential nominee? The *Wall Street Journal* was guilty of *ad hominem* argument.

Ad hominem argument is not always fallacious. A lawyer who attacks the testimony of a courtroom witness by questioning his moral character, and thus his truthfulness, argues *ad hominem* but does not commit a fallacy. For courtroom witnesses, doctors, auto mechanics, lawyers, and other experts often present opinions against which we, as nonexperts, are unable to argue directly. In such cases, claims about an expert's character may well be an important kind of evidence to use in deciding whether to accept or reject his opinion.

In these cases we certainly do not prove by *ad hominem* argument that expert opinion is incorrect. At best, *ad hominem* argument provides grounds only for canceling or disregarding the opinion of an expert. It cannot provide good grounds for assuming his view is false. If a doctor who advises operating on a patient turns out to be a quack, it is rash to conclude that no operation is necessary. In disregarding his opinion, we don't thereby assume his claim is false, but only that his holding that view says nothing significant in its favor.

Nevertheless, in the vast majority of cases, attacks on a person rather than on what he says are fallacious. And such attacks can be rather subtle. Here is *Time* magazine reporting on Yale chaplain William Sloan Coffin, Jr., and the New Haven Black Panther murder trial:[3]

The climate was such that Yale chaplain William Sloan Coffin, Jr., saw no unreason in characterizing the murder trial as "legally right but morally wrong." . . . How to explain such logic? The answer is that the New Haven Panthers have ample white guilt going for them at Yale.

---

[2]From a speech delivered in New Orleans, October 19, 1969.

[3]*Time,* May 4, 1970, p. 59.

Time's argument was *ad hominem* because it attacked Coffin himself through his motives and not his argument. *Time* gave a psychological motive (white guilt) for Coffin's alleged error in reasoning, rather than an argument to demonstrate that he in fact reasoned incorrectly. Even supposing *Time* was correct in saying that a motive of white guilt was at work, what is wrong with Coffin's idea that the murder trial was "legally right but morally wrong"? *Time* erred in failing to answer that question, thus failing to support its implication that the statement is illogical.

One of the more important variations on *ad hominem* arguments is **guilt by association.** Many people believe that a person is to be judged by the company he keeps. But many also hold that you should not judge a person by his associates, any more than you judge a book by its cover. Which view is correct?

The answer is that it *is* rational under certain circumstances to judge a person by his associates. However, only rarely will such a judgment have a *high degree of probability* attached to it. In the absence of other evidence, a man frequently seen in the company of different women known to be prostitutes is rightly suspected of being connected with their occupation in a way that casts doubt on his moral character. Similarly, a person who associates frequently and closely with men known to be agents of a foreign government is rightly suspected of being an agent of that government himself.

But we must always be cautious in using this kind of evidence. For it is both indirect and circumstantial. Its best use is as evidence leading to further investigation, not as evidence leading to firm conviction. Direct evidence is preferable and almost always takes precedence. The man who frequently associates with prostitutes may be a sociologist conducting an investigation or even a minister shepherding his flock. The close associate of spies may be a counterspy or an innocent cover being taken advantage of by his "friends".

Nevertheless, when judgments must be made solely on the basis of indirect evidence, as they sometimes must, it may be reasonable to judge on the basis of a man's associates.[4]

Indirect evidence of this kind is misused much more often than it is used correctly. In particular, this applies to politics, where the "guilty" association can be quite remote. An example is the tactic employed by Connecticut Republican State Chairman Howard E. Hausman against the 1970 Democratic candidate

---

[4]This fact generates important moral and political problems. It often is true that in the absence of direct evidence a man's qualifications for obtaining insurance or being hired for a job are most rationally judged on the basis of indirect statistical evidence. Thus, insurance companies may refuse to insure Negroes who live in the black ghettoes of large cities or they may charge them much higher rates on the grounds that statistically the risk is higher in such cases. The same is true with respect to auto insurance for single males under 25 years of age. But, although it is rational to assume the risk is higher, there is a question as to the morality, or at least the political advisability, of permitting actions·on the basis of such rational assumptions. For actions based on gross statistical classifications of this kind are inevitably unfair to those who most deserve fair treatment. An example is a reliable Negro denied insurance simply because he resides in a certain undesirable area. By acting on indirect statistical evidence, the insurer does him an injustice and helps to perpetuate the conditions that produced the statistics in the first place.

for the U.S. Senate, Reverend Joseph Duffey.[5] Hausman questioned Duffey's patriotism on the grounds that Duffey associated with Georgia State Representative Julian Bond, who was quoted as saying that patriotism is a "stupid idea". What Bond had said was this: "We must reject this stupid idea of patriotism that has made us first in war, last in peace and last in the hearts of our countrymen." Hausman's comment was, "I can't believe that the people of Connecticut want as their next Senator a man who is associated with the view that patriotism is stupid."

But Hausman argued fallaciously. First, the evidence that Duffey was associated with the view that patriotism is stupid is *indirect,* and thus discountable given the abundant *direct* evidence indicating candidate Duffey was as patriotic as the next man. And second, the charge constituted a particularly nasty form of *guilt by association* in which the opinion of a man's casual associate was judged to be his opinion. As Duffey himself pointed out, we cannot hold a person responsible for the opinions of everyone he ever associated with. To do so surely is to commit the fallacy of *guilt by association.*

2.   *Two Wrongs Make a Right*

Just as it is almost second nature for politicians to attack their opponents by means of *ad hominem* argument, so also it is natural for them to defend themselves against the charges of others by using the fallacious idea that **two wrongs make a right.** The erroneous rationale behind this fallacy is that if the "other side" does it, or some other evil, then it's all right if we do it also.

Here is a rather mild but otherwise typical example, concerning the apparent difficulty the two major political parties have in finding qualified black lawyers to serve as judges in the South:[6]

> Georgia Republicans say they don't know of a single black Republican lawyer who could be appointed to a judgeship. They add smugly that if the Democrats couldn't find a Negro judge in all those years, how can anybody expect the Republicans to find one now?

The fallacy here is setting up the Democrats as a standard of conduct. Past Democratic errors in no way justify current Republican errors. Two wrongs simply do *not* make a right.

An Associated Press dispatch, which attempted to explain the atmosphere in Vietnam before the American massacre of civilians at My Lai 4, contained a more subtle version of the fallacy *two wrongs make a right.*[7]

---

[5]Reported in the *New Britain* (Conn.) *Herald,* September 10, 1970, p. 4.

[6]"Picking Judges in Georgia," *New Republic,* August 15, 1970.

[7]Seymour M. Hersh, *My Lai 4: A Report on the Massacre and Its Aftermath* (New York: Random House, 1970).

In Vietnam the killing of civilians was a practice established by the Viet Cong as a major part of the war long before the first U.S. ground troops were committed in March 1965.

The implication was that if they do it, then it is all right if we do it, too.

When we stop and think, the fallacious nature of such an implication is clear. But in daily life it often doesn't strike us as fallacious, especially when we seem to be giving "them" back nothing but a taste of their own medicine.

But the taste-of-their-own-medicine attitude in these cases is misguided. This would be true even if there were some validity to the "eye for an eye and tooth for a tooth" version of justice, a conception of justice many rational men reject. The babies killed at My Lai, for example, could not have been the same Viet Cong who murdered civilian Vietnamese. The fact that some Viet Cong have engaged in civilian murder cannot possibly justify our doing the same thing. We are not less evil by being copycats.

Senator Robert Dole, then Republican National Committee Chairman, was guilty of *two wrongs make a right* when he defended President Nixon against charges of impropriety in the ITT case. (The charge was that ITT had received favors in an important antitrust suit in return for their huge donation to Nixon's 1972 reelection campaign.) Dole's counterattack was to schedule a news conference to disclose ". . . improper activities involving the Democratic National Convention involving vast sums of money improperly received from big business". Dole hoped his attack would take some heat off Nixon, and it did until the Watergate scandal brought ITT back into the public eye.

Ladislow Dobor, leader of the Brazilian Popular Revolutionary Vanguard was guilty of the fallacy *two wrongs make a right* in his statement concerning the Vanguard's kidnapping of foreign diplomats in Brazil to barter for the release of political prisoners from jail:[8]

We see nothing "unfair" in kidnapping an "innocent person", since the authorities arrest not only revolutionaries but many ordinary people as well.

But the fact that the Brazilian government has engaged in immoral acts does not justify their revolutionary opponents in doing so.

George McGovern was guilty of *two wrongs make a right* in his defense against the charge of 1972 campaign fund impropriety. He defended himself by pointing to many other political campaigns that also ended with bad debts owed to corporations, arguing that no question had been raised about those donations. "Why," he asked, "does this standard practice become an abuse in my campaign?" The answer is that the practice is illegal, and illegal for good reason.[9] Two wrongs do not make a right.

---

[8]Reported in *Ramparts,* October 1970.

[9]As McGovern himself believed, since he favored its illegality. See the *Boston Globe,* July 5, 1974, pp. 1, 8.

This particular variation on *two wrongs make a right* occurs so frequently it has received the special name **common practice.** The fallacy of common practice occurs when an alleged error is defended by claiming that it was after all, just common practice, standard operating procedure, and therefore not to be faulted. But common practice may well be wrong, as it was, for instance, when slavery was commonly practiced in the United States. So mere appeal to common practice is generally fallacious.[10]

Big business executives are guilty of this fallacy when they attempt to justify salaries of over $100,000 per year on the grounds that almost all top executives of large firms are paid such princely sums. So are college professors when they attempt to justify their use of departmental secretaries for private correspondence by pointing out that their colleagues do the same thing.[11] And so are those who reply to vegetarian arguments about the immorality of meat-eating by pointing out that almost everyone eats meat.

The Socialist Workers Party (Trotskyist) has launched a hue and cry for "special measures" to apprehend the persons responsible for the February 4 bombings of their Los Angeles headquarters. The SWP has accused the L.A. police of foreknowledge of the incident, collusion with the CIA, and laxity in performing their investigations. Such a situation is ironic in several respects.

First, it is somewhat out of character for the SWP to be condemning terrorism. Trotsky conducted the infamous "red terror" which allowed Lenin to consolidate power after the Bolshevik revolution; and though the SWP does not find terror to be tactically advisable in the U.S. at the present time, it is affiliated with South American terrorist groups and has no opposition to using terror here in the future when conditions change.

Typical occurrence of *two wrongs make a right.*

---

3.   *Tokenism*

When action is clearly called for but is politically inexpedient, politicians frequently turn to **tokenism.** That is, they make a token gesture (do a very little of what is required) and then shout about it as loudly as they can.

---

[10]The connection between *common practice* (and thus *two wrongs make a right*) and *traditional wisdom* (and thus *appeal to authority*) should be obvious. In *common practice* the appeal is to the authority of established practices, which are generally in conformity to traditional wisdom.

[11]This proves that college professors and business executives are guilty of the same fallacy, but obviously not that their "crimes" are equally serious, any more than a worker's theft of a hammer would rival the theft of millions of dollars by General Electric executives in the famous price-fixing conspiracy.

On May 31, 1970, an earthquake in Peru killed about 50,000 people, and left an emergency of major proportions in its wake. (It is unlikely that so many people have been killed in the United States in all the earthquakes, hurricanes, and tornadoes in our history.) Relief aid was desperately needed by the Peruvians. The American response was a trip to Peru by Mrs. Nixon (widely publicized—a picture of Mrs. Nixon hugging a little earthquake victim appeared on page one in many newspapers around the country). But very little effective aid ever reached Peru from the United States.[12] Clearly, our hearts were not really in the relief venture: the American efforts were only a token gesture designed to pacify the few in the United States who wanted to aid the Peruvians.

The American relief efforts in Biafra, both during and after the Nigerian war, also exhibited this kind of tokenism. In this case, the American government (under both Johnson and Nixon) seemed perfectly willing to relieve the mass starvation in Biafra, but was unwilling to do so against Nigerian objections, and unwilling to exert the pressure necessary to change the Nigerian government's position on relief aid. So the government did the "natural" thing and gave token aid to the church groups, the Red Cross, and UNICEF, the agencies attempting to get food into blockaded Biafra.[13]

The fallacy involved in *tokenism* is this: if you mistake the token gesture for the genuine article, you commit a fallacy. Judging from the lack of complaints from Americans after Mrs. Nixon's visit to Peru, for example, it is reasonable to assume that a great many Americans committed this fallacy at the time.

Professional politicians are not the only ones who attempt to mislead via *tokenism.* Ralph Nader has pointed out that Consolidated Edison of New York paid its board chairman more in one year than it spent on pollution control in five (this was roughly during the period 1965 to 1970). At the same time, General Motors spent about ten times more on advertising per year than it did on pollution research. Its pollution research budget was about 0.1 percent of its gross annual sales.

The token nature of big business and government actions frequently is masked in large-sounding figures. The average American cannot hope to earn a million dollars in an entire lifetime. So when he hears that a large corporation will spend $20,000,000 on antipollution efforts, he is impressed with the apparent size of the venture. He may not notice that the amount is to be spent over a period of years. And he forgets, if he ever knew, that the corporation has yearly sales in the billions, and spends millions per year just on its corporate image. (Indeed, much spending on pollution during the period 1968 to 1975 looked suspiciously like image-building, given the immense fanfare that accompanied each project and the widespread use of antipollution themes in institutional advertising.) The average American forgets also that the federal government's budget now is measured in hundreds of billions of dollars per year.

---

[12]See Roger Glass, *New Republic,* September 19, 1970.

[13]The fact that this token American aid did save thousands of lives, even if only temporarily, is irrelevant to the charge of *tokenism,* in view of the grisly grand total of over one million deaths by starvation.

4.   *Hasty Conclusion*

In many textbooks, the fallacies about to be discussed are set apart from those just dealt with and are characterized as **inductive fallacies.**[14] But this standard division is not very useful. Almost all of the fallacies discussed in this text, including *slippery slope, ad hominem,* and *false dilemma,* are primarily inductive fallacies, for the simple reason that it is rare in daily life to claim deductive certitude for the conclusion of an argument.

The fallacy of **hasty conclusion** is generally described as the use of an argument which presents evidence relevant to its conclusion, but insufficient by itself to warrant acceptance of that conclusion. In a sense, a great many of the fallacies so far considered satisfy this criterion. *Ad hominem* and *appeal to authority* are good examples. But the trouble with *ad hominem* arguments or fallacious appeals to authority is that their evidence is insufficient because *a better kind* of evidence (generally more direct) is available or required. More of the same kind (such as another attack on the man rather than on his argument) would not make the argument any better. Let's restrict the term *hasty conclusion* to fallacies in which the fault is not in the type of evidence but in the lack of sufficient evidence.

A news story on a local flurry of flag-stealing quoted a local citizen:[15]

> They took both the flag and the pole. This just thoroughly demonstrates the lack of law and order.

But all by itself, it just doesn't. In the best of times there will always be some lawbreaking, especially of this minor variety. The evidence *is* relevant, and more like it might establish the conclusion. But taken alone, it cannot possibly do so.

Another example of *hasty conclusion* comes from an article which argued that medical treatment is less and less worth the money.[16]

> . . . increased treatment by . . . doctors . . . has shown steadily declining results. Medical expenses concentrated on those above forty-five have doubled several times over a period of forty years with a resulting 3 percent increase in life expectancy in men.

Does this prove the point? No, the conclusion that we're not getting our money's worth is a bit too hasty. There are all sorts of reasons why life spans might

---

[14]Roughly, the essential property of a *valid deductive argument* is that if its premises are true, then its conclusion cannot be false. In contrast, a *valid inductive argument* provides good but not conclusive grounds for acceptance of its conclusion or, to put it another way, its premises provide good grounds for acceptance of its conclusion but do not guarantee its truth. Here is an example of a valid deductive argument: All politicians are con artists, and Edward Kennedy is a politician, so Edward Kennedy is a con artist. And here is an example of a valid inductive argument: I've contributed to 20 political campaigns so far and never backed a winner, so I guess this contribution I'm about to make to McGovern's campaign will not back a winner either.

[15]*New Britain* (Conn.) *Herald,* October 1970.

[16]*New York Review of Books,* July 2, 1970.

have *decreased* over the last forty years had it not been for the new expensive improvements in medical care. Cigarette smoking, pollution, increased tension, rapid social change, less exercise, and poorer diets are several such reasons. So it may be that doctors have had to fight just to keep us as healthy as we used to be, much less make us healthier. (The argument is a poor one for other reasons also. It fails to take account of the fact that in the last forty years prices have more than tripled. And it overlooks the likelihood that beyond a certain point extremely complicated devices and sophisticated drugs are required to increase a person's life span by even a small amount. But a small increase, and 3 percent isn't all that small, may well be worth the added expense and effort.)

Most of President Nixon's term in office was plagued by both high inflation and unemployment, leading his opponents to pin the negative label "recession" onto then-current economic conditions. (Sometimes the economy was in recession during that period, usually it was not, although growth was slower than during most of the post-World War II period.)

Here is Senator Mike Mansfield, Democrat from Montana, trying, in 1970, to pin the recession label onto the economy:

. . . the country is mired in inflation, unemployment, and war, and . . . whether the term is used or not, these words spell recession.

What he meant was that these conditions *prove* the existence of a recession. But they don't, although rising unemployment is good evidence of a recession. (War, in fact, is indirect evidence, although surely not proof, that an economy is not in recession, since most recent wars have been accompanied by an expanding economy.)

5.   Questionable Classification

Hasty conclusion is a special variety of a wider species we might call **questionable classification,** or **false classification.** The fallacy of *questionable classification* occurs when we classify something incorrectly, given the evidence we have or could have. For instance, Senator Mansfield's classification of the 1969–1970 business slowdown as a recession was a questionable one, since the evidence he presented didn't prove the slowdown warranted that label.

Robert Waters reported in one of his newspaper columns that the U.S. Chamber of Commerce had classified 152 U.S. congressmen as "big spenders" because each of them had voted to override President Nixon's vetoes of four bills he had labeled "excessive spending bills".[17] The four bills, for domestic matters,

---

[17]Robert Waters, "Washington Scene," *Hartford Courant,* September 3, 1970.

appropriated a total of about 2.5 billion dollars more than the 40.5 billion Nixon had asked for.

But the Chamber's classification of these congressmen as "big spenders" was a bit hasty. Many of them had attempted to reduce expenditures for other matters, such as the outer space program, the SST, and ABM, as well as many other military programs. So they weren't necessarily big spenders. They might more accurately have been classified as people who wanted to spend money *differently* than did the Nixon administration. But it would have been politically unproductive to brand them as *spend-it-differently* men, while it was politically expedient to brand them as *big spenders*.

The program of NOW (National Organization of Women—a women's liberation group) once included in its list of recommendations for securing equality of the sexes the proposal that facilities be established to rehabilitate and train divorced *women*. They further recommended that the ex-husbands in question, if financially able, should pay for the education of divorced *women*.

But stated this way, their recommendation exhibited *questionable classification* (to say nothing of female chauvinism). The group in need of rehabilitation clearly was not divorced women, but divorced *persons,* or better yet divorced *homemakers*. For if a man happened to be the partner who took care of the home while his wife earned the bread, surely he would be entitled to help in the event of a divorce just as a woman would in the same situation. Of all groups, NOW, with its concern for equality between the sexes, should not have classified the needy group as divorced *women*.

This is a particularly interesting example of *questionable classification* because the correct and incorrect classes (divorced homemakers and divorced women) are close to being identical in membership. There are relatively few divorced males in the United States who fit the classification divorced homemaker. Close overlap of this kind is frequent when the fallacy of *questionable classification* occurs, and is a major reason why this fallacy is so common.

But it also is a major reason why avoiding questionable classifications is so important. In some areas of the United States, the overwhelming majority of "deprived children" (whatever that means) are nonwhite (whatever *that* means). Deprived children, as a group, do less well in school than nondeprived children. Hence, nonwhites do less well than whites. But to classify backward students as nonwhites leads naturally to the conclusion that their being nonwhite is the *cause* of their backwardness. And we are all familiar with the way in which this conclusion has been used to defend racially segregated schools in the United States.

6.   Questionable Cause

You are guilty of the fallacy of the **questionable cause,** or **false cause,** if you label a given thing as the cause of something else on the basis of insufficient evidence.

The fallacy of *questionable classification* frequently entails *questionable cause,* because we classify partly in order to determine causes. For instance, once we classify slow learners as mostly nonwhite, it is easy to take the next step and conclude that their being nonwhite is the *cause* of their being slow learners.

But even in cases where the *classification* is correct, it does not follow that we have discovered a causal connection; the connection we have discovered may be *accidental.*

Here is an example from the logic-textbook-writer's best friend, Spiro Agnew. He was speaking of Lawrence O'Brien, Democratic Party Chairman who had been Postmaster General under Lyndon Johnson and then became president of a Wall Street brokerage firm after Johnson left office:[18]

> Under his [O'Brien's] adroit management, the firm collapsed, and it is presently being liquidated. Isn't that a splendid credential for a man who would advise the president of his country on economics?

The implication of Agnew's comment is that O'Brien's lack of ability *caused* the brokerage firm to collapse. Now there is no doubt that the classification is correct; O'Brien does belong in the unenviable class of those who have presided over a business firm as it went under. The question is whether this proves that he was unreliable on economic theory or even as a businessman. In other words, the question is whether the firm went under *because* he lacked business ability.

And put this way, the answer is obvious; the conclusion is much too hasty. There are many cases of financial disaster presided over by first-rate business people who have at other times proved their business acumen. The Edsel was one of the biggest financial disasters in American business history. But it would be foolish to conclude from its failure that Henry Ford II, the man who rescued the Ford Motor Company from the brink of disaster after World War II and increased Ford's share of the highly competitive automobile market, didn't know how to run a business.

In addition, Agnew was guilty of the fallacy of *suppressed evidence.* O'Brien's firm went under at a time when brokerage firms as a group suffered great losses. His was by no means the only firm that was forced to liquidate. (Indeed, it is ironic that Agnew should have mentioned the matter, since it was commonly charged at the time that Wall Street's losses were the result of President Nixon's economic measures that were supposed to cure the inflation problem.)

Another *Newsweek* story (August 31, 1970) quotes Charles Morgan, Jr., of the American Civil Liberties Union:

> The Uniform Code of Military Justice is uniform, is a code, and is military—and *therefore* has nothing to do with justice.

---

[18]Reported in *Newsweek,* August 31, 1970.

But even if it's true that "justice" is not what results from actual applications of the Uniform Code of Military Justice, it doesn't follow that the particular features of this code that Morgan cites are the cause of that condition. We know these features alone are not sufficient to *cause* injustice, because there have been other social systems in which enforcement of uniform military codes resulted in a brand of justice at least as good as any other generally available in that culture.

The same article in *Newsweek* contains still another example of the fallacy of the *questionable cause*. It asks concerning the My Lai massacre:

> . . . should the G.I.'s be punished for, in effect, *trying too hard*—by gunning down civilians in a village long sympathetic to the Viet Cong?

Forgetting what might justify the commission of such a massacre, is it reasonable to say that the *cause* of the massacre was too great effort on the part of the soldiers in question? Firsthand accounts of the massacre contradict such a simplistic view.[19]

Statistical fallacies are not discussed until Chapter Four, but let's anticipate a bit and consider one statistical version of the fallacy of *questionable cause*.[20] Dr. K. S. Sitaram, a University of Hawaii mass media researcher, claims that television programs displaying a great deal of violence may *cause* reckless and irresponsible driving. He drew his conclusion after interviewing 293 "bad" drivers (convicted of traffic violations) and 54 "good" drivers, and comparing their tastes in television programs.

But even if bad drivers watch more television violence, this doesn't prove that watching television *causes* bad driving. It may be, for instance, that poor driving and a tendency to watch television violence both are caused by some third element, such as a desire for excitement, so that, say, forbidding bad drivers from watching television violence would have no effect whatever on their driving habits.

7.   *Questionable Analogy*

We reason by analogy for much the same reason that we classify and assign causes, namely to understand and control ourselves and our environment. In fact, analogical reasoning is a common way in which we reason to causes.

In analogical reasoning, we infer from the fact that two or more items share certain *relevant* properties to the conclusion that they will share another property one of the items is known to have already. For example, we might reason from the fact that history courses taken so far have been boring memory ordeals to the conclusion that the course we just signed up for, a U.S. history course, will also be boring.

---

[19]Those who have read no firsthand accounts of the incident will have to rely on the word of this book's author or that of the *Newsweek* writer. Whether in doing so the reader commits the fallacy of *appeal to authority*, given the availability in book form of such testimony, is a question best left to the reader.

[20]*Houston Chronicle*, May 18, 1972.

But analogical reasoning can go wrong in much the same ways as general reasoning about causes. And when it does, the result is the fallacy of **questionable analogy,** or **false analogy.**

It is very difficult to say precisely when analogical reasoning is fallacious, just as it is difficult to determine exactly when any kind of generalization is fallacious.[21] Nevertheless, it's not hard to spot fairly clearcut cases of *questionable analogy.*

A hairdresser, Marc DeCoster, complained that some of his customers tried to save money by shampooing their own hair before getting a DeCoster set:[22]

> Some are trying to wash their hair at home and then ask why I charge them for a shampoo. So I ask them, *do you bring your own salad to the restaurant?*

Spelled out, DeCoster's analogy is this: Washing your hair at home before getting a set at the beauty parlor is like bringing your own salad to a restaurant before eating their roast beef. It would be wrong to bring your salad to the restaurant; so it's wrong to shampoo your hair first at home. Therefore, claims DeCoster, it's not unfair to charge for the shampoo he doesn't give you, when he does give you a set.

But DeCoster's analogy is not apt. Shampooing your hair at home before going to the hairdresser is more like eating your own salad *at home* before going to the restaurant than it is like bringing your own salad to the restaurant to eat there before eating their roast beef. The two cases he considers thus differ in a relevant way. So the analogy fails.

Here is a portion of an article discussing the refusal of a father to reveal the whereabouts of his hippie daughter on grounds that the parent–child relationship should be legally privileged, just as is the husband–wife relationship:[23]

> But should there be such a privilege [contrary to present law]? . . . There is, of course, a counter-argument. As Mr. Schaefer says [Philip Schaefer, New York lawyer who helped draft domestic relations legislation], *"What if the child the parent is protecting is Jack the Ripper?"*

The argument for a special parent–child relationship is an analogical one based on the resemblance between the parent–child and husband–wife relationships. Presumably, Mr. Schaefer favors the special privilege of not having to testify against one's spouse granted in the husband–wife relationship. Yet a husband is just as likely as a child to turn out to be a Jack the Ripper. Mr. Schaefer failed to describe a relevant difference between the two relationships and so failed to show what is wrong with the analogy, which on its face (and in view of other material in the article) has much plausibility. His fallacy might be said to be that of incorrectly rejecting a plausible analogy.

---

[21]For more on this, see Howard Kahane, *Logic and Philosophy,* 2d ed. (Belmont, Calif.: Wadsworth Publishing Co., 1973), pp. 255–257.

[22]*New York Times,* December 12, 1971, p. 57.

[23]*New York Times,* January 3, 1971, p. 6E.

Analogies are used for different purposes, two in particular: (1) to explain; and (2) to provide reasons or justifications for some conclusion. The person who says that, say, the poor in twentieth century America are like the indentured servants of seventeenth century America illustrates the former. The person who says not to bring pornography into her house because that's like bringing in contaminated food illustrates the latter. If you are *persuaded to a belief* by the former, rather than just to a better *understanding* of a point being made, then you reason fallaciously.

In analogical reasoning, we *compare* two or more items with respect to a particular property. So when we use an analogy *fallaciously,* we are guilty of what might be called **faulty comparison.**[24]

A *3-in-1* Oil television commercial pictured a saw oiled with *3-in-1* Oil outperforming an unoiled saw—the intended conclusion being that you should use *3-in-1* Oil on your saws. But the comparison was faulty. It should have shown a saw oiled with *3-in-1* outperforming a saw oiled with some other standard oil brand. Otherwise, all it proves is that oiled saws work better than unoiled ones, not that saws oiled with *3-in-1* Oil work better than those oiled with a competing product. In other words, their faulty comparison gave no "reasons why" you should use their brand rather than another.

Summary of fallacies discussed in Chapter Two

1. *Ad hominem argument.* Attacking the arguer rather than the argument.

   Example: Senator Randolph dismissing women's liberationists as "a small band of bra-less bubbleheads."

   a. *Guilt by association.* Unfairly judging a man by the company he keeps or is alleged to keep.

   Example: Judging senatorial candidate Duffey to be unpatriotic because of something a casual political acquaintance said about patriotism.

2. *Two wrongs make a right.* Just what the name implies.

   Example: The AP report which implied that since the Viet Cong killed civilians in South Vietnam, it wasn't so bad if we did too.

---

[24]*Faulty comparison* is a broader category than *questionable analogy.* But here we can think of them as pretty much the same.

a. *Common practice.* Claiming that something is not wrong, or at least is excusable, because it is commonly done.

Example: Justification of huge salaries on the grounds that all top business executives are paid a great deal of money.

3. *Tokenism.* Mistaking a token gesture, usually ineffective, for an adequate effort.

Example: Accepting General Motors spending of 0.1 percent of its gross annual sales on air pollution research as a genuine effort at pollution control.

4. *Hasty conclusion.* Use of relevant but insufficient evidence to reach a conclusion.

Example: A newspaper's claim that the theft of a flag and a flag-pole "thoroughly" demonstrated a lack of law and order.

5. *Questionable classification.* The incorrect classification of something, given available evidence.

Example: The classification of those congressmen who voted to override the president's veto of some domestic spending programs as "big spenders", although many of these same congressmen had sought to reduce military expenditures.

6. *Questionable cause.* Labeling something as the cause of something else on insufficient evidence, or contrary to available evidence.

Example: A magazine's suggestion that Vietnamese civilians were massacred by American soldiers because the soldiers were "trying too hard", although available evidence suggested a more complex cause of the massacre.

7. *Questionable analogy.* Use of analogy where the cases seem relatively different.

Example: DeCoster's analogy between washing your own hair at home before going to the beauty parlor and bringing your own salad to the restaurant to eat before ordering roast beef.

Exercise I for Chapter Two

Determine which fallacies (if any) occur in the following passages, and state the reasons for your answers.

*1. It's all right for President Ford to impound funds voted by the Congress. Every recent president—Nixon, Johnson, Kennedy—did so. In fact, Nixon did so on a grand scale.

2. *Toni:* Why didn't I get that Indian bracelet for Christmas?
Judy: Because you don't believe in Santa Claus any more, and Santa doesn't bring presents to anyone who doesn't believe in him.

3. Hartford Courant, *December 21, 1970, AP story on Soviet efforts to crush political dissent in Russia:* Minister of Culture Yekaterina Furtseva publicly berated

an American correspondent for "poking his nose into our internal affairs" when he asked a question related to the case of disgraced novelist Alexander Solzhenitsyn. "If you cannot punish the killers of your government leaders, you have no right to be interested in such questions," the [Soviet] culture minister retorted.

*4. *Judy:* The U.S. government is making great strides in alleviating hunger in the United States.
John: Well, it's about time. What's the government doing?
Judy: President Ford appointed a fact-finding commission to study the problem and make recommendations directly to him.

5. *Newspaper story:* Thor Heyerdahl has done it again, crossing the Atlantic in a papyrus raft designed according to ancient Egyptian tomb carvings. Landing in the Western Hemisphere on the island of Barbados, he was greeted by the Barbados Prime Minister, Errol Barrow, who declared, "This has established Barbados was the first landing place for man in the Western world."

6. *UPI story:* Mrs. Martha Mitchell (Attorney General Mitchell's former wife) blames American educators for destroying the country. "They are totally responsible for the sins of our children."

*7. Hartford Courant, *Sunday Parade, August 20, 1972:* [There was] a judge in Salisbury, Rhodesia, who had never driven a car. Someone in his court wanted to know how [he] could rule on motor accidents without firsthand knowledge of driving. "It's really no handicap," the magistrate explained. "I also try rape cases."

8. *Judy:* The philosophy of communal living used to appeal to me. But it doesn't any more.
John: Gee hon, what made you change your mind?
Judy: I got my head out of the clouds and looked carefully at the people selling that communal line.

9. *New Jersey State Attorney George F. Kugler, Jr.,* New York Times, *August 17, 1970:* "I'm not saying there are no abuses." . . . but [he] added that the problem of obtaining justice for poor persons was a problem everywhere in the U.S.

10. *John:* Thank God President Nixon was forced out of office. If he'd been in much longer the Constitution would have been good only for confetti.
Judy: Yes, I'm glad too. That'll show students our system does so work, after all.

11. I would no more permit filthy reading material in my own home than I would serve food from a contaminated kitchen.

12. Of course Patty Hearst's father doesn't understand what his daughter did. He's a millionaire capitalist, isn't he? You must have gone soft in the head to think otherwise.

13. *Anthony Lewis, in his column,* New York Times, *August 1, 1974, p. 29:* Representative John Seiberling, Ohio, House Judiciary Committee, on a motion to recommend impeachment of President Nixon for the secret bombing of Cambodia: ". . . we should not use our impeachment power . . . [when] other presidents have taken the same sort of action and . . . Congress bears a very deep measure of responsibility."

*14. *John:* Get out Dr. Spock's baby book—Norman's sick again.
Judy: Oh no you don't. We're not using that book any more. Did you know that the Dr. Spock who wrote that book is Benjamin Spock, the radical nut who's always demonstrating against the government?
John: No, I didn't realize that. How about using Gesell?

15. *Susan:* Look, we've got Howard Samuels scheduled to appear at the orphans' home from 10:00 to 12:00 tomorrow. But kissing babies is a waste of time. Let's use that time to make some TV spots.
Ted: But campaigners always pose with little kids. It's my decision, and I say he goes to the orphanage.

*16. People who live in glass houses shouldn't throw stones.

17. *Jack Newfield,* Village Voice, *October 1, 1970:* I agree it was unfair the way [Richard] Ottinger was able to outspend Paul O'Dwyer in the primary, but it strikes me as a hollow issue. Any politician who has money will spend it . . . And I didn't hear too many complaints about Lindsay outspending Procaccino in 1969.

18. *Judy:* It's disgraceful how little they pay college teachers. Of course *your* opinion on that subject is worth exactly zilch, given the prejudice of a person of his (O.K., *or her*) own profession. If you were a typist or something, instead of a college teacher, I might listen to you on that.

19. Houston Post, *September 30, 1972:* The U.S. has supported UN economic sanctions against Rhodesia as an alternative to a violent solution to the controversy over independence for the white minority ruled country. We were criticized when Congress exempted from the sanctions our imports of such strategic materials as chrome ore. This act, open and official, gave rise to criticism that we were ignoring the UN sanctions. The fact is that far more extensive trade with Rhodesia has been carried on by industries in other countries whose governments ostensibly observe total embargoes.

20. *John:* You admire my good looks and tall figure, and I appreciate that. But you're always trying to manipulate and dominate me.
Judy (shocked): Why John, what ever do you mean?
John: Well, just a few little examples: We vacation where you want to, play tennis instead of squash, give money to your charities, and even use your brand of shampoo.
Judy: O.K., what brand of shampoo do you like?
John: Now you're talking, lady.

21. *Article critical of President Nixon by Robert W. Dietsch,* New Republic, *September 12, 1970:* Suggestions are piling up on White House desks (not the President's, of course, he keeps his neat).

*22. *Private letter:* The concern for the Japanese killed by atomic weapons at Hiroshima and Nagasaki is misplaced. My brother was killed by the Japanese in the Bataan Death March of World War II, in which the Japanese inflicted terrible punishment on wounded and starving American soldiers. The Japanese are barbarians and don't deserve our concern.

23. *George McGovern's secretary, Kirby Jones, during the 1972 Ohio presidential primary, in response to Senator Henry M. Jackson's criticism that McGovern had supported Henry Wallace for President in 1948 (Wallace was considered "soft on Communism"):* Senator Jackson's attacks on Senator McGovern are just acts of political desperation.

*24. *Presidential press conference, July 1, 1970: Questioner:* Do you feel that in the modern world there are situations when a president must respond against a very tight deadline when he cannot consult with the legislative branch? [The question was general, but in context had specific reference to the incursion into Cambodia, which was taken without prior consultation with the Congress.]
President Nixon: Well, another good example, of course, is the Cuban missile crisis. President Kennedy had a very difficult decision there and two hours and a quarter before he ordered the use of American men to blockade Cuba, he told the Senate and Congressional leaders. I can assure the American people that this President is going to bend over backwards to consult the Senate and consult the House whenever he feels it can be done without jeopardizing the lives of American men. But when it's a question of the lives of American men, or the attitudes of people in the Senate, I'm coming down hard on the side of defending the lives of American men.

25. Houston Chronicle, *August 14, 1972:* . . . McGovern said that the Administration's own documents prove President Nixon knew of a North Vietnamese "signal" that Hanoi was willing to negotiate seriously. McGovern referred to a study put together by presidential aide Henry A. Kissinger in February, 1969, which noted that during the summer and fall of 1968 some North Vietnamese fighting units had withdrawn from South Vietnam. The North Vietnamese withdrawal was "a sign that they were willing to ease off militarily and they were expecting us to respond then with generous offers of negotiation," McGovern said in a televised interview Sunday.

26. *Column by John Cunniff, July 1970:* Do Americans eat well in comparison with other nations? Millions of Americans still have poor diets, but generally speaking most Americans can afford to eat well. In the U.S. and Canada less than 20 percent of all "personal consumption expenditures" are for food. In less developed countries, the figures are much higher.

27. *Nicholas von Hoffman,* New York Post, *October 1, 1974:* The trouble with such propositions [that there was another gunman in the Robert Kennedy murder]

is that . . . they are seldom able to give us much of a clue as to who the "real" killer may be. It is for that reason that nobody has been able to discredit the Warren Commission report. If Lee Harvey Oswald didn't murder President Kennedy, then who did?

28. The universe, like a watch, must have a maker.

29. *Kerner Commission Report (Report of the National Advisory Commission on Civil Disorders), p. 236:* The hostility of Negro parents and students toward the school system is generating increasing conflict and causing disruption within many school districts. But the most dramatic evidence of the relationship between educational practices and civil disorder lies in the high incidence of riot participation by ghetto youth who have not completed high school. Our survey of the riot cities found that the typical riot participant was a high school dropout.

30. *William F. Buckley, Jr.,* The Governor Listeth *(New York: Putnam, 1970), p. 226, explaining how American soldiers could have murdered at My Lai after only a few months in uniform:* [A] society deprived of the strength of religious sanctions . . . hugely devoted to hedonism . . . to an indifference to authority and the law . . . I would contend that [an] . . . explanation for what happened, according to this analysis, is—not Vietnam, but, to reach for a symbol— Berkeley.

31. Hartford Courant, *July 11, 1972, UPI story:* A study completed by four University of Rhode Island researchers shows vitamin E may be a key to the secret of youth. . . . The research team said the vitamin, . . . may be at work normally in humans to prevent aging. Working with a group of experimental rats, the scientists learned animals deprived of vitamin E seem to age faster and even become senile. Dr. Harbrans Lal of URI said that although the aging process is still a mysterious event, an "interesting relationship" had been found in the rats between the lack of vitamin E and old age.

32. *From the* American Sociological Review, *October 1950:* One of woman's most natural attributes is the care of children. Since the ill and infirm resemble children in being physically weak and helpless as well as psychologically dependent and narcissistically repressed, women are also especially qualified to care for the sick.

Exercise II for Chapter Two

Find examples in the mass media (newspapers, magazines, radio, and television) of fallacies discussed in Chapter Two and explain why they are fallacious.

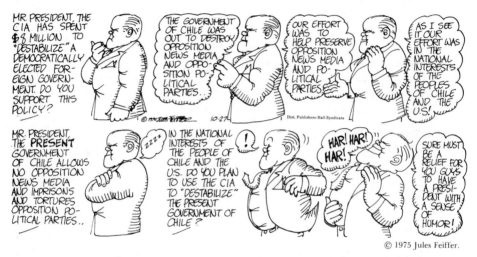

© 1975 Jules Feiffer.

This Feiffer cartoon illustrates an *inconsistency between our words and actions* in Chile. If we say we interfered in Chile at one time to "preserve opposition news media and political parties" then we ought to have been prepared to do so again in like circumstances. We weren't, leading Feiffer to conclude that our stated reasons were window dressing to conceal our real reasons. This is often the case where there is an inconsistency between words and actions, which is why spotting such inconsistency is so important.

Before the Watergate scandal, embarrassing follow-up questions of the kind depicted were considered very bad form, and the few reporters (such as Dan Rather) who asked them were punished in one way or another. (For example, CBS reassigned Rather away from the White House.) As Watergate recedes into the background, the old polite rules are again taking hold.

Chapter Three

Fallacious Even
If Valid

So far, we have considered arguments that are fallacious precisely because they are invalid. But arguments may be fallacious for reasons other than invalidity —even *valid* arguments may be fallacious. Thus we have the fallacy category *fallacious even if valid*.

1. Suppressed Evidence

When arguing, it is human nature to present every reason you can think of that is favorable to your own position, while omitting those that are unfavorable. Nevertheless, anyone who argues in this very human way argues fallaciously. Let's call this the fallacy of **suppressed evidence.** Anyone convinced by such an argument who might reasonably be expected to think of the suppressed evidence can be said to reason fallaciously by way of *suppressed evidence*.

William S. White, the well-known biographer, was guilty of the fallacy of *suppressed evidence* in the following passage about Lyndon Johnson:[1]

> . . . as early as March of 1949, as the very new and junior Senator from Texas with a plurality of less than a hundred votes in his pocket, he [Johnson] had gone on record [against racial discrimination]: "Perhaps no prejudice is so contagious or so unreasoning as the unreasoning prejudice against men because of their birth, the color of their skin or their ancestral background . . ."

Mr. White wanted to portray Johnson as having been a champion of civil rights in 1949, at some risk to his political career. But as I. F. Stone pointed out,[2] White suppressed the fact that the quotation is taken from a speech in defense of a filibuster against civil rights legislation, in which Johnson also stated:

[1] William S. White, *The Professional, Lyndon B. Johnson* (Boston: Houghton Mifflin, 1964).

[2] I. F. Stone, *In a Time of Torment* (New York: Random House, 1964).

I say frankly that the Negro . . . has more to lose by the adoption of any resolution outlawing free debate in the Senate than he stands to gain by the enactment of the civil rights bill. If the law can compel me to employ a Negro, it can compel that Negro to work for me.

Since most of us tend to suppress evidence when it suits our purposes, it is surprising how often we fail to suspect others of doing the same thing. This is true in particular when an argument is designed to misdirect our attention. A series of television commercials extolling Shell gasoline and the ingredient Platformate provides a good example. In these commercials the automobile using Shell with Platformate always obtained better mileage than autos using gasoline without this ingredient. What was the suppressed evidence? Simply that just about every standard brand of gasoline at the time contained Platformate or a similar ingredient. Thus, Shell pitted its gasoline against a decidedly inferior product most auto owners did not use. The viewer's attention was directed away from this fact by the way the claim was worded and also by the general presentation of the commercial.

Experts often trade on our ignorance of or forgetfulness about details in perpetrating the fallacy of *suppressed evidence*. (The person so taken in commits a fallacy only if he should have suspected that evidence was being suppressed.)

The 1969 American Bar Association House of Delegates came out against no-fault auto insurance in part because of:[3]

the moral values which underlie the almost instinctive feeling that persons guilty of wrongful conduct . . . ought to be required to pay.

We should be on our guard when experts argue on matters about which they have a large financial interest (like auto accident lawsuits). In this case, what the ABA hoped you would forget is this: (1) many accidents involve no moral or legal guilt (for example, accidents caused by mechanical defects or "acts of God"); and more importantly (2) the very point of automobile insurance is to spread the risk of accidents, so that the person who has the accident pays no more than anyone else (the insurance company pays, not the person who has the accident). Note also the *ambiguity* in the phrase "wrongful conduct". Our feeling, right or wrong, is that *immoral* wrongful conduct ought to be paid for, not illegal wrongful conduct.

In early 1971, Democrat John Connally, ex-governor of oil-rich Texas, testified before the U.S. Senate Finance Committee concerning his nomination as Secretary of the Treasury. He testified that the allegations of his "vast wealth" in oil and gas were false and that his total wealth in oil and gas was $7240. But when the *New York Times* then revealed that Connally had received money from the Richardson Foundation (set up by the late Texas oil millionaire Sid Richardson),

---

[3]"The ABA: The Rhetoric Has Changed but the Morality Lingers On," *Washington Monthly,* January 1974, p. 23.

Connally admitted he had been paid $750,000 by the Richardson Foundation for services rendered to Richardson's estate.[4]

This example illustrates how a man may attempt to conceal evidence while not actually lying. Connally's original testimony conveyed the impression that he had not profited from his proximity to vast oil wealth. And he managed to convey that impression without committing what is politely called an "error of commission" (that is, he did not actually lie). But his suppression of the very kind of information that he knew his questioners were looking for did amount to an "error of *omission*" (that is, he did mislead by omitting the kind of information he knew the Committee was seeking).

Finally, here is H. R. Haldeman, Assistant to President Nixon, arguing that President Nixon was *not* isolated from public opinion during the demonstrations in Washington against the 1970 American "incursion" into Cambodia:[5]

> . . . President Nixon himself went to the Lincoln Memorial at sunrise on Saturday, May 9, to talk with young people who had come to Washington for that day's demonstrations.

Haldeman conveyed the impression that the president and the "young people" had had a heart-to-heart talk about Cambodia, Vietnam, and foreign policy. But no. The (suppressed) fact is that the President (in what might be called his "Lincoln Memorial Caper") talked mostly about football and surfing.

2. Questionable Premise

The fallacy of the **questionable premise** is simply the fallacy of accepting premises in an argument that are both questionable and inadequately supported.

Until about a week before he resigned from office, President Nixon repeatedly asserted his innocence with regard to the Watergate coverup. He claimed that information he could not then reveal supported him on this. A great many Americans chose to believe him, although under the circumstances they ought to have doubted. They thus committed the fallacy of the *questionable premise*.[6] (Nixon, of course, also committed this fallacy, not because he reasoned fallaciously as did so many in his audience, but rather because he *argued* fallaciously.)

Students often ask how a teacher knew to doubt a particular statement or suspect suppression of evidence. They want to know why *they* often aren't suspicious when they should be. The answer is to be found in the way most of us reason

---

[4]For more details, see the *New Republic*, February 13, 1971.

[5]At U.C.L.A., September 9, 1970. Quoted in U.C.L.A. *Benchmarks*, Summer 1970. Even if the event had happened precisely as depicted by Haldeman, it still would have amounted just to *tokenism*.

[6]This is the fallacy of the *questionable premise* because the conclusion Nixon wanted us to draw is that he should not be forced out of office. (Premise: I have evidence proving I'm innocent. Conclusion: Don't fire me.)

when confronted with new information or arguments. We tend to evaluate the new in terms of what we already know or believe—our background beliefs (including our overall "world view"), as they enter consciousness through the emotional filters of loyalties, desires, and habits.

In the Nixon example, all of these influenced many Americans to believe Mr. Nixon. First, they accepted the "official myth" as to how our political and social institutions function. For according to that myth, presidents do not lie to the American public, except perhaps for very highminded reasons (the point of the George Washington cherry tree myth is to reinforce that idea).

Second, heads of state automatically function as benevolent authority figures. It is as difficult for a person to believe the leader of his nation is a liar as it is for a child to believe this of a parent.

Third, our feelings get bound up with issues and personalities, making it hard for us to be objective. (Gamblers know, for instance, that in a stadium sports crowd you can get better odds betting *against* the home team.) Thus, the feelings of those who voted for Nixon became bound up with his innocence. It's hard, after all, to admit you voted for a liar.

Fourth, we tend to deceive ourselves in ways that favor our own narrow interests. Nixon, like any president, favored certain social and economic interests over others. Selfish desire led some people who had those interests to deceive themselves into believing in his innocence.

Fifth, many tend to hang on to beliefs out of tenacity or loyalty, even in the face of contrary evidence. Some diehard Nixon supporters didn't want to become "quitters" or "fair weather friends", and thus believed the President long after overwhelming evidence of his guilt was available.

And finally, most of us tend to reason as we do (that is, poorly) about these gut issues because of ignorance, lack of training (or poor training), or plain old sloth. Nixon *should* have been doubted because of his past record (think of his inconsistencies over the years on Vietnam) and because of the implausibility of his account of his role in the Watergate scandal. Yet many Americans didn't doubt him, in part because they're not skilled in *critical* reasoning, they're not in the habit of putting two and two together to get four, at least not when thinking about gut political, social, religious or moral issues. For all their formal education, they have not been trained to think critically about these topics.

The person who wants to be an effective, cogent thinker should learn to be on guard against the psychological tricks we all play on ourselves (like self-deception), and try to acquire and use more and better background information (for instance, a good understanding of the mixed quality of human nature). Those who tend to believe what it's comfortable to believe or uncritically accept what they were brought up to believe are the natural prey of rhetorical con artists.

There are several important subclasses of the fallacy *questionable premise.* (Note that these subclasses are *not* mutually exclusive.)

Quotation of the Day

"It's the protection of American personnel. You don't need any more author-ity than that. It's sufficient, it's complete, and total. There should be no question about it." (Secretary of Defense Melvin R. Laird, discussing the authority invoked by the president for the bombing of North Vietnam, in the *New York Times,* April 19, 1972)

Questionable premise: The conclusion was that Nixon had the authority.

---

a.   Unknown fact   The first is the fallacy of the **unknown fact.** This species breaks down further into those "facts" that are more or less *unknowable by anyone* (such as the number of snowflakes that fell in the blizzard of '88) and those that might be known by someone at some time or other but in fact are not known by the person committing the fallacy. Naturally, it is the second category, dealing with things knowable in principle, that is of major interest here.

Here is an example from a political column by John Chamberlain:[7]

> But the Moscow imperialists—and they remain just that—have certain fish to fry, and the continued blockage of the Suez Canal does not consort with the number one Soviet priority, which is to prepare for a possible mortal struggle with the Red Chinese.

Ignoring the likelihood that the Soviets had many other reasons for unblocking the Suez Canal, how could Mr. Chamberlain know the number-one Soviet priority at that time, even supposing the Russians *had* a number-one priority? We have here a clearcut case of the fallacy of the *unknown fact.*

Sometimes the unknown fact is *implied,* but not quite stated. Here is an example from a column by Rowland Evans and Robert Novak:[8]

> Law enforcement authorities have lost the scent of ex-UCLA professor Angela Davis, charged with murder in the San Rafael shootout. Like most of the Weathermen terrorists now being sought, Miss Davis could be almost any-where, shielded by the hippie subculture.

---

[7]John Chamberlain, *New Haven Register,* August 24, 1970.
[8]*Lawrence* (Kan.) *Daily Journal World,* August 24, 1970.

Although Evans and Novak didn't quite assert that Miss Davis was "shielded by the hippie subculture", their implication that this was the case is clear enough. Yet, at the time no one who was talking seemed to have any idea where Miss Davis was; and Evans and Novak provided no evidence that she was being "shielded by the hippie subculture".[9]

Another example of *unknown fact* is furnished by Tom Hayden:[10]

Nixon's promise to withdraw from Cambodia did have a temporary cooling effect, but it also blew away many lingering illusions about peace in Asia. The government had served notice to all but the most blind that its intention was to win the war through escalation—even with nuclear weapons, if necessary.

Obviously Mr. Hayden, of all people, was not privy to one of the most intimate secrets of the Nixon administration (whether that administration would or would not use nuclear weapons). He thus stated something as a fact which he could not possibly have known and hence was guilty of the fallacy of the *unknown fact*.

b.   Questionable evaluation   A perhaps even more insidious species of *questionable premise* is that of the **questionable evaluation,** where what should be questioned is a judgment about *values* (as opposed to facts).

Time magazine was guilty of the fallacy of *questionable evaluation* in its report of a charge made by the National Association for the Advancement of Colored People (N.A.A.C.P.) that the Nixon administration had adopted a ". . . calculated policy to work against the needs and aspirations of the largest minority of its citizens":[11]

One *accurate* assessment of the controversy was offered by former Attorney General Ramsey Clark, who told the N.A.A.C.P. convention that he "hated to believe" that the Administration was anti-black. "It's not that they are aginners," he said, "but rather they are do-nothingers. They are guilty of neglect, not malice."

Time furnished no evidence for its judgment that Mr. Clark's evaluation was "accurate". Yet the question of its accuracy was of great importance at the time in evaluating the Nixon administration on crucial racial issues.

This quotation is interesting because it illustrates how one word (the word "accurate") can be used to slant the viewpoint of a whole article and put the reader into a frame of mind receptive to the writer's message. The fact that only one word was used to do the job makes it all the harder to detect the fallacy.

---

[9]She wasn't, which became evident after her capture.

[10]Tom Hayden, "All for Vietnam," *Ramparts*, September 1970, p. 27.

[11]*Time*, July 13, 1970, p. 11.

In the above example, *Time* at least used an out-and-out value term, the term "accurate". But more frequently the key words express both *facts and values,* thus tending to hide the fact that a value judgment has been made.

Marquis Childs does this in an interesting column in which he writes:[12]

> . . . university [of California] officials estimate that 4,500 [nonstudent hippies] are *holed up in the warrens* along Telegraph Avenue.

The *fact,* shorn of all value tinge, is that university officials estimated that 4,500 nonstudents *resided* along Telegraph Avenue. But written this way, the line loses its power to conjure up an image of students living like rabbits in foul nests along Telegraph Avenue (an image for which Mr. Childs presents no supporting evidence) and thus loses its power to prejudice the reader against the 4,500 nonstudents.

Incidentally, in the next paragraph Mr. Childs makes use of the fallacy of the *unknown fact:*

> Living . . . partly as remittance men and women given an allowance by their parents *on condition they do not come home,* they are an unfailing potential for violence and upheaval.

Again, evidence for the alleged fact is not forthcoming; one suspects that it is the sort of thing about which a newspaper columnist could not possibly have had accurate information.

c.   *Straw man*   A person who misinterprets an opponent's position to make it easier to attack, or who attacks weaker opponents while ignoring stronger ones, is guilty of the fallacy of the **straw man.** Politicians running for office frequently use this fallacy, hoping, of course, that the unthinking will be led to favor them over their opponents. Richard Nixon used *straw man* as the cornerstone of his rhetorical style in every campaign he ever waged. (He usually used it in conjunction with *ad hominem* argument and—as we'll see later—the fallacy of *false dilemma.*)

Nixon always tried to associate his opponents' views with unpopular positions they did not hold (although a tiny handful of their supporters sometimes did). The early Nixon distorted his opponents' positions to make them seem "pinko", or Communist. He even did this in his 1952 campaign for Vice President, when he called the Democratic presidential candidate, Adlai Stevenson:

> Adlai the appeaser . . . who got a Ph.D. from Dean Acheson's College of Cowardly Communist Containment.

Dean Acheson was President Truman's Secretary of State and a fervent anti-Communist. But he had earlier been branded "soft on Communism" by Nixon,

---

[12]Marquis Childs, "Student Revolution Brings a Counter Revolution," *New Britain* (Conn.) *Herald,* August 17, 1970, p. 14.

Senator Joseph R. McCarthy, and others; so in the above quote Nixon was trying to make voters think of Stevenson as soft on Communism also.

In 1950, when he ran for the Senate against Congresswoman Helen Gahagen Douglas, Nixon's speeches and political ads were full of *ad hominem* and *straw man* arguments. Here is an example from a political ad:[13]

> The real import of the contest between Mr. Nixon and Helen Gahagen Douglas is whether America shall continue to tolerate COMMUNIST CONSPIRACIES within our own borders and Government, persist in condoning BUREAUCRATIC PROFLIGACY and appeasing TOTALITARIAN AGGRESSION, or whether America shall victoriously resist these deadly dangers.

The later Nixon played down Communism in distorting his opponents' positions, preferring instead to associate them in the public eye with the views of "radical liberals", hippies, the youth counterculture, and militant left-wing groups like the Weathermen. Here is an example from his acceptance speech at the 1972 Republican Convention:

> Let me illustrate the difference in our philosophies. Because of our free economic system, what we have done is build a great building of economic wealth and might in America. It is by far the tallest building in the world, and we are still adding to it. Now, because some of the windows are broken, they say tear it down and start again. We say, replace the windows and keep building. That's the difference.

The "they" was the radical left; Nixon wanted voters to think the position of his opponent, George McGovern, was just like that of the radical left, because Nixon's version of the radical left position was so easy to caricature and then attack. Nixon rarely mentioned the specifics either of McGovern's program or actual record. The straw McGovern was, after all, such an inviting target.

Why are *ad hominem* argument and *straw man* so powerful in the hands of a skilled practitioner like Richard Nixon? One reason is that voters rarely do the small amount of work necessary to discover that the position attacked is a straw one—a distortion of the position actually held. Those who fail to follow through on the facts are condemned to be easy marks for the clever politicians who hawk *straw man* and other fallacies as their stock in trade.

Here is a simple example that shows how simple the "switch" can be and still be effective—*if* the electorate fails to get the details that make all the difference. This is from a political advertisement:[14]

---

[13]For more on early Nixon campaign rhetoric, see the October 1973 article on Helen Gahagen Douglas in *MS* magazine, and the book *The Strange Case of Richard Milhous Nixon* (New York: Popular Library, 1973) by former Congressman Jerry Voorhis, Nixon's opponent in 1946.

[14]*New Britain* (Conn.) *Herald,* November 4, 1972.

There is a woman running for Congress who voted *against* voluntary school prayers.

> Citizens for Public Prayer
> Rev. Robert G. Howes
> National Coordinator

The switch was quite simple. The school bill voted against would have instituted *compulsory* prayers, which is quite different from permitting voluntary prayers.

Here is an example from a speech by Vice President Spiro Agnew (on a Western congressional campaign trip during 1970) in which the *straw man* was manufactured out of thin air:[15]

> The issue [in the November elections] is whether a free people operating under a free and representative system of government will continue to govern the United States, or whether they will cede that power to some of the people—the irresponsible people, the lawbreakers on the streets and campuses and their followers, the sycophants, and the people who subscribe to their activities behind the scenes, the radical liberals.

The issue Agnew raised was a straw one. There was not the slightest chance that Agnew's "radical liberals" would be ceded power via the 1970 elections for the U.S. Senate and House.

Now, let's hear Al Capp on a remark made by New York Mayor John Lindsay about serving in the Army. Capp quotes Lindsay as saying:[16]

> The Americans I have unending admiration for are the guys who say, I simply will not serve in the Army of the United States and I am willing to take the consequences. Those are the guys who are heroic.

Capp then remarks:

> And so, if Lindsay is elected, his first act as commander-in-chief will, no doubt, be to withdraw the Army from everywhere. . . .

This illustrates the fallacy of the *straw man* because, as Capp well knew, Lindsay was referring to service in *Vietnam;* he was not advocating pacifism in general. (Incidentally, another printed version of Lindsay's comment included the two crucial words, "in Vietnam", that do not appear in Capp's version.)

Here is an example of the successful use of *straw man*. After President Nixon sent ground troops into Cambodia in June 1970, touching off a great deal of

---

[15]The *New York Daily News* used this speech as a "Guest Editorial" on September 12, 1970.

[16]See his column, "Al Capp Here," *New York Sunday News,* August 30, 1970, p. C23.

unrest throughout the country, Princeton University adopted a plan whereby the university would schedule no classes for a short period before the November 1970 elections, enabling students to campaign for political candidates if they wished. For a while, it looked as though the Princeton plan would spread to many other campuses around the country.

Then, Senator Strom Thurmond of South Carolina entered the picture. He attacked the plan and asked the Internal Revenue Service to determine how the plan would affect the tax-exempt status of educational institutions that adopted it.

The result was much agitation and, finally, a report by the American Council of Education which was sent to member institutions around the country warning colleges to be careful about campus political activity which might lose them their tax-exempt status. The report warned colleges against any ". . . political campaign on behalf of any candidate for public office" and stated that a person making a gift to a college would not be allowed a tax deduction if the college violated I.R.S. rules.[17]

All of this made college administrators think twice; very few colleges adopted the Princeton plan. The University of Kansas was one of the schools that did not adopt it (although the plan was well supported on the K.U. campus), and Thurmond's *straw man* seems to have played an important role. The *Lawrence* [Kansas] *Daily Journal World*, June 22, 1970, after quoting K.U.'s Chancellor E. Laurence Chalmers, Jr., to the effect that K.U. would not give time off for political campaigning in the fall, reported that the Kansas Board of Regents had adopted "with the unanimous approval of the chief administrators of the schools" a policy requiring Board approval of all state college calendar changes. This policy, said the *Journal World*, ". . . is designed to protect the tax-exempt status of the institutions, and that status would be jeopardized by partisan political activity".

This incident illustrates an extremely common use of *straw man* in political infighting. Internal Revenue Service regulations prohibit tax-exempt institutions from engaging in *partisan political activity*. But Senator Thurmond knew or should have known that adoption of the Princeton plan could in no sense be considered partisan political activity by a college or university. (Granting students time off for their own political activities no more constitutes partisan political activity than granting students time off for their own religious activities constitutes partisan activity in favor of a particular religion.) Nevertheless, as Thurmond characterized the Princeton plan (his *straw* plan), there was danger of loss of tax-exempt status. This fact came out in the AP article titled "Warning to Colleges", which appeared in the *Kansas City Star* on June 21, 1970:

---

[17]The American Council on Education report received wide press coverage. See, for example, the AP story printed in the *Kansas City Star,* June 21, 1970.

A project linked with Princeton University to help elect doves and defeat hawks in Congress was attacked last month by Senator Strom Thurmond (R.-S.C.). The senator said he would ask the Treasury to investigate.

The result was that colleges across the country reacted to the Princeton plan as though it really were a college project "to help elect doves and defeat hawks" and thus really did constitute a threat to their tax-exempt status.[18] They reacted to Thurmond's *straw man,* not to the true Princeton plan.

The fallacy of the *straw man* is perpetrated by distorting the argument of one's opponent and then attacking that distorted version. However, distortion itself is not necessarily bad or fallacious. In the form of **exaggeration,** for instance, it is a time-honored literary device used by most great writers with satirical or poetic effect. Great satirists, such as Jonathan Swift, have used exaggeration in order to shock people into seeing what they take to be man's true nature, and in an attempt to reduce that strange gap in most of us between mere belief and belief that serves as an impetus to action.

So exaggeration in itself is not fallacious. The purpose of the exaggeration determines whether or not a fallacy is committed. A satirist who exaggerates the evil in human nature doesn't intend us to believe that human beings are as bad as he portrays them. He exaggerates to help us realize the actual extent of human evil. But when his intent is to make us believe that the exaggeration is literally true, then the fallacy of the *straw man* enters into the picture.

Exaggeration can be accomplished easily, with a single word or a short phrase, so it often slips by unnoticed. Here is an example:[19]

Since the beginning of a *massive* airlift on January 23, the United States has flown 113 jeeps and trucks to Nigeria.

The airlift was intended to help overcome the truly *massive* starvation following the collapse of the Biafran attempt to gain independence from Nigeria. Those threatened with starvation numbered in the millions. So the 113 airlifted jeeps and trucks could hardly be said to represent a *massive* airlift in comparison, for instance, with the amount of material flown into Berlin *every day for months* during the Russian blockade of Berlin in 1948. The word "massive" was used to exaggerate the importance of what was in fact a miniscule effort to reduce Biafran deaths by starvation.

---

[18]The more cynically inclined suspected at the time that worried administrators seized on Thurmond's straw man as a welcome excuse for not adopting a plan that was sure to anger already quite angry taxpayers and alumni.

[19]*New York Times,* February 15, 1970, p. 10.

In the case of Richard Nixon, he got where he got by . . . dogged and intelligent perseverance: *ten million* town hall appearances for local candidates over a period of 20 years. (William F. Buckley, Jr., *N.Y. Post,* October 1974)

We don't want to be foolishly strict in labeling items fallacious. Obviously, Buckley did not intend readers to take the ten million figure literally. So he is not guilty of the fallacy of *exaggeration,* although he surely did exaggerate. He used exaggeration to impress on us that Nixon made an unusually large number of appearances for local candidates, and in fact Nixon did do just that.

Finally, here is an example that uses two words to accomplish its deception:[20]

The U.S. government has already demonstrated its willingness to attempt *subtle genocide* in Vietnam under the pretense of waging a "war of attrition".

It is now generally agreed that we killed a great many civilians in Vietnam. But neither Hayden nor anyone else has provided evidence to support the claim that we either attempted or intended to attempt genocide, subtle or otherwise.

d.   False dilemma   The fallacy of **false dilemma,** also called the **either-or fallacy,** occurs when the number of possible positions or alternatives with respect to some question is erroneously reduced.[21] Usually the improper reduction is to just two alternatives (which accounts for the name **black or white** often given to this fallacy).[22]

Here is a newspaper editorial, which manages to commit *false dilemma* and one other fallacy in near-record time:[23]

Alternative?

One suggestion to those who don't care much for policemen is that the next time they get in trouble, call a hippie!

The writer of this editorial is guilty of the fallacy of the *false dilemma* because he implied that those who don't care much for policemen (exactly which policemen is left vague) have as their alternative *no policemen whatever* (the implication of

---

[20]Tom Hayden, "All for Vietnam," *Ramparts,* September 1970, p. 27.

[21]*False dilemma* is a species of *questionable premise* because any statement that sets up a *false* dilemma ought to be questioned.

[22]But the name "black or white" also is used for another fallacy, namely that of failing to distinguish matters of degree correctly; the person who defended American soldiers involved in the My Lai massacre on grounds that civilians always get killed in war is guilty of this fallacy, because he overlooked the *degree* to which My Lai fell short of the goal of no civilian deaths in war.

[23]*Lawrence* (Kan.) *Daily Journal World,* June 25, 1970. Reprinted with permission.

the phrase "call a hippie"). Clearly, there are many other alternatives. London bobbies, who ordinarily carry no weapons, are an example.

False dilemma frequently occurs in conjunction with other fallacies which help set up the false alternative. The hippie–policeman editorial is an example since it also argued against a *straw man*. Lawrence residents who didn't care much for local policemen certainly did not advocate having *no* police whatever; they simply wanted a different kind of policeman (less likely to shoot to kill, for instance). Hence the "no police" position constituted a *straw man*.

The oversimplification inherent in *false dilemma* is a stock-in-trade of most politicians. A recent master of this art is Richard Nixon. One of his frequently used rhetorical strategies was this: use *ad hominem* argument to brand your opponent with a derogatory label (Communist, "pinko," hippie), then use *straw man* to characterize your opponent's *position* as just like that of members of an unpopular group, and finally use *false dilemma* to convince voters the choice is between Nixon's position and the straw position alleged to his opponent. Here is an example of *false dilemma* taken from a Nixon speech on welfare:[24]

> After a third of a century of power floating from the people and from the states to Washington it is time for a new federalism in which power, funds and responsibility will flow from Washington to the states and to the people.

Nixon thus characterized the choice as between two extremes, one championed by his opponent, the other by himself. He overlooked the vast middle ground between the two extremes in which it is overwhelmingly likely the best solution lies. Commented Hinds and Smith: "A reasonable position would suggest that any brand of federalism demands that power, money and responsibility be shared. The situation simply cannot be totally one way or the other." Some power should flow one way, and some the other way, with the balance differing from case to case. (Incidentally, Nixon's characterization of the past third of a century is so oversimplified that it amounts to nothing better than a caricature of the truth. In addition, he failed to mention that for almost one-fourth of that third of a century, he was Vice President under Eisenhower, a president with whom he professed to agree on all basic issues.)

e.   Begging the question   When arguing, it is impossible to provide reasons for every assertion. Some of what we say or do must go unjustified, at least for the moment. But if, in the course of an argument, we endorse without proof some form of the very question at issue, we are guilty of the fallacy generally called **begging the question.**[25] This fallacy is much more common than might be sup-

---

[24]See the article "Nixspeak: Rhetoric of Opposites," *The Nation*, February 16, 1970, by Lynn Hinds and Carolyn Smith.

[25]The fallacy of *begging the question* falls into the category *fallacious even if valid* because arguments that beg the question can be cast into the form p /∴q, or p and q /∴p, both of which are valid. And it falls into the category *questionable premise* because a statement questionable as a conclusion is equally questionable as a premise.

posed; in particular, the radical left and right seem prone to it. Here is an example from the left:[26]

> [Richard Pough, President of the Open Space Institute] . . . was asked what he would have said to a British scientist who pooh-poohed concern over DDT in a recent TV debate [by saying] "Why should we care about the state of penguin fat?"
>
> With soft anger, Pough said he would have reminded the scientist that DDT is in us too.
>
> In contrast, . . . a young marine biologist from Columbia, a student participant in the DDT debate, . . . [said of] the British scientist [, . . . he] "shouldn't be in a position of power and influence."
>
> Another generation. Another answer.

True. But which answer exhibits better logic? Mr. Pough's, because his answer does not *beg the question. Why* shouldn't the British scientist be in a position of power and influence? Because his opinions are incorrect? Surely that is what the marine biologist had in mind. But she failed to provide *reasons* for believing his opinions were wrong, and so she *begged the question* at issue.

Question-begging occurs frequently in disputes between partisans of extremely different positions. Thus, the rejoinder "But that amounts to socialism!" often is heard in disputes over public medical care, even though the other side is perfectly aware of this fact, and may even be attracted to the proposal precisely because it *is* socialistic. To avoid *begging the question,* the antisocialist must present *reasons* for rejecting anything that smacks of socialism.

Similarly, so-called "black militants" frequently speak (without proof) of the "oppression" of blacks when arguing with whites who deny that blacks still are oppressed in the United States. To avoid *begging the question,* they should present evidence of actual cases of current oppression of blacks in the United States.

Almost every political speaker, of whatever stripe, is guilty of at least minor instances of question-begging. Here is an example from a Spiro Agnew speech on radicals and violence given on May 2, 1969, a time of great campus unrest and some violence over civil rights, Vietnam, and other problems of the times:

> Aside from self-claimed romantic charisma, the radical's appeal is highly suspect *in a democracy which responds to the electorate's demands.*

But his radical opponents were vehement in denying that *our* democracy at that time responded to the electorate's demands, exactly the justification they gave for their radical actions.

f.   Inconsistency   The fallacy of **inconsistency** consists in arguing or reasoning from inconsistent (contradictory) premises, or reasoning to inconsistent conclusions. Obviously, if two premises contradict each other, one of them must be false. So even if the argument in which they occur is *valid,* we commit a fallacy in

---

[26]Quoted by Anna Mayo, *Village Voice,* July 30, 1970.

accepting its conclusion. (Similar remarks apply to the case in which we reason to inconsistent conclusions.)

Politicians are famous for being inconsistent, but their inconsistency rarely is overt, explicit, or even exact. Perhaps this is true because politicians rarely speak with enough precision to be 100 percent inconsistent. At any rate, politicians frequently are more or less inconsistent in several different ways. One way is to say one thing at a particular time and place and something quite different at another time and place (without either explaining the change or retracting the former statement).

The following statements by President Nixon on American Vietnam policy illustrate this version of the fallacy of *inconsistency*. He made the first statement on September 13, 1966, while he was out of office and campaigning for Republican candidates before the 1966 congressional elections:

> He [President Johnson] owes it to the people to come clean and tell them exactly what the plans are; the people should be told now, and not after the elections.

But on March 10, 1968, now himself a candidate for President of the United States, Mr. Nixon stated:

> No one with this responsibility who is seeking office should give away any of his bargaining position in advance. . . . Under no circumstances should a man say what he would do next January.

And then on May 8, 1968:

> Let's not destroy the chances for peace with a mouthful of words from some irresponsible candidate for President of the United States.

Famous Lost Words

Washington (AP)—The White House said Monday there may be a need for additional consultations with the North Vietnamese beyond the "one more" negotiating session outlined last month by Presidential adviser Henry A. Kissinger. . . .

The press spokesman [Ronald Ziegler] denied this was a shift from the statement Kissinger made last month in which he predicted that "what remains to be done can be settled in one more session with the North Vietnamese negotiators, lasting I would think no more than three or four days." *(New York Post,* November 14, 1972)

Inconsistency over time (confirmed in the very attempt to deny it).

The Vietnam War also furnishes another famous (and disputed) example of this version of the fallacy of *inconsistency,* this time by President Johnson. During the election year 1964, President Johnson implied, and even appeared to say directly, that if elected he would neither enlarge the scope of the war nor send large numbers of American soldiers to Vietnam to fight. He repeatedly used expressions such as the following (uttered on June 23, 1964):

The United States . . . seeks no wider war.

(But notice the "weasel word": the United States *seeks* no wider war.)

One statement in particular (made on August 29, 1964) became quite famous, and was used over and over in the 1964 presidential campaign:

I have had advice to load our planes with bombs and to drop them on certain areas that I think would enlarge the war and escalate the war, and result in committing a good many American boys to *fighting a war that I think ought to be fought by the boys of Asia to help protect their own land.* And for that reason I haven't chosen to enlarge the war.

But, of course, the Johnson administration did commit a good many American "boys" to fighting in that war. So occasionally it was necessary for the White House to make announcements which in general were *inconsistent* with the above statement. Here is one issued by the White House on February 12, 1965:

On February 11 United States air elements joined with the South Vietnamese air force in attacks against military facilities in North Vietnam used by Hanoi for the training and infiltration of Vietcong into South Vietnam.

These actions by the South Vietnamese and United States governments were in response to further direct provocations by the Hanoi regime.

While maintaining their desire to avoid spreading the conflict, the two governments felt compelled to take the action described above [air strikes on North Vietnam].

A second way in which politicians can be inconsistent and (usually) get away with it results from the fact that large organizations such as governments are composed of many people. Thus the President of the United States can say one thing, while eminent and responsible officials in his administration say (or do) the contrary.

At about the time President Johnson was stressing his policy against enlarging the Vietnam War, his Assistant Secretary of State, William P. Bundy, stated (on June 18, 1964):

We are going to drive the Communists out of South Vietnam even if that eventually involves a choice of attacking countries to the north. If Communist forces get the upper hand in Laos, the only response we would have would be to put our own forces in there.

But, of course, the Democrats have no monopoly on *inconsistency* with regard to Vietnam. On April 30, 1970, Republican President Richard Nixon made interesting use of a third common variety of *inconsistency*, which is to *say* one thing while *doing* another. Here are excerpts from his April 30, 1970, announcement that the United States was sending ground troops into Cambodia:

In cooperation with the armed forces of South Vietnam, attacks are being launched this week to clean out major enemy sanctuaries on the Cambodian–Vietnam border. . . .

He then went on to virtually contradict himself by saying:

We shall avoid a wider war. . . .

An act that widened the war is thus portrayed as one that avoided a wider war.

Nixon used this same technique later, when immersed in the Watergate crisis. While stating publicly that he wanted the speediest possible conclusion to any impeachment process that might be necessary, his lawyer, James St. Clair, was doing everything possible to slow down the action. (Nixon's best hope then was to drag things out to the point of public exhaustion with Watergate.)

Of course, neither Nixon nor St. Clair described St. Clair's public actions as part of a slow-down. But it was obvious to anyone who cared to look that this was almost certainly their intent, and was surely their effect. Yet some Americans failed to put two and two together, even though the evidence of inconsistency between words (Nixon's) and actions (St. Clair's) were staring them in the face. They thus themselves committed the fallacy of *inconsistency*.

Of course, high government officials are not the only ones whose words are inconsistent with their actions. Cigarette smokers who argue against smoking marijuana on the grounds that marijuana is unhealthy are inconsistent in this way. And so are those women's liberationists who argue against different "roles" for each sex yet play the feminine role when it's in their interest to do so (for instance, expecting men to pay on dates, drive on long trips, buy them expensive engagement rings, or spank errant children).

Politicians often are forced by circumstances to commit the fallacy of *inconsistency* when, by rising in office, they come to represent different constituencies with different viewpoints. Similarly, they often commit this fallacy in order to "keep up with the times"; what is popular at one time often is unpopular at another.

Lyndon Johnson's position on civil rights legislation is a good example of *inconsistency* in an effort to keep up with the times. As a congressman and for a while as a senator from Texas, he consistently voted and spoke *against* civil rights legislation. But when he became a power in the Senate his tune modified, and as president it changed completely. Here are two quotes that illustrate Johnson's fundamental *inconsistency over time* on the question of race and civil rights legislation. The first statement was made in 1948 at Austin, Texas, when he was running for the Senate:

> This civil rights program (part of President Truman's "Fair Deal"), about which you have heard so much, is a farce and a sham—an effort to set up a police state in the guise of liberty. I am opposed to that program. I have fought it in Congress. *It is the province of the state to run its own elections.* I am opposed to the antilynching bill because the federal government has no more business enacting a law against one form of murder than another. I am against the FEPC [Fair Employment Practices Commission] because if a man can tell you whom you must hire, he can tell you whom you cannot employ.

But in 1964 Johnson was President of the United States. He had a larger constituency, and, more importantly, the average American's views on race and civil rights had changed. In that year Congress passed an extremely important civil rights act *at his great urging.* And in 1965 he delivered a famous speech at the predominantly black Howard University, in which he said in part:

> . . . nothing in any country touches us more profoundly, and nothing is more freighted with meaning for our own destiny than the revolution of the Negro American.
>
> In far too may ways American Negroes have been another nation; deprived of freedom, crippled by hatred, the doors of opportunity closed to hope.
>
> In our time change has come to this nation, too. The American Negro, acting with impressive restraint, has peacefully protested and marched, entered the courtrooms and the seats of government, demanding a justice that has long been denied. The voice of the Negro was the call to action. But it is a tribute to America that, once aroused, the courts and the Congress, the President and most of the people, have been the allies of progress. . . . we have seen in 1957 and 1960, and again in 1964, the first civil rights legislation in this nation in almost an entire century.
>
> As majority leader of the United States Senate, I helped to guide two of these bills through the Senate. And as your President, I was proud to sign the third. And now, very soon *we will have the fourth—a new law guaranteeing every American the right to vote.*
>
> No act of my entire administration will give me greater satisfaction than the day when my signature makes this bill, too, the law of this land.

And on August 6, 1965, he did sign the Voting Rights Act into law. But he did not explain why it was no longer ". . . the province of the state to run its own elections". He did not explain his about-face on civil rights legislation.

Andy Capp by Reggie Smythe, © 1974 Daily Mirror Newspapers Ltd.
Courtesy of Field Newspaper Syndicate.

Humorous use of *inconsistency between words and actions.*

During the hearings held before President Ford's confirmation as Vice President, he was asked: "If a President resigned his office before his term expired, would his successor have the power to prevent or to terminate any investigation or criminal prosecution charges against the former President?" His reply was: "I do not think the public would stand for it," a clear indication that he would not use such power.

And then, eleven days before issuing the pardon, when asked if he intended to pardon Mr. Nixon, he replied that until legal procedures had been undertaken, ". . . I think it's unwise and untimely for me to make any commitment."

In the absence of an explanation of his change of mind, it's clear that President Ford was guilty of the fallacy of *inconsistency* when he pardoned Richard Nixon.

It is important to remember that in everyday life the fallacy of *inconsistency* is rarely encountered in its purest form. There are many degrees of inconsistency and many ways in which its occurrence is veiled. Everyday talk is usually not sufficiently precise to enable the listener to say positively that the fallacy has been employed.

In discussing the American effort to put a man on the moon, President Kennedy addressed himself to the question of *why* we should engage in such an effort. One of his answers was this:

We have vowed that we shall not see it [space] governed by a hostile flag of conquest, but by a banner of freedom and peace.

But in that same speech, as I. F. Stone pointed out, President Kennedy also said:[27]

. . . there is no strife, no prejudice, no national conflict in outer space.

This is *not quite* inconsistent with his first remark. But it comes so close that the two remarks can be considered to be inconsistent for all practical purposes.

---

[27]*I. F. Stone's Weekly,* September 24, 1962.

Now, consider this newspaper account of starvation in Biafra following the Biafran defeat by Nigeria:[28]

> Doubt is expressed by several experts involved in relief work that the new government of East Central State [in the region formerly Biafra] can take on the job [feeding and medical care of three million war-weakened Ibos—the Ibos being the largest ethnic group in Biafra]. . . .
>
> Although Biafra's secession came to an end in January and starvation no longer is a serious threat, hardships prevail because many people lack money to feed themselves, the experts say.

As it stands, the statement is not inconsistent. But when we add the simple fact that free food was generally unavailable (there were almost no reserves, and, as suggested in the article, relief agencies were not able to feed all of those in need), we do arrive at what is at least close to a contradiction, namely that "starvation is no longer a serious threat" although *sufficient conditions* for it exist.

One last word on this all-important fallacy. We are *all* inconsistent to some degree at some time or other. Even those (for instance philosophers) who spend a lifetime on some systematic program usually fail to root out a particular kind of inconsistency that occurs quite frequently (usually unnoticed). It's very difficult for most people to face this sort of inconsistency, which arises roughly as follows. We all appeal from time to time to a stock of individually very plausible general principles which unfortunately are inconsistent when taken together. It often happens, then, that if we want to do some action A, we appeal to one plausible principle, while if we want to do B, we appeal to another. That the two principles are inconsistent generally is not noticed.

For instance, many of those who applauded the pardon granted President Nixon on grounds of compassion were absolutely against amnesty for Vietnam draft evaders on grounds of the general principle of equality before the law. At the same time, some who felt that amnesty should be granted on grounds of compassion were opposed to Nixon's pardon on grounds of equality before the law. In both cases, inconsistent principles were appealed to, for we cannot make exceptions to the principle of equality before the law and still uphold it.

When two initially plausible principles contradict each other, one principle may not be as plausible as the other and can therefore be overridden. Or, it may turn out that both principles can be retained by *qualifying* them in some way. Thus, we might hold on to both of the principles just mentioned—compassion and equality before the law—by qualifying the equality principle to say that in all cases of a certain kind (for instance, when the law is broken as a moral protest or to avoid immoral actions) the principle of compassion takes precedence. This second way to avoid inconsistency often is the right but more difficult way—difficult because it is usually hard to discover an *acceptable* noncontradictory blend of initially plausible yet contradictory principles. But no one ever said cogent thinking is easy.

---

[28]*Kansas City Star,* June 28, 1970.

ABORTION PASTORAL

VARIATIONS ON A THEME

Few of the many comments on the unfortunate contrast between the strong stand of American bishops on the matter of abortion and their silence on the question of Vietnam have been as striking as that of one priest of the archdiocese of New York. After reading from the pulpit Cardinal Cooke's pastoral letter marking Right-to-Life Sunday and preaching on its contents, the priest added that "respect for life in one direction demands respect for life in another." He reread the letter with only slight modifications such as those below. He made no other remarks, nor were any necessary.

My Friends in Christ:

Today, America needs to be reminded of the guiding principles upon which it was founded. Respect for all human life is fundamental to our national existence. In recent years, however, we have seen a steady erosion of respect for life in our society. .

The ~~New York State Abortion Law of 1970~~ *war in Vietnam* has drawn our society far down the road to open contempt for human life. Since I wrote to you on behalf of the Bishops of the State last December, we have seen the situation grow worse daily. New ~~abortion clinics~~ *fronts* have opened with increasing frequency. Both as Catholics and as citizens we must speak out against this tragedy of ~~abortion~~ *war*.

Some say that Catholics should not speak on this issue. "~~Abortion~~ *The war* is only a ~~social~~ *political* matter," they claim; "religion should not enter into it." Such a position disenfranchises men of certain religious convictions. It says, in effect, that certain citizens may not have a voice on particular issues.

Anyone who is convinced, be he Catholic or not, that ~~abortion~~ *the war in Vietnam* is an attack on human life has the right and the duty to say so. Every human person is a member of society and has a serious social responsibility to shape the values of that society as they are expressed in its laws.

~~In New York State,~~ we have moved far beyond a mere debate on personal values. ~~One hundred thousand unborn children~~ *Hundreds of thousands of lives* have been destroyed in ~~New York alone. New York is already the abortion capital of the nation.~~ *Indochina.*

Not only Catholics, but men and women of many diverse religious backgrounds believe that, by the ~~Abortion Law of 1970, New York State~~ *war in Vietnam, the United States* has alienated what the Declaration of Independence calls the "inalienable" right to life.

We urge each person, young or old, who believes in the right of every ~~child to be born~~ *person to life*, to enter the public forum and work for the ~~repeal~~ *end* of this tragic ~~law~~ *war*.

There are bills in ~~Albany~~ *Congress* right now that would stop this slaughter of the innocent ~~unborn~~. I suggest that you write, phone, telegraph and speak to all our ~~state's~~ *nation's* lawmakers and make your support of life known to them in a very clear manner.

I join in prayer with you that the tragedy of ~~abortion~~ *the war in Vietnam* may be removed from our society.

Faithfully yours in Christ,
TERENCE CARDINAL COOKE,
Archbishop of New York

From *Commonweal*, May 14, 1971. Reprinted by permission.

Selective use of principles constitutes a kind of inconsistency. In the above case, Cardinal Cook argued against abortion on grounds that it is "an attack on human life". But the cardinal did not argue against the Vietnam war on these grounds, even though it too was an attack on human life.

3.   *False Charge of Fallacy*

At this point, let's digress for a moment in order to clear up an important point that may be bothering many readers. When a person makes a statement at one time and a contradictory statement later, he is not automatically guilty of the fallacy of *inconsistency;* he may have rational grounds for changing his mind.

Take the person who argues, "I used to believe that women are not as creative as men, because most intellectually productive people have been men; but I've changed my mind because I believe now (as I didn't then) that *environment* (culture, surroundings), and not native ability, has been responsible for the preponderance of intellectual men." Surely, he (or she!) cannot be accused of *inconsistency,* since he (or she) has presented new evidence to explain the change in opinion.

The trouble in the above Johnson and Nixon examples is that neither man ever explained *why* his statements changed from one time to another or even *admitted* that they had changed, for they wanted to play both sides of the street as much as possible.

In contrast, consider the charge that the philosopher Bertrand Russell was guilty of *inconsistency.* Soon after World War II, he advocated attacking the Soviet Union if the Russians failed to conform to certain standards, and yet in the fifties he supported the "better Red than dead" position.

Russell *would* have been guilty of *inconsistency,* were it not for the fact that he had, and stated, what he took to be good reasons for changing his mind about how to deal with the Russians. He felt, and stated, that Russian acquisition of the atomic bomb made all the difference in the world. Before they had the bomb, he believed it to be rational to deal with them in ways that became irrational after they had acquired such great power. Hence, Russell was not guilty of the fallacy of *inconsistency.*

On the contrary, it is his critics who are guilty of a fallacy, which we might as well call the **false charge of fallacy.** For it is fallacious to charge an opponent with being inconsistent *merely* because he has changed his position.[29]

Summary of fallacies discussed in Chapter Three

1. *Suppressed evidence.* The omission from an argument of known relevant evidence (or the failure to suspect that relevant evidence is being suppressed).

   Example: The failure of Shell Platformate commercials to indicate that all other standard brands of gasoline contain the ingredients of Platformate.

2. *Questionable premise.* The use of questionable evidence to reach a conclusion.

   Example: President Nixon's many statements from June 1972 to the time of his resignation that he had no part in the Watergate coverup.

---

[29]The cases of *false charge of fallacy* dealt with here are examples of false charges of *inconsistency;* but any unjustified charge of fallaciousness, whether of *inconsistency, begging the question, straw man,* or whatever, can be said to constitute a *false charge of fallacy.*

a. *Unknown fact.* The use or acceptance of questionable evidence about matters of fact.

   Example: Tom Hayden's statement that President Nixon would use nuclear weapons in Vietnam if all else failed to win the war.

b. *Questionable evaluation.* The use or acceptance of doubtful statements about values.

   Example: Time magazine's unsupported statement that Ramsey Clark's assessment of a racial controversy was "accurate".

c. *Straw man.* Attacking a position similar to but significantly different from your opponent's position.

   Example: Senator Thurmond's attack on the so-called Princeton plan as a project "to help elect doves and defeat hawks in Congress".

   (1) *Exaggeration.* Distortion by exaggeration.

   Example: Characterizing the sending of 113 jeeps and trucks to Nigeria as a "massive airlift".

d. *False dilemma.* Erroneous reduction of alternatives or possibilities, usually a reduction to just two.

   Example: The editorial that implied we have a choice between two alternatives—police as they are and hippies (that is, no police at all).

e. *Begging the question.* Failure to support the very question at issue.

   Example: The student's response to a scientist's unconcern about the harmful effects of DDT: "He shouldn't be in a position of power and influence," which implied the begged conclusion that the scientist was wrong to be unconcerned.

f. *Inconsistency.* The use or acceptance of contradictory statements to support a conclusion or conclusions. These statements may be presented (1) by one person at one time; (2) by one person at different times (without explaining the contradiction as a change of mind and providing evidence to support the change); or (3) by different spokesmen for one institution. It also is committed by someone who *says* one thing but *does* another.

   Example: Lyndon Johnson's stand on racial questions as a candidate for the U.S. Senate and his stand on racial questions as President of the United States.

3. *False charge of fallacy.* Exactly what the name implies.

   Example: The charge that Bertrand Russell was inconsistent in advocating the use of force against the Russians at one time, while adopting a "better Red than dead" position at another; Russell explained this switch several times as being due to changing circumstances, and thus he was not guilty of a fallacy.

Exercise I for Chapter Three

Determine which fallacies (if any) are committed by the following, and explain why you think so.

*1. *Joan:* Most men who have never been married are obsessed with sex.
Eugene: Oh? I don't know.
Joan: Well, I do, because I know all bachelors are.

2. *Governor George Wallace of Alabama:* Now this busing. I said many years ago, either we stop the federal takeover of schools or there'd be chaos. Well, what've we got? Chaos.

3. *Judy:* We shouldn't do away with the death penalty.
John: Why not?
Judy: Because we need it as punishment when someone takes a human life.
John: That needs explanation.
Judy: Oh, honey, you're just teasing me. You know anyone who takes a human life *deserves* to forfeit his own life as punishment.

*4. *William F. Buckley, Jr.,* The Governor Listeth *(New York: Putnam, 1970):* The Beatles are not merely awful, . . . they are God-awful. They are so unbelievably horrible, so appallingly unmusical, so dogmatically insensitive to the magic of the art, that they qualify as the crowned heads of anti-music. . . .
[Several paragraphs later] Suddenly . . . riding in the back of the car, you look up, startled. That was *music* you just heard, blaring out of the radio. . . . not long after, you hear it again . . . and you realize, finally, that indeed, rock is here to stay.

*5. *Political comment:* Liberals have been consistent on Interior Secretary Walter Hickel. They disapproved of his appointment *and* his removal.

6. *Judy:* I wouldn't vote for him for less than a hundred bucks.
John: Why not?
Judy: He wants to legalize pornography, and I'm not about to let *my* children see nothing but sex films at the Elgin, look at lewd photos in shop windows, and read dirty books in their school libraries.

7. *Teacher:* I said I'd have the exams by today, but I'm not finished grading them.
Student: Good. We're even. I haven't finished Chapter Three yet either.

8. *Soviet sociologist Geunadi Gerasimov (quoted in* Village Voice, *May 5, 1975, p. 19):* . . . communism will replace capitalism because private ownership of the means of production is obsolete.

9. a. *Spiro Agnew, Cleveland, Ohio, June 20, 1970:* We are not going to heed the counsel of the Harrimans and Vances and Cliffords [important Democrats], whom history has branded as failures. . . .

b. *Lawrence O'Brien, Democratic National Chairman, Washington, D.C., in reply to the above:* You'd think that of all people, Mr. Agnew would know the difference between a donkey and an ass.

*10. *John:* Capitol Federal is the best place to keep your money, because their deposits are insured by an agency of the federal government.
Judy: Yes, I know. That's why I wouldn't put my money anywhere else.

11. *Radio announcer:* President Nixon today announced another troop withdrawal of 25,000 men from Vietnam, and pointed out that he would continue to confound his critics by continuing his scheduled withdrawal of troops. He also reemphasized the importance of our defense of the Saigon Government, pointing out that the prestige of the United States is at stake: We simply cannot afford to let the Communists take over in Vietnam.

12. *Editorial,* Hartford Times, *September 11, 1970, on the topic of an extra twenty minutes of school time for teachers; the extra time was objected to by the teacher's union:* Insisting that teachers be in school [twenty minutes] longer than children may seem to some teachers like a factory time-clock operation, but it probably troubles the conscientious teacher far less than those who leave school at the final bell.

13. *Al Capp, in his column,* New York Daily News, *September 13, 1970:* Mayor Lindsay of New York and Senator Ribicoff of Connecticut are usually in perfect agreement on such issues [as] that college students are forced to blow up buildings and people because Spiro Agnew is so mean to them, and that looters and arsonists are blameless: it's the police who are sent in to save the community from them who cause all the trouble.

14. Time, *July 13, 1970 (in a story on President Nixon's white paper on the Cambodian invasion, in which* Time *agreed that Nixon was right to have invaded Cambodia):* He [Nixon] claimed convincingly that U.S. and South Vietnamese troops had (1) conducted an effective military operation, (2) captured or destroyed a substantial amount of enemy supplies, (3) diminished any immediate threat of a major enemy assault on the Saigon area from sanctuaries in Cambodia, and (4) complicated Hanoi's problem of resupplying its troops.

15. *Explanation of why Senator McGovern went from about even to approximately 20 percent ahead of Senator Humphrey in the 1972 California primary:* One factor is that McGovern was on the rise; he had momentum.

16. *Editorial,* Hartford Courant, *September 1, 1970:* The United States Senate is scheduled to vote today on the Hatfield-McGovern amendment that would set a timetable for closing out the war in Vietnam. . . . [The Senate is] being asked . . . to invade the rights and responsibilities of the executive branch of government. Whether the Senate enjoys it or not, the President is the Commander in Chief of armed forces and so designated in the Constitution.

17. *Column by James J. Kilpatrick, September 1970:* . . . A revulsion against the temporary may create a vast market for things that endure. A society gorged upon sex may rediscover love.

*18. *Rowland Evans and Robert Novak in a political column, August 1970, on Hanoi's opposition to Mideast ceasefire proposals and the Soviet-West German treaty; the statement was used later in drawing further conclusions:* Apart from again revealing their ideological differences with Moscow, the North Vietnamese are venting morbid premonition in Hanoi that the Kremlin may yet forcibly end the Vietnam war short of total victory.

19. New Britain [*Connecticut*] Herald, *October 15, 1970:* Manchester Mayor Nathan Agostinelli . . . seized a demonstrator's flag Monday when President Nixon was in Hartford and stomped on it. Nixon, according to published reports, sought Agostinelli out and praised him for his actions.

20. New York Times Magazine, *August 30, 1970:* The new constitution foisted on Japan by the U.S. after WW II contained a "no war" clause, forbidding Japan to rearm. But [General Douglas] MacArthur, himself a principal architect of the Constitution, restored the Japanese army, calling it first a "National Police Reserve", and then "Self Defense force".

21. Houston Chronicle, *December 1972, in an editorial, "Farmers are a Source of Strength":* [C. G.] Scruggs [of the Progressive Farmer magazine] is of the opinion that when Russia and China became aware of their impending food shortages and knew that they would have to buy from the United States, this could well have been the clincher that persuaded them to start disengaging from the North Vietnamese cause.

22. Although China gave idealistic reasons for their veto of the entry of Bangladesh into the U.N., their real reason was to maintain power in Pakistan.

*23. *John F. Kennedy:* Why, some say, the moon? Why choose this as our goal? They may [as] well ask why climb the highest mountain? Why thirty-five years ago fly the Atlantic? Why does Rice play Texas?

*24. *David Ogilvy in* Confessions of an Advertising Man *(New York: Atheneum, 1963), p. 32:* I always showed prospective clients the dramatic improvement that followed when Ogilvy, Benson and Mather took accounts away from old agencies—"in every case we have blazed new trails, and in every case sales have gone up." [The period referred to was roughly the post-war period 1946 through 1962.]

25. People who want us to negotiate an end to the Vietnam war must want a Communist takeover there. After all, in war there can be only one winner. If we don't win, then the other side must.

26. *Judy:* I'm against capital punishment.
    John: Why? It deters people from committing serious crimes, doesn't it?
    Judy: Well, I don't know if it does or doesn't. All I know is that murder, under any circumstances, is wrong.

*27. All those people who rant and rave against Detroit and the automobile don't know what they're talking about. One-eighth of the economy rests on the auto in one way or another. So if we did away with automobiles, we'd have a depression that would "curl your hair". And imagine the terrible bus, train, and subway crushes. But I trust the American people. They won't go for any crazy plan to abolish cars. They'll prefer what we have now, for sure. Don't sell that G.M. stock yet.

28. *Television interviewer:* What makes you think 18-year-olds are qualified to vote? *Eighteen-year-old:* Have you looked lately at the hacks older adults have voted into office?

29. New York Times, *March 10, 1972, story on the alleged bribe involved in the I.T.T. $400,000 contribution to the 1972 Republican National Convention:* Inquiry here indicates that, although there may be no actual "rejection" of the I.T.T.-Sheraton commitment—since that might be construed as a confession of guilt and wrongdoing—Republican party leaders in Washington are urging the local fund raisers and convention planners to "get out from under" the I.T.T. arrangement as quickly as can be done.

30. *Nutrition expert Frederick Stare, answering the charge that flaked dry cereals—Wheaties, Corn Flakes, and the like—are not sufficiently nutritious* (New York Daily News, *August 5, 1970):* Stare said cereals with milk "provide approximately the same amount of protein and calories as a bacon-and-eggs breakfast. And they also provide substantially more calcium, riboflavin, niacin, thiamin, and iron and substantially less saturated fat. . . . Popeye's spinach doesn't begin to compare with the over-all nutritional worth of breakfast cereal—any cereal. . . ."

31. [*Texas*] Advocate, *December 7, 1972, story on proposed "shield law" granting reporters immunity from prosecution if they refuse to reveal their sources to the police or courts:* Contempt of court is a crime for an ordinary citizen. Since it is a crime for every citizen, it ought to be a crime for a news reporter who refuses to disclose his sources to a court which has subpoenaed him.

*32. *George Meany, American Federation of Labor President,* New York Times, *August 31, 1970:* To these people who constantly say you have got to listen to these younger people, they have got something to say, I just don't buy that at all. They smoke more pot than we do and if the younger generation are the hundred thousand kids that lay around a field up in Woodstock, N.Y., I am not going to trust the destiny of the country to that group.

*33. *John:* I can prove to you that some sound arguments are invalid. *Judy:* How? *John:* Well, some sound arguments—not many, of course—have inconsistent premises. But since all sound arguments are not only valid but must have true premises, it follows by the rules of logic that some sound arguments (again only a few) are invalid. *Judy:* No one else is as brilliant as my John.

34. *Evans and Novak column:* More serious, however, was [University of Michigan President Robben] Fleming's acceptance of a 10 percent Negro enrollment goal, the major demand of the March student strike. Substantive arguments against the 10 percent quota . . . are formidable. To raise black enrollment from the present 3.5 percent would leave precious little in scholarship funds for poor white students.

35. *House Appropriations hearings on the 1971 supplemental, pp. 609–610, released December 8, 1970. Reported in* I. F. Stone's Bi-Weekly, *December 28, 1970:*
    Congressman Frank T. Bow, Republican, Ohio: How did this so-called leak get out with regard to Kent State?
    FBI Director, J. Edgar Hoover: That did not come from the FBI. But it did cause me great concern. The first time I knew of it was when the *Akron Beacon-Journal* had a great headline—it is part of the Knight chain of newspapers—saying "FBI: No Reason for Guard to Shoot at Kent State." I knew this was untrue. We never make any conclusions. . . . There were certainly extenuating circumstances which caused the guard to resort to the use of firearms. Perhaps they were not as completely trained as they should have been, but certainly some stated they feared for their lives and then fired; some of the students were throwing bricks and rocks and taunting the National Guardsmen.
    Congressman Bow: Do you mind this being on the record?
    Hoover: Not at all.

36. Houston Chronicle, *September 18, 1972, editorial on minority group quotas:* . . . hasn't there been previous discrimination because of race, sex, religion, or age which was just as unfair [as quotas] and should be corrected? Certainly. Can correction be effectively accomplished without some form of quota-like pressure? Probably not. . . . But eventually the nation is going to have to settle on the only really true answer—a free and open competition for whatever is at stake. That may be idealistic and might require a lot of people's thinking to change, but it is the only workable solution. Enforced quotas, in whatever situation and by whatever else they are called, will create more problems and more injustice than any virtue they can claim.

37. *Judy:* I love you John, you handsome dog, but it's too bad you're not religious, like me.
    John: I'd believe in God, go to church, and all that, if you could give me one good reason for thinking there's a God.
    Judy: Oh? Well how about this: Millions of people go to church every week and worship God. Right?
    John: Right.
    Judy: Well. He couldn't be worshipped if he didn't exist, could he?
    John: Hmm. Let me think about that one for awhile.

38. A magazine article (*New Times,* May 30, 1975, p. 13) on the Catholic Church reported its efforts to reduce the divorce rate among Catholics by instituting rules that prospective couples must satisfy to gain the Church's blessing for their marriage. A church spokesman stated that the right to marry is a

natural right, but restrictions are justified when the proposed marriage "poses a threat to the common good of society".

*39. *Senator Jacob Javits, New York, October 5, 1971, on Senator Mike Gravel's amendment to cut off funds for bombing Indo-China:* I have decided to vote against the amendment [which he then did], because on balance, I think it would be a mistake to single out this one aspect of U.S. military activity in Indochina. . . . I want to make it clear that my decision to vote against the Gravel amendment in no way lessens my deep, anguished concern over the continuing ravage being rained on civilians throughout Indochina through the massive U.S. bombing program. I want this war to end now.

40. *Thomas A. Porter, Dean, School of Arts and Sciences, Central Connecticut State College, in a November 1970 report titled "School of Arts and Sciences: 1970–1980":* Each department of the school should begin at once to plan how to utilize various instructional patterns and/or new instructional techniques so as to make quality instruction available to all students who seek it. The problem of closing students out of classes which they want and need can only become more serious as our enrollments increase. Efforts in this direction by departments may include the creation of large lecture classes (not always at the lower division level) and utilization of TV, auto-instructional labs, and other technological aids. It can be argued, of course, that this approach sacrifices individual communication between faculty and student and dehumanizes education. On the other hand, nothing sacrifices communication so much as being closed out of a class entirely.

41. *From a student exam:* If you ask whether *all* men have free will, I would say "no". But there are exceptions. It is up to the individual and solely the individual whether he does or doesn't have it.

42. *Naval Investigative Service director, reported by AP, January 3, 1971:* A Naval Investigative Service office will not initiate any investigation . . . when the prediction [predication? provocation?] for the investigation is mere expression of views in opposition to official U.S. policy. . . . Nothing herein is intended to inhibit or preclude normal reporting of information . . . on those individuals whose expressed controversial views may be adjudged to have a potential for embarrassment to the Department of the Navy.

43. *Judy:* Well, if he isn't a Communist, why is one of his friends a Communist?
John: Gee, I don't know. But did you know that President Nixon claimed to be a friend of Nikita Khrushchev, who certainly was a Communist?
Judy: So what? You don't judge a book by it's cover, do you?

*44. *Advertisement showing U.S. flag, below which is written:*

Made in Japan

Has your job been exported to Japan yet?
If not, it soon will be.
Unless you buy the products of American workers who buy
from you. . . .

45. *Testimony before the Senate Foreign Relations Committee, November 24, 1970, and reported in* I. F. Stone's Bi-Weekly, *December 14, 1970:*

Senator Church: What do you expect the bombing will accomplish?

Secretary Laird: The bombing, I think, will stop the violation of these understandings [that the United States could fly unarmed reconnaissance planes over North Vietnam unmolested].

Church: Has the bombing in the past ever caused the enemy to acquiesce in our demands or to make concessions?

Laird: Yes it has.

Church: It has? When did it have that effect in the past?

Laird: Well, the last protective reaction flight [i.e., bombing] that was flown in the North was in May, and after that strike there was an indication by the other side that they would abide by those understandings, and they did until the month of November when they shot down an unarmed reconnaissance plane. . . .

Church: Was this the only attack upon a reconnaissance plane that occurred or were there a series of attacks on reconnaissance planes?

Laird: We had attacks upon our planes, Senator Church. But this was the first plane shot down.

Exercise II for Chapter Three

Find examples in the mass media (newspapers, magazines, radio, and television) of fallacies discussed in Chapter Three, and explain why they are fallacious.

1. For some time now, Premier Fidel Castro's brother, Raoul, has been "the power in Cuba". During this coming year (1970–1971), Fidel Castro will be "physically removed from Cuba".

2. Starting in 1971, the U.S. will begin a great and successful drive to eliminate pollution in this country.

3. Defense budget reductions will result in a "serious arms shortage" in the U.S., like the one suffered by Britain in World War II after Dunkirk.

4. A crash program to utilize cosmic energy for peace and war, costing 10% of our national research budget, will lead to a "major breakthrough in armaments".

5. The next ten years will bring two great scientific discoveries. One will harness electromagnetic forces and result in almost limitless cheap power. The other will use outer space and its vacuum to manufacture goods and will be the "key to a new industrial age".

6. Ambassador Sargent Shriver will run for governor in 1970 and win—a steppingstone in his plan to become president.

7. The My Lai affair will be seen as a well-executed Communist plot to blacken our image around the world, as was the Pueblo incident.

1. In 1979, four years from now, Jackie Onassis will learn of a current plot to cheat her out of part of her inheritance. She will become "bitter and frustrated" in her relationship with the Onassis family.

2. In December 1975, she and her daughter Caroline will fight over Caroline's romance with an older man, an "ordinary working man". Jackie will get Caroline away from him by sending her on an extended trip.

3. A serious kidnapping threat against the Kennedy children will take place in about March 1976.

4. Beginning sometime next year (1976), Jackie will start going out on dates frequently again, mostly with wealthy attractive art patrons. But serious romance will wait for 1979–1980.

5. Jackie will prove in the next few years that she is an excellent businesswoman, and in fact through business will become one of the richest women in the world.

6. She'll again be the admired and imitated "darling of America" that she once was.

Statistics: Statistics are just numbers. And numbers can be used to count anything. In the case of alleged seers or prophets, like Jeane Dixon, they should be used to count the number of successful (correct) predictions compared to the total number of predictions made. The predictions of Jeane Dixon on the left (above) are taken from a set of about 100 she made in late 1969 (for the year 1970), which appeared in her book *My Life and Prophecies* (as told to Rene Noorbergen, New York, Bantam Books, 1970). The predictions on the right (above) were made by her in 1975 and appeared in the *National Enquirer* (April 25, 197́, p. 5). Most of the 1970 predictions were vague, ambiguous, or futuristic, and thus hard to tally. The ones listed above were chosen because they were easier to assess, and also to show that she does make lots of incorrect predictions. Her overall success rate was *at best* about what one would expect from a normally informed viewer of the scene; more likely she did less well than such an informed person would have done. The 1975 predictions were selected solely for clarity and ease of assessment. As time passes, readers of this text will be in a better position to assess her success rate on these 1975 predictions. But it surely must already be clear that those of her followers who fasten on her successes to the exclusion of her failures are guilty of the fallacy of *biased statistics* (discussed in Chapter Four). If a person really does have prophetic vision, it should show in a higher success rate than is obtained by those who predict in the normal way (that is, from past experience). Jeane Dixon does not have a higher success rate, so we ought to conclude that (probably) she does not have prophetic powers. Statistics prove that.

Chapter Four

Statistics and Fallacies

There are lies, damn lies, and statistics.
Benjamin Disraeli

Figures don't lie. But liars figure.
Old saying

Statistical fallacies are just ordinary fallacies in which numbers play a central role. Nevertheless, they merit special attention because so many of us are more likely to fall for statistical fallacies than for the nonstatistical variety.

1. Examples

a. Suppressed evidence The statistical fallacy most frequently encountered is simply the suppression of known and relevant data (a variation on the fallacy of *suppressed evidence*).

Republican victory claims in the nationwide 1970 U.S. Senate races furnish a typical example. These claims were based on the fact that in off-year elections (years when no president is being elected), the party of the incumbent president almost always loses Senate seats. In the 1970 elections, the Republicans *gained* two Senate seats.

In this case, the suppressed evidence is quite simple. In the first place, Republicans suppressed the fact that a victorious presidential candidate usually carries a comfortable majority of senators of his own party along with him and that the larger the majority, the greater the loss two years hence (on the average). But in 1968, President Nixon, elected by the tiniest of margins, failed to carry a Republican Senate in with him. So only a very small Republican loss would be expected in any case.

Even more important is the suppressed fact that 25 Democrats and only ten Republicans were up for reelection, due to the Johnson landslide of 1964. Such an imbalance of risk is almost unprecedented. Once we take it into account, the Democratic showing begins to look quite respectable, and Republican claims of victory out of order. Having risked fifteen more seats, it is not surprising the Democrats lost two more races than did the Republicans.

And, finally, the two-seat improvement looks even less like a victory when it is observed that two of the Democratic losses (those in New York and Connecticut) may have resulted from unusual three-way races which hurt the Democrats more than they did their opponents.

Notice again that this fallacy could not be detected by the uninformed; they always are fair game for the slick operator. The political professionals who crowed victory for the Republicans were in a position to know that pertinent information was being suppressed; it was the uninformed man in the street who was misled.

The battles surrounding the Massachusetts no-fault insurance law provides another case in which the man in the street should have known (but generally didn't) that information was being suppressed. One of these battles centered on attempts to lower auto insurance premiums by 15 percent. The response of the insurance industry was a vast campaign in which they claimed that bankruptcy was possible. Typical was the article in the *New Britain Herald* (October 12, 1970, by David L. Walter) on the problems of the insurance industry, and their need to raise rates:

> Over the past ten years, the insurance industry has paid out $2 billion more in claims than it has collected in premiums, says a spokesman for the Insurance Information Institute. . . .

The impression given is that without a rate increase, insurance companies would soon be unable to pay insurance claims.

But this conclusion was not warranted by the facts, as the spokesman for the I.I.I. and the writer of the article ought to have known. Insurance companies don't just put premiums in a vault; they *invest* them, and use investment profits along with premiums to meet insurance claims. So the pertinent figures were *total* income and total outgo, which yield total profits. During the ten years in question, the insurance industry took in comfortably more in premiums and investment profits than it paid out in claims and operating expenses.

b.   Unknowable statistics   Statistics always seem precise and *authoritative*. But statistical facts can be just as unknowable as any others. Here is a letter received several years ago. It contains examples of **unknowable statistics** that would be hard to top:

> Dear Friend: In the past 5000 years men have fought in 14,523 wars. One out of four persons living during this time have been war casualties. A nuclear war would add 1,245,000,000 men, women, and children to this tragic list.

It's ludicrous to present such precise figures as facts. No one knows (or could know) the exact number of wars fought up to the present time, to say nothing of the number of war casualties. As for the number of casualties in some future nuclear war, it would depend on what kind of war, and in any event is a matter on which even so-called experts can only speculate.

c.   Questionable statistics   But it is not just *unknowable statistics* which should be challenged. Business statistics, while in theory knowable, in fact often are questionable. Or at least there are those who think so.

Take the statistics published by the U.S. government on business conditions in the United States. Oskar Morgenstern is one expert who argues that these statistics are very questionable indeed.[1]

One of the major problems with government statistics is that their margin of error (not usually reported) is greater than the "significant" differences they often report. We read in the newspapers that the economy grew in a given month at a rate amounting to 5 percent a year, perhaps an increase of 1 percent over the previous year. Everyone is pleased at this increase in the growth rate of the economy. But the *margin of error* on government growth rate statistics very likely is much greater than 1 percent, as Morgenstern indicated, citing one of the government's own revisions:

> If the rate for the change [in growth] from 1947 to 1948 was determined in February, 1949, when the first figures became available, it was 10.8 percent. In July, 1950, using officially corrected figures, it became 12.5 percent; in July, 1956, it fell to 11.8 percent—a full percentage point. All this for the growth rate from 1947 to 1948!

Add to this the fact that even the officially corrected figures cannot take account of the deliberately misleading or false figures businessmen sometimes provide the government (to cover their tracks or to mislead rival companies) and it becomes clear that the margin of error on figures for the gross national product has to be fairly large.

In addition, there is the problem arising from the need to use a base year (because of price fluctuations):

> If a year with a high (or low) gross national product is chosen as base year, this will depress (or raise) the growth rate of subsequent years. . . . An unscrupulous or politically oriented [!] writer will choose that base year which produces the sequence of (alleged) growth rates best suited to his aims and programs. . . . These are, of course, standard tricks, used, undoubtedly, ever since index numbers were invented.

In other words, if you want to show that a given year had a high rate of growth, choose a low base year, and vice versa for a low growth rate. Meanwhile, the true rate of growth remains unknown, except for broad, long-term trends.

Government statistics may report confidently on things that are not *known* with such precision, but at least they bear some resemblance to the truth. Many statistics, however, don't even have that virtue. An example is the statistical

---

[1]Oskar Morgenstern, *Qui Numerare Incipit Errare Incipit* (roughly, "He who begins to count begins to err"), *Fortune,* October 1963.

evidence obtained from surveys which ask "loaded" or biased questions. In general, the technique is to ask a question in such a way that you are more likely to get the desired answer.

Henry A. Bubb, President of Capital Federal Savings and Loan Association, asked the following loaded question of the readers of his column in Capital Federal's *News and Views:*

> Do you think that we should continue to lose precious lives and spend $26 billion a year for the war in Vietnam while we only spend $1.9 billion a year to relieve poverty and riots at home?

The response, in case you're in doubt, was "yes"—18 percent, "no"—82 percent, a figure he could have more or less reversed simply by asking the question this way:

> Do you think we should stop wasting $1.9 billion per year on slackers in the U.S. who won't work and won't support themselves adequately while at the same time we increase our $26 billion expenditure in Vietnam and thus strike a greater blow against the atheistic communists who threaten our Democracy?

Here is another Bubb masterpiece from the same survey:

> Should the government's program for aid to dependent children, which has skyrocketed from $1.6 million to $3.7 million per year in the last decade, continue unchecked?

The vote? "Yes"—27 percent, "no"—73 percent. It takes a strong person to vote for a program which has "skyrocketed unchecked", even if it's for the kiddies.

Reprinted by permission of *National Review*, 150 East 35 Street, New York, NY 10016

Polls also are used to determine consumer preferences and habits. Of course, statistics compiled from such surveys need not be worthless; it is possible to construct reliable surveys, although it's generally expensive and takes trained personnel. But all too frequently, surveys of this kind are worthless. Here is an example which was intended to prove that exact point:[2]

> A sidewalk researcher in New York City asked passers-by what books they preferred to read from a specified list of paperbacks. The winners were: Shakespeare, the Bible, and a few classics.
>
> After each interviewee answered, the researcher told him to select one of the listed books as a gift to be sent for cooperating. . . . The book most people selected was *Murder of a Burlesque Queen* by Gypsy Rose Lee. The researcher stated: "The biggest trap you can fall into is believing what people tell you they want."

Yet this is exactly what most surveys, including political surveys, report.

d.   Hasty conclusion   Statistics often seem more significant than they are, leading to commission of the fallacy of *hasty conclusion* in its statistical version.

The *Saturday Review* (February 9, 1974) ran an article stating that college entrance scholastic aptitude test scores are going down in America, indicating, according to the article, that students in the United States are not as bright (or well-educated) as they used to be.

But their conclusion was hasty. For it fails to take account of the fact (mentioned in the article) that the percentage of the total high school population taking these tests has increased—many more academically poor students now take them.

During the 1970 race for governor of Connecticut, it was pointed out that Emilio Daddario missed 119 roll calls on bills before Congress in the previous session, whereas his opponent, Thomas J. Meskill, missed only 112. Daddario defended himself by claiming he didn't miss *important* roll calls, a defense objected to by Meskill on the grounds that Daddario had missed votes on a drug-control measure, on railroad legislation, and on organized crime.

While Meskill's statistics are pertinent to the charge that Daddario didn't do a good job in Congress, they don't come close to proving the point, even forgetting that voting on bills is only one of the important jobs of a congressman. For merely missing a roll call, even on an important bill, is not necessarily significant. The bill may have been doomed to failure or certain to pass without a particular congressman's vote. He may pass up a vote in such a case so as not to annoy certain power groups among his constituents by voting against their narrow interests. In addition, it is impossible to tell from the subject matter whether or not a bill is important. Some railroad legislation, for instance, can be fairly trivial in nature.

---

[2]Sam Sinclair Baker, *The Permissible Lie* (Cleveland and New York: World Publishing Co., 1968), Chapter 10.

Finally, in assessing the 119 to 112 ratio, we have to bear in mind that committee votes often are much more important than those on the floor of the House. In addition, the import of a particular vote often cannot be determined even by carefully reading a particular bill. Here is a rather complicated illustration:

Before Senate defeat of a bill providing a $290 million subsidy for the proposed U.S. supersonic transport plane (SST), backers of the bill tried to line up support for it by blunting one of the main objections to the SST, namely sonic boom. They did this by passing a motion banning supersonic flights over land in the United States. As a result, some senators who felt that sonic boom was a greatly overplayed issue found themselves voting *for* the bill banning supersonic land flights, even though they were against the content of the bill: They did so hoping that as a result the $290 million SST appropriation would be passed by the Senate the next day.

The SST vote also illustrates the difficulty of assessing failure to vote on a measure. Senator Magnuson attached an amendment to the overall transportation budget bill (of which the SST appropriation was a part) which stipulated that the Portland, Oregon, International Airport would get no funds until detailed and exhaustive environmental studies were completed. Oregon's Senator, Mark Hatfield, tried to get the amendment removed, but was told that Magnuson might be willing to strike his amendment *after* the SST vote was taken. Hatfield was thus in a bind. He was known to be opposed to the SST. Yet if he voted against the SST appropriation, Magnuson's amendment would not be withdrawn, and Portland would lose its airport funds. On the other hand, it would look bad to vote for the SST appropriation, since he was a well-known opponent of it. He did the only thing he could under the circumstances and announced he had a long-standing speaking engagement elsewhere. An Oregon voter who *merely* noted the missed vote simply failed to grasp the problem, and completely missed Hatfield's attempt to save Portland's airport money.[3]

e.   Small sample   Statistics frequently are used to project from a sample to the "population" from which the sample was drawn. This is the basic technique behind all polling, from the Gallup Poll to the Nielsen television ratings. But if the sample is too small to be a reliable measure of the population, then to accept it is to commit the fallacy of the **small sample,** a variety of the fallacy of *hasty conclusion.*

This fallacy is committed frequently at election time, because a sufficiently large representative sample generally is quite expensive and difficult to obtain.

---

[3]The SST story actually is even more complicated than that. In December 1970, the Senate voted against the $290 million appropriation for the SST. But anyone who rated his state's senators solely on their votes up to that time again was guilty of *hasty conclusion.* For the vote came late in the year and some senators may have known what was coming next on the issue: a beautiful squeeze play by the House. The House passed an amended Department of Transportation bill, which included three months' additional funding for the SST, and then adjourned for the year. A Senate vote against this bill would have cut off all funds for air traffic controllers (thus grounding all commercial planes) and for DOT employees. So the Senate voted for the bill and thus to extend SST funding for three months more. So another "crucial" vote came up in March 1971. A citizen interested in the SST thus had to keep up with the topic for some time in order to determine how his representatives in Washington really affected the issue. (Senator Hatfield, incidentally, voted against continued funding for the SST in the March 1971 vote.)

There is a great deal of controversy about how large a sample has to be, but there should be little argument about the following examples.

An Evans and Novak column (October 1970) contained the following on the 1970 Connecticut Senatorial race: "In the blue-collar neighborhoods of this old factory town, the Rev. Joseph Duffey is losing—and losing badly—his audacious bid to weld a neo-Rooseveltian coalition. . . ." Their statement was based on a poll of 67 Bridgeport voters in normally Democratic Italian-American working-class precincts, which showed Senator Thomas Dodd with 43 percent of the vote, Rep. Lowell Weicker with 27 percent, and Duffey with only 11 percent. This obviously was too small a sample on which to base more than tentative conclusions.[4]

The *Hartford Times* (September 13, 1970), in a story on University of Connecticut "Hard Hats" (conservative faculty members), stated that "hardliners" tend to teach at the University of Connecticut in the physical sciences, while more liberal types tend to teach liberal arts. This conclusion was based on a study of the voting pattern on three resolutions concerning punishment for disruptive students. The trouble is that the three votes constitute too small a sample from which to draw more than a tentative conclusion.

f.   Unrepresentative sample The survey just referred to also was defective in lacking what is called *instance variety,* thus constituting an **unrepresentative sample** of the population as a whole. In this case, the population was all relevant attitudes of University of Connecticut faculty members; the survey checked only attitudes on punishment for disruptive students. A man who voted to punish disruptive students may not have been a "hardliner" on other issues.

An Evans and Novak column *(Toronto Star,* July 19, 1974) argued that "well-heeled" American suburbia had lost its faith in President Nixon, and wanted him out of office. Their conclusion was based on a survey of fifty-four registered voters in one district of Mamaroneck, New York, a Westchester County suburb of New York City.

But their conclusion was fallacious. In the first place, the sample size was much too small, even as a sample of the New York area, much less the nation as a whole. And second, the sample was not *representative*—we know after all that suburban areas in other parts of the country differ from Westchester County in their political makeup. Evans and Novak should have tried to make their sample representative of all suburban areas.

g.   Questionable cause And then there are the statistical variations on the fallacy of *questionable cause.* A *New York Times* article on marijuana, which argued that

---

[4]Duffey did lose the election, and he lost primarily because he failed to pile up margins in cities like Bridgeport. But the election figures for Bridgeport show that Duffey lost there to *Weicker,* not Dodd. The figures were Duffey 18,273, Weicker 21,674, and Dodd only 5,909, a far cry from the sample cited by Evans and Novak. (Of course, the actual results are irrelevant to the charge of *small sample.* The sample would have been too small even if, luckily, it exactly mirrored the election results.)

THERE ARE MORE PEOPLE IN PRISON THAN EVER BEFORE—

MAYBE THE POLICE ARE GETTING BETTER—

MAYBE THE LAWYERS ARE GETTING WORSE—

Washington Star Syndicate, Inc.

1-26 BRICKMAN

Reprinted by permission of the Washington Star Syndicate, Inc.

It's not easy to determine what is the cause of what.

marijuana is harmful to health, cited a report that twelve American soldiers in Vietnam had been reported to have smoked marijuana and to have had acute psychotic reactions. The implication was that marijuana-smoking *caused* the psychosis.

But the statistic cited is not significant by itself. Statistics linking one thing with another rarely are. In this case, we need to know at least the incidence of psychosis among U.S. soldiers in Vietnam who had not smoked marijuana. The horrors of war, after all, may well have been responsible for the psychosis, not marijuana.

h.   Faulty comparison   Statistics have such an authoritative ring that it seems possible to do just about anything with them and get away with it. One trick is to juxtapose otherwise valid statistics in a way that *seems* to yield significant results, but actually does not, because the statistics are not of comparable types or because a more important comparison has been overlooked. Let's call this the fallacy of **faulty comparison.** (The chief variety is sometimes referred to as **comparing apples with oranges.**)

The U.S. Chamber of Commerce magazine, *Nation's Business,* ran an article "Big Tax Reform Myth of 1972", which pointed out that although 107 millionaires paid no taxes in 1971, the remaining 15,323 having adjusted gross incomes over $200,000 did pay taxes, and a whopping 44.1 percent of adjusted gross income, much higher than ordinary taxpayers pay on their income.

The catch, which they suppressed, was that *adjusted* gross income is not total income—it's total income minus lots of things, such as one-half of capital gains (a very large item for millionaires). *Nation's Business* led its readers to commit the fallacy of *faulty comparison*—to compare the percentage of *total* income paid in income taxes by average taxpayers with the percentage of *adjusted* gross income paid in income taxes by millionaires.

Aaron Go Bragh[5]

by David Markson

If I couldn't care less, do they have to keep shoving it down my throat?

Henry Aaron is an essentially drab, durably proficient baseball player who has lasted 20 full years, and there are at least 15 other baseball players who have hit more home runs in a single season than Henry ever did. Aaron's ass sticks out when he digs in, which certain quirky souls might find as endearing as the memory of Ottie's flapping right foot, or Stash's high-tension swivel, and my son's "Who's Who in Baseball" shows no asterisks for any major Aaron injuries ever. (Cf. Williams, Theodore: 1950, broken elbow; 1954, broken shoulder.) A foolish consistency, as Emerson suggested, is the hobgoblin of little minds—and of sportswriters with space to fill.

Seven-fourteen. Give Teddy Ballgame back those five years in the marines, he'd have caught Babe Ruth somewhere late in the Eisenhower administration. Give Willie back his two years in the army, he'd be there too.

Where? Give Ruth back the years he spent pitching.

Seven-fourteen. When Ruth quit, the man in second place was more than 300 behind; that, now, is not unimpressive. Matter of fact, Gehrig had 378 at the end of that summer, and the only others above 300—just above—were Foxx and Hornsby. Today, last I checked, Norm Cash's mother-in-law was somewhere in the 430s.

There is only one astonishing home run record. In 1920, with 54, Ruth hit exactly *twice as many* as any other player before him. Wake me up for the season when Aaron hits 122.

The only real fingernail to chew this month is Nolan Ryan and those 382 Koufax strike-outs.

Longevity is for old buildings.

One sports fan's opinion. But is it truth or *faulty comparison?*

In 1970, the Consolidated Edison Company of New York wanted to double the capacity of its power plant in Astoria (an area of Queens, a borough of New York City). Antipollutionists were against this expansion. In trying to combat the pollution charge, Con Ed's Jerry V. Halvorsen, Environmental Affairs Coordinator, argued that the expanded plan would actually reduce pollution:[6]

---

[5]*Village Voice,* September 13, 1973, p. 21. Copyright © 1973 The Village Voice, Inc. Reprinted by permission.

[6]Quoted by Anna Mayo in the *Village Voice,* August 13, 1970.

Let 5 stand for the existing capacity of the Astoria plant. Multiply by 1, the percentage of sulfur in the fuel we use now. And you get 5. Now let 10 stand for the proposed double capacity of the plant. Multiply by .37, the percentage of sulfur in the fuel we will use in the future. You get 3.7. And 3.7 is less than 5.

The conclusion he wanted the reader to draw was that pollution would be reduced even though power capacity would be doubled. But he obtained this result by comparing *apples with oranges.* (He also was guilty of a bit of *suppressed evidence.*) For if low-sulfur fuel was to be used in the new expanded plant, then it could be used in the plant already in existence. Doubling capacity would after all double pollution, as Anna Mayo was quick to point out.[7]

The fallacy of *faulty comparison* may also be committed when statistics from one time or place are compared with those from another. For the *quality* of such statistics often differs a great deal. Crime statistics are a good example. In many parts of the country, apparent increases in the crime rate can be achieved simply by changing the recording habits of police officers, for instance, by recording minor crimes by blacks against blacks, Chicanos against Chicanos, or Indians against Indians. In New York City, police can increase the crime *total* simply by walking down almost any main street and arresting hot dog, pretzel, or ice cream vendors; if a decrease is desired, they simply become blinder than usual to these everyday violations of the law. The same is true of prostitution, gambling, and homosexual activity, areas of crime in which the police generally have a special interest.

Statistics on parking violations in many big cities suffer from this same fault. A big city policeman who ticketed every illegally parked car he saw would have little time for anything else. Police statistics simply do not accurately reflect the actual incidence of lawbreaking. Hence, if we compare figures on lawbreaking for one place or time with those for another, the result is apt to be ludicrous.

Equally silly are many of the statistical comparisons which fail to take account of inflation or (occasionally) deflation. A piano ad touted Steinway pianos as a "growth investment", on the statistical grounds that many older Steinways were selling for as much or more than their original cost. Now this does prove that buying, say, a $3000 Steinway is less expensive in the long run than buying a $3000 Pontiac, since in ten years the Pontiac will be worth next to nothing.

---

[7]The fallacy also might be construed as that of *ambiguity.* For pollution would be less than before, even though more than if low sulfur fuel now were used.

In a *Time* magazine article (Canadian edition, July 28, 1975, p. 40), rising food costs were attributed primarily to supermarkets not being as efficient as generally supposed. Statistics were used to justify the introduction of controversial new electronic systems: "[What we have at present is] a costly, cumbersome system that, for example, adds 24.3¢, *or 69%*, to the price of a pound of chicken between farm and checkout counter (see chart)." In context, this made supermarkets look very inefficient indeed. But if *Time* had wished to make them look efficient, they could have used other figures from the same article to do so. For instance, they could have said instead that the 12.4 cents supermarkets add to the retail price of a pound of chicken (a statistic on their chart) is only about 20 percent of the retail price, which is reasonably low, although not quite as low as a few years ago.

But it doesn't prove Steinways are a *growth* investment, since the dollars of twenty or thirty years ago, or even ten, were worth much more than those of today. Steinway should have tried to convert the figures to a neutral basis (a tricky business) before making a comparison.

Perhaps the classic inflation example is the one inadvertently furnished by Marvin Kitman in his book, *Washington's Expense Account* (New York: Simon & Schuster, 1970). Mr. Kitman was trying to prove that George Washington had lived relatively high on the hog during the Revolutionary War, which is true,[8] and also that he padded expense accounts, which is possible but not proved by Kitman's figures.

Washington's accounts were kept primarily in Pennsylvania pounds. Mr. Kitman translated them into dollars via the Continental (Congress) dollar, equating 26 Continental dollars with one Pennsylvania pound. The trouble is that the value of the Continental dollar fluctuated widely, mostly downward, eventually becoming just about worthless (the origin of the phrase "not worth a Continental").

Kitman listed Washington's total expenses as $449,261.51 (note the aura of authority in that last 51¢!). An "expert" (who preferred to remain anonymous— perhaps because of the amount of guesswork involved) suggested $68,000 was a better figure.

---

[8]But you won't find this truth in many history textbooks, because it runs counter to an official myth. See Chapter Nine for more on this sort of textbook shenanigans.

In these examples, the comparisons themselves are faulty. Often, however, while the comparison is on the up and up, the *conclusion* is misleading. It is frequently stated that the American Indian has less to complain about than is usually supposed, that we can't have treated the Indian all *that* badly in the United States, since there are more Indians in the United States now than when Columbus "discovered" America. (This is disputed by some experts, who think the standard estimates on the Indian population in 1492 are too low. But in any event, the population then was probably not greatly different from what it is now.)

But even supposing the cited figures are correct, what do they prove? A more significant figure would be this (but still not terribly significant, given the immense amount of direct evidence that white men mistreated Indians). Take the number of whites and blacks in the United States in, say, 1783 (the end of the Revolutionary War), and compare that to the number of their descendants alive today (that is, don't count later immigrants and their progeny—a good trick because of interbreeding, but not impossible to estimate). Now compare this increase with that of the American Indian. What we would no doubt find is that the white and black populations doubled many times over, while the Indians' remained fairly stable.[9] If we had no direct evidence, then this comparison would be significant; but it would support the idea that the white man did, after all, mistreat the Indian.

i.   Ambiguity   Statistics would seem to be the last place in which to encounter the fallacy of *ambiguity;* numbers, after all, are so very precise. But what numbers are used to *count* may not be so precise.

In 1970, Attorney General John Mitchell stated before the International Association of Chiefs of Police that the federal government placed only 133 taps during the first seven months of 1970. But (as pointed out in the *New Republic,* October 24, 1970) he must have had in mind only one kind of wiretap, for his figures did not include taps used in "internal security" cases, 48-hour "emergency" taps, or bugs, as opposed to wiretaps. The latter was especially deceptive, because Mr. Mitchell could expect police officers to know the difference between a wiretap and a bug, but not his wider audience (the general public) to which his statement ultimately was addressed. The public could be expected to assume that 133 was the total on electronic eavesdropping by the federal government. (Of course, if caught in the act, Mitchell could always have said he was speaking loosely, a defense that it is hard to counter, because life is short and in daily life we do tend to save time by speaking loosely.)

2.   Statistical Fallacies in Context

It is relatively easy to spot statistical fallacies when they're extracted from surrounding material. But it's another matter when a batch of statistics is thrown

---

[9]Actually, Indian population steadily declined until the Indians were completely conquered at the end of the nineteenth century. But in the past fifty years or so, their number has increased.

at you in a whole article or column. Here is a political column which contains at least two statistical fallacies. The reader is invited to do his own analysis before reading this writer's opinion:[10]

Inflation Notes

New York (AP)—The cost of a college education is going to be higher again this fall. Parents have become so accustomed to this statement that it no longer has any shock effect. But the figures, nevertheless, are rather numbing.

The median charges for tuition, fees and room-board are expected to total about $2,502 in private coeducational colleges, up $200 from the 1969–1970 academic year.

Private women's colleges will be about $234 higher at $2,737, and private men's schools higher by $211 at $2,840. But those are the medians, meaning the figures half way between the highest and the lowest.

And what are the extremes? Well, at Bennington College in Vermont you must figure on total expenses of $4,325, which is $5 more than the price at Sarah Lawrence. Radcliffe, Tufts, Monterey Institute of Foreign Studies and several other schools will cost $4,000 or more. But students at public schools, such as the New York city colleges, may pay as little as $60.

The figures were compiled by the Life Insurance Agency Management Association to convince the public that they need to save well ahead to meet tuition costs—preferably through an insurance program.

At the rate prices are rising, however, the industry may find a good many families borrowing the cash value of their policies.

Once upon a time inflation was at the rate of only a couple of percentage points a year and most people hardly noticed it at all. But now it's 6 percent or more and few families can ignore it.

In an effort to show how damaging this can be if permitted to continue, the U.S. Savings and Loan League figured out that 30 years from now a man would have to earn $57,435 to equal his present $10,000 salary.

A $20 bag of groceries, 1970 style, would cost $114.87 in the year 2000. A $500 color television set would sell for $2,871, and a $3,000 automobile would carry a price tag of $17,230. A $25,000 home would be priced at $147,000.

Shocked? You should be. But don't forget either that these figures are not likely to be approached. Most economists would tell you that in all probability the economy would collapse long before 2000.

The statistics, some of them, are interesting and informative. But the conclusions, stated or implied, are another matter. Let's start with the comparison between

---

[10]The column is by John Cunniff. © 1970, the Associated Press. Reprinted by permission.

private school costs and those of public schools. In the first place, we are given the *average* for private schools, as well as two of the highest figures, but only the lowest figure for public schools. Thus, we are invited to commit the fallacy of *faulty comparison.*

But second, and more important, the figures for private schools cover room and board, while the $60 figure quoted for public schools does not—another example of comparing apples with oranges.

The column also quotes scare statistics on how damaging it would be if a 6 percent inflation rate continued into the future. A $25,000 home would cost $147,000, a $20 bag of groceries $114.87. But mere inflation proves nothing. The question is how *income* rises in comparison. If prices 30 years from now are six times higher than at present, then anyone making more than six times his present salary will be better off financially than now, and anyone making less than six times his present salary will be less well off. It's as simple as that.[11]

The average person tends to see issues in simple terms. He doesn't want to get down to the nitty-gritty details or read the fine print. This usually results in his being taken, no matter what the field. But in the case of *business politics,* where statistics are king, it results in deceit on a grand scale.

One of the classic ploys of this type was detailed in an article by *Ramparts* magazine.[12] American Telephone and Telegraph Co. (A.T. & T., the Bell Telephone system) is one of America's largest military contractors, its particular baby being the ABM. In one case, its subsidiary, Western Electric Company, took a profit of $113 million on an Army ABM contract of $1.6 billion. This amounts to "only" 7.9 percent, and those satisfied with outward appearances no doubt looked no further, satisfied that 7.9 percent was not very far out of line.

But in fact, the profits to Western Electric and thus to Bell Telephone were immense and grossly out of line. The above figures served only to conceal suppressed data, which *Ramparts* magazine brought to the surface. For Western Electric itself did only $359 million of the work, including $82 million for administrative expenses. So its profits at the very least were 31.3 percent, a tremendously exorbitant profit rate.

Here is roughly how it worked, so that everyone profited but the federal government (and thus you and me). Western Electric subcontracted $645 million of the contract to Douglas Aircraft, which took a profit of $46 million (7.6 percent). Douglas then subcontracted all but $103 million, so that its profit on actual work done was 44.3 percent. Of course, the sub-subcontractors. Consolidated Western (a division of U.S. Steel) and Fruehoff Trailer Corporation, also took their profits.

So the government ended up paying profits to Consolidated and Fruehoff, profits on profits to Douglas, and profits on profits on profits to Western Electric.

---

[11]Of course, the effect of inflation on economic activity is another matter, and one concerning which economists differ.

[12]*Ramparts,* November 1969. Notice that it is a *nonmass* media magazine that ran this exposé.

The details of a particularly flagrant overcharge on part of this contract illustrate the care that must be exhibited in handling profit and loss statements. Here is the *Ramparts* account of this detail:

> Probably the greatest chutzpah shown by Western, however, was in the scrupulous insistence on paying rent of $3 million to the government for the use of two surplus plants where much of the Nike production work was done. Ordinarily the government would have simply donated the use of the plants, but Western insisted on paying. Then again, Western has to make a buck too, so it added the $3 million to its "costs." The government had to turn around and give the rent money back as a reimbursement, plus $209,000 profit on it. Nothing excessive, just about seven percent. A reasonable profit.

Finally, it ought to be pointed out that military contracts are different from many others only in degree. Bell, for instance, uses the same profit on profit system in its purchases of telephones from—surprise—Western Electric. First, Western Electric takes a profit on the "sale" of the telephones to Bell, and then Bell takes a profit on the "cost" of telephones purchased from its own subsidiary, Western Electric.

Summary of fallacies discussed in Chapter Four

Statistical fallacies are variations on the kinds of fallacies considered in earlier chapters. The varieties discussed in Chapter Four are:

1. *Suppressed evidence.*

   Example: The cited suppression of the fact that insurance companies *invest* premiums, and thus have income in addition to the premiums themselves with which to pay claims.

2. *Unknowable statistics.*

   Example: The letter stating there have been 14,523 wars in the past 5000 years.

3. *Questionable statistics.*

   Example: Government business statistics calculated down to tenths of a percent.

4. *Hasty conclusion.*

   Example: The Republican claim that Congressman Meskill had a better record in Congress than Congressman Daddario because Daddario missed several more House roll calls than Meskill.

5. *Small sample.*

   Example: The Evans and Novak use of a sample of 67 Bridgeport voters to prove Duffey would lose in his race for the Senate.

6. *Unrepresentative sample.*

Example: The Evans and Novak use of a sample from one district of Mamaroneck, New York, to prove that upper middle suburbia overwhelmingly wanted Nixon out of office.

7. *Questionable cause.*

Example: The implication that marijuana caused American soldiers in Vietnam to have acute psychotic reactions.

8. *Faulty comparison.*

Example: Uncritically comparing crime statistics from one time or place with those from another.

9. *Ambiguity.*

Example: Attorney General Mitchell's use of the word "tap" to mean only one kind of electronic eavesdropping (not covering so-called bugs, for instance) in reporting statistics on government surveillance, correctly assuming that most people would construe the term more widely to include *all* electronic surveillance.

Exercise I for Chapter Four

Explain what (if anything) is wrong with the uses of statistical evidence in the following items:

*1. *Judy:* It's more dangerous to drive a car now than in the 1930s.
John: Really? How do you know?
Judy: Well, there were about 30,000 auto deaths per year in the U.S. then, and now it's about 50,000 a year.
John: You learn something new every day.

2. An Evans and Novak political column rated the chances of State Senator Sander Levin, Democratic nominee for governor of Michigan, as poor, on the basis of a poll of sixty-four blue collar suburban workers of Warren, Michigan. The poll showed 36 percent for Levin's opponent, 42 percent for Levin, and 22 percent undecided, in a normally very heavily Democratic stronghold. Later evidence showed that the poll correctly predicted the outcome of the election.

3. *John:* It's actually healthier in the Navy than in New York City.
Judy: Oh, cut it out. You're pulling my leg.
John: No, honestly. The death rate in the Navy is only 9 per 1000 per year, while in New York it's 16.
Judy: That why you got out of the Navy?

*4. Smoking marijuana definitely leads to heroin use. A report by the U.S. Commissioner of Narcotics on a study of 2,213 hardcore narcotic addicts in the Lexington, Kentucky, Federal Hospital shows that 70.4 percent smoked marijuana *before* taking heroin.

5. U.S. Customs officials justify their method of solving the heroin problem (catching drug smugglers) by citing the fact that heroin seizures are up sharply, from 210 pounds seized in 1969 to 346.8 pounds in 1970, to a staggering 1308.85 pounds in 1971.

*6. *Column by James J. Kilpatrick, August 1970, in which he argued for more action on the drug problem:* J. Edgar Hoover released his 1969 Crime Report a week ago. Last year, for the first time, there were more arrests in the U.S. for violations of drug laws than for violation of liquor laws—223,000 drug offenses against 213,000 liquor offenses.

7. *Judy:* It's safer taking a long trip than going into Hartford to shop.
John: What? You're kidding.
Judy: No, I'm not. Half of all auto accidents occur within five miles of home.

8. *John:* I've been reading the latest sex-book bestseller, and it says less than 2 percent of all adult females have vaginal climaxes, a figure that seems to remain fairly constant in all cultures—so it isn't cultural, it's biological. The authors claim that women who have such orgasms are abnormal, perhaps even nymphomaniac. Do you think the 2 percent figure could be correct?
Judy: If anything it's too high. The vaginal climax is an invention of male chauvinist psychologists, like Freud.

9. *Reported by Dan Nimmo in his book* The Political Persuaders *(Englewood Cliffs, N.J.: Prentice-Hall, 1970). Mr. Nimmo presented this view and then argued against it:* . . . students of politics . . . point out that factors shaping voting choices are affected only marginally by campaign appeals. The principal factor consistently related to voting decisions is the party loyalty of the voter. . . . So long as a substantial portion of the electorate is committed to a party (and studies indicate that proportion to be four out of five voters), campaigns will have little effect on voting patterns.

*10. *Judy:* I'm reading a fascinating article in *Women's Home Journal.* Ten years ago, they conducted a survey and discovered that 39 percent of those interviewed stated they were happy with their lives. A follow-up last month showed—get this, John—48 percent now were happy, up 9 percent in ten years. They conclude things are getting better in the United States pretty rapidly.
John: Do I discern a note of doubt about our plans to chuck it all and buy a subsistence farm in Vermont?
Judy: Well, if Mainstream America is getting happier, why leave it?

11. *John:* Did you know four-cylinder engines are more efficient than six?
Judy: No. Not that I cared. But how do you know?
John: I checked the mileage ratings of every car sold in the United States, and four-cylinder cars get far better mileage than sixes.
Judy: Guess what, John? You've committed what that logic book calls the

fallacy of the *questionable cause.* Most four-cylinder cars are made in foreign countries; sixes are mostly made in the United States. Right? You thought I wouldn't know that, didn't you? So the truth is that *foreign-made engines* are more efficient than American-made. Admit it, John. I got you this time.

12. *Article in* Boston Globe, *June 26, 1974, on youth, drugs, and alcohol:* "We're seeing a tremendous switch back to alcohol." Dr. Chafetz (of National Institute on Alcohol Abuse) cited a recent national survey of 15,000 boys and girls, aged 11 to 18, in which 92% reported alcohol use but only 38% said they smoked marijuana.

13. New York, *September 12, 1972, article on alcoholism:* A genetic biochemical deficiency could be the reason some persons become alcoholics while others don't. Dr. Stanley Gitlow, President of the American Medical Society on Alcoholism, [stated] that more than 80% of the alcoholics he has seen had a blood relative who also was an alcoholic.

*14. Hartford Courant, *October 29, 1970, story by Jack Zaiman on a poll of 842 people, conducted by Research Associates for Senator Dodd. (Weicker won the election, Duffey was second, and Dodd third.)* Poll Question: Which candidate do you favor for election to the United States Senate? "Senator Dodd led with 30 percent . . . Duffey followed with 28 percent and Weicker trailed with 23 percent. . . ." Twenty percent of the voter interviews were conducted in the home. The majority were conducted in shopping areas and work areas on a random basis.

15. *Judy:* You may not like driving at lower speeds, but it does save lives. I got a letter from a friend who's police chief in a small upstate N.Y. town—oh, about 10,000 people live there—and he says auto deaths in his town are down 33⅓ percent since the lower speed limit was instituted.
    John: I'd still rather tool along at 65 m.p.h.

16. Richard C. Gerstenberg, General Motors Board Chairman, arguing against more stringent auto exhaust emission standards, stated that the Clean Air Act passed by Congress would force auto makers to put out a car which ". . . would emit fewer hydrocarbons per day than would evaporate from two ounces of enamel you might use to paint your shutters."

17. *Judy:* It's male chauvinism that causes rape. Another reason to be a woman's libber.
    John: Oh, come on, Judy. You think male chauvinism is responsible for everything.
    Judy: Smirk all you want. But I just read a survey which showed that rape is higher in areas of high male chauvinism.
    John: Who conducted the survey?
    Judy: Some women's organization.

18. *John:* I know we have it pretty soft these days, but you know, sometimes I think we were happier when I was a kid.
    Judy: You've got to be kidding, John old man. Everyone knows the standard

of living in America is *way* up since World War II. I was reading just the other day how we eat more, and more expensive, food, have more autos per capita, more swimming pools, telephones, bathtubs—all sorts of things. They didn't even have TV then. Statistics don't lie.

John: Yeah. I suppose memory tends to make the past better than it was.

19. Vancouver *(British Columbia)* Sun, *July 10, 1975:* Britain has a strong socialist tradition more preoccupied with the distribution than the production of wealth. But distributionist preoccupations are a luxury for rich nations, which Britain no longer is. Since 1945, while world living standards tripled and productivity increased more than it did in the preceding 10,000 years, Britain went from being the second richest nation in northwest Europe (behind Sweden) to being the second poorest (behind Ireland).

20. Newsweek, *July 31, 1972, article on a government program to give rent money directly to the poor to find their own housing:* Financially, the program is a definite success, because the cost to the government has averaged out at only $1500 a year per family—a hugely favorable comparison with $25,000 per unit cost of new low-income housing.

Exercise II for Chapter Four

Check the media use of statistics and find examples of the statistical fallacies discussed in this chapter. (Explain *why* they are fallacious.)

D. C. REDEVELOPMENT LAND AGENCY

M E M O R A N D U M   May 4, 1972

TO : SEE ATTACHED DISTRIBUTION LIST

FROM: Harold D. Scott

SUBJ: Intra-Agency Communication

        In order to avoid negative re-
flections as a result of dysfunctional
internal communications, and in order to
enhance the possibilities of coordinated
balances I am strongly urging that any
item having a direct or indirect affect
on the NW#1 Project Area be made known
to me before, rather than after it's oc-
curence, when possible.

        Your cooperation in achieving a
better communication channel relative to
NW#1 would be greatly appreciated.

Attachment

Doublespeak, jargon, bureaucratese, governmentese, newspeak. Government memos often use jargon to hide (relative) triviality—to make communications seem more important than they really are (in addition to protecting the writer by getting a document "on the record"). The above memo, translated into plain English, seems to say simply this: *Please let me know when something is going to happen which concerns NW#1 Project Area before it happens rather than after, when it's too late.* But it all sounds so much more important and professional in doublespeak.

Chapter Five

Language

1. Emotive and Cognitive Meaning

If the purpose of a sentence is to inform, or to state a fact, some of its words must refer to things, events, or properties. Some of its words thus must have what we shall call **cognitive meaning.** The sentences in which they appear also may be said to have cognitive meaning—provided, of course, that they conform to grammatical rules and have no nonsense terms.

But words also may have **emotive meaning**—that is, they also may have positive or negative overtones. The emotive charges of some words are obvious. Think of the terms used in expressing prejudices against members of certain groups, like "nigger", "wop", "kike", "queer", or "fag". Or think of four-letter sex words, which even in this permissive age rarely appear in textbooks.

The emotively charged words just listed have negative emotive meanings. But lots of words have positive emotive overtones. Examples are "freedom", "love", "democracy", "springtime", and "peace".

On the other hand, many words have either neutral or mixed emotive meanings. "Pencil", "hydrogen", "run", and "river" tend to be neutral words. "Socialism", "automobile", "politician", and "whiskey" tend to have mixed emotive meanings.

In fact, almost any word that is emotively positive (or negative) to some may be just the opposite to others, perhaps because one man's meat is another man's poison. "God", for instance, has quite different emotive overtones for a sincere believer and for an atheist. Similarly, "dictatorship", a negative word for most Americans, in some contexts has positive overtones in the Soviet Union. And "black" now is beautiful in the eyes of many, although not all.

Even terms that on first glance appear neutral often turn out to be emotively charged, perhaps because the charge is fairly small. But even if the charge is quite large, we may fail to notice it because of prejudice or provincialism, or because the obvious sometimes gets overlooked. The words "bureaucrat", "government official", and "public servant", for instance, all refer to roughly the same class of people, and thus have roughly the same cognitive meaning. But their emotive meanings, usually overlooked, are quite different. Of the three, only "government official" is close to being neutral.

It is sometimes claimed that emotive meaning gets in the way of rational "objective" thought. According to this view, serious intellectual uses of language should be stripped of their emotive content so that we can deal rationally with their cognitive content. Thus, newspapers, textbooks, political rhetoric, even advertisements, on this view, should be written in emotively neutral language.[1]

But it isn't at all clear that this view is correct. For one thing, the emotive meanings of terms differ from person to person. For another, it is extremely difficult, perhaps impossible, to write, say, history books, news articles, or political speeches using only emotively neutral terms. And for another, it is debatable whether such writing can be read easily or with profit.

For it isn't only in poetry or literature that the emotive element gives language its charm, interest, and even importance. Newspapers and books would be extremely dull if written only in emotively neutral language. And relating what we read to problems in our daily lives would be very difficult.

No, the point of becoming aware of the emotive side of language is to become aware of how this otherwise *useful* feature of language can be used to con us into accepting fallacious arguments. The point is to understand this language tool—a tool that can be, and is, used for both good and evil purposes.

2.   Emotive Meaning and Con Artistry

Con artists take advantage of the emotive side of language in two very important ways: (1) They use emotive meaning to mask cognitive meaning—to whip up emotions so that *reason* gets overlooked; and (2) they use emotively neutral terms, or euphemisms (less offensive terms used in place of more offensive ones), to dull the force of what they say and thus make acceptable what otherwise might not be.

New York Daily News editorials are famous for their use of emotively charged expressions (partly because most newspapers, including the competing *New York Times*, tend to avoid emotional language, ending up with dull editorials). A relatively mild *Sunday News* editorial (September 8, 1974) on a campaign reform bill started with the title "A Snare and a Delusion" (compare that with the emotively less charged "An Unsatisfactory Bill", or even "A Misguided Bill"). It then referred to the bill's "*ogreish* feature" and the idea of "*saddling* the taxpayers with the cost of campaigns" (compare: "assessing the taxpayers . . ."), finding the saddling "*obnoxious*" (not just "ill advised" or "wrong"). Some other emotively charged expressions it used were "well-disciplined *band of zealots*", "*grab* control", "*ridiculous*", and "increase the clout". (See the exercise in Chapter Six for another *Daily News* editorial using lots of colorful language.)

---

[1]Proponents of this view usually associate all evaluative language with emotive meaning, including that of ethics and aesthetics. This assumes that evaluative terms such as "right" and "good" as used in sentences such as "Killing is sometimes morally right" and "That is a good painting" are basically emotive terms, a conclusion many would deny.

What *is* in a name?

Slow Down[2]

By James S. Kunen

I don't know when it started, but names are going to hell.

I felt at home in the world when shampoos had names like "Halo," and football teams were called the "Philadelphia Eagles," and bands went by handles like the "Del Vikings." Now I'm supposed to live with shampoos called "Gee Your Hair Smells Terrific," and football teams with singular tags like "The Philadelphia Bell," and bands with post-psychedelic-derivative names like "Mahogany Rush"; and I don't like it.

That's why I'm happy to tell you about a couple of naming competitions—two chances for us to strike back.

It seems last November a man by the name of Alex Parker bought the Allied Chemical Tower, né the Times Tower, a.k.a. No. 1 Times Square, and at midnight on New Year's Eve, he smashed a bottle of champagne on it and un-named it. It is now dubbed the No Name Building, and though I think that's a pretty good moniker, Mr. Parker wants to rename it again, and he's going to announce a public competition to do it. Whoever submits the winning name will win some sort of prize, though the real prize, I should think, would be the satisfaction of naming the building which dominates the Square which used to be called The Crossroads of the World.

It has also come to my attention that NASA has decided it needs more "catchy" names for its projects. They renamed the Earth Resources Technology Satellite Program "Landsat," and their oceanographic satellite program "Seasat." At that point they decided they needed help. They're soliciting new names (send 'em to NASA Headquarters, Washington) for the "Space Shuttle," a reusable vehicle to ferry men and machines to earth orbit and back. Leave aside for the moment whether the Shuttle program should exist at all. (A lot of things that don't exist have names: the International Communist Conspiracy, the Free World, the Free Enterprise System, to name a few. As a matter of fact, when things don't exist is when their names are most important. But that's another story.) We're putting a lot of money into the Shuttle, and we're going to hear a lot about it. It may as well be easy on the ear.

What chance have you got, in a naming competition, against the market research technocrats and their computers, you ask? A *good* chance. You're the solution. *They're* the problem. The degeneration of nomenclature is the fault of the pointy heads in the name game, who work by process of elimination, thinking names down, instead of thinking them up.

When Standard Oil (New Jersey) decided they needed a single name to replace the regional trademarks "Esso," "Enco," and "Enjay," their experts in linguistics, design, psychology, and statistics toiled for three years. They started out with 10,000 names, some produced by computer. They studied the world's principal languages to avoid objectionable meanings or connotations. ("Enco" was eliminated because in Japanese it means "stalled car.") They examined 15,000 telephone directories lest they pick something already taken. They did linguistic studies of 55 languages to make sure *everybody* would be able to pronounce the new trademark. They interviewed 7,000 people, doing word association tests to find a trademark that sounded "positive and progressive." They noted that a double x would be distinctive, because, except in proper names, it occurs in no language except Maltese. Finally, they set up prototype signs on an abandoned airstrip in a remote area of South Carolina, and drove executives past them at various speeds, at night and in daylight, to judge how the name looked. After all that labor—and at a cost (including implementation of the changeover) of something like $100 million—they brought forth the wondrous new name "Exxon." This from a company which in the past 90 years had used and discarded such truly mellifluous brand names as "Polarine," "Stanacola," "Aladdin," "Eupion," and "Astral" Oil.

Exxon! For this they needed a computer? We'll be better off sticking with the traditional methods of arriving at a name: individual genius, luck, and Divine Inspiration.

George Eastman—*he* didn't have computers, but he was smart. He wanted to coin a trademark for his pocket camera which "must be short, incapable of being misspelled, with a vigorous and distinct personality," he wrote. "The letter 'k' has been a favorite with me. It seems a strong, incisive sort of letter." It was also the first letter of his mother's maiden name. Filial devotion served him well.

A certain Dr. Bunting—*he* didn't have computers, but he was on fortune's good side. A Baltimore pharmacist, 50 years ago he was selling a new vanishing cream, which he called "Dr. Bunting's Sunburn Remedy." One day a customer declared, "Your cream *knocked* my *eczema!*" The rest is history.

Or take Harley Proctor. *He* didn't have computers, but a name *came to him*. The manufacturer of a slow-selling product then named "White Soap," Proctor was sitting in church one Sunday in 1879 when he heard Psalm 45 read. Verse 8 struck him like a thunderbolt: "your robes are all fragrant with myrrh and aloes and cassia. From *ivory* palaces stringed instruments make you glad." A star was born.

Somewhere in the language there lurk great names for the building and space project. I suppose changing names is not what you'd call dealing with the substance of our problems. But substance isn't everything. Until we change the world, we can at least make it sound good.

Government officials and other politicians tend to be masters of emotive con games. In fact, they have invented a whole new language to take advantage of the emotive side of language, in particular, by employing emotively neutral expressions rather than highly charged ones.

War, for instance, is hell. So government officials soften the emotive force of the war language they employ. We no longer have a *War Department* in the United States—it's now called the *Department of Defense.*

During the Vietnam war, we used particularly nasty weapons (for example, fragmentation bombs and napalm) in areas where they were certain to kill thousands of civilians. We dropped far more bombs on that tiny nation than on Germany and Japan combined in World War II. To make all this palatable, a "doublespeak" language was developed. Here are a few examples (with translations):

Pacification center	Concentration camp
Incursion	Invasion (as in "Cambodian incursion")
Protective reaction strike	Bombing
Surgical strike	Precision bombing
Incontinent ordinance	Off-target bombs (usually used when they kill civilians)
Friendly fire	Shelling friendly village or troops by mistake
Specified strike zone	Area where soldiers can fire at anything—replaced "free fire zone" when that became notorious
Waterborne logistic craft	Sampan (as in "waterborne logistic craft sunk")
Interdiction	Bombing
Air support	Bombing
Strategic withdrawal	Retreat (when our side does it)
Advisor	Military officer (before we admitted "involvement" in Vietnam) or C.I.A. agent
Termination	Killing
Termination with prejudice	Assassination

Enemy infiltration	Movement of enemy troops into the battle area
Reinforcements	Movement of friendly troops into the battle area
Selective ordinance	Napalm (also similarly "selective" explosives)

Here are a few ordinary doublespeaks, with emphasis on Watergate language:

Inappropriate	Illegal
Entry	Burglary (as in "the entry into Democratic headquarters")
Electronic surveillance *or* Intelligence gathering	Wiretapping *or* Illegal eavesdropping
Indicated	Said (usually when what was said was a lie or politically risky)
Thrift shop	Day-old bakery store
Terminal objective	Goal
Destabilize	Overthrow (as in "We intended to destabilize the communist government in Chile.")
Termination	Any kind of ending (for example, of a relationship; in military and spy circles generally restricted to death)
Life insurance	Insurance against an early death
Terminology, Nomenclature	Name
The War Between the States	The Civil War
Zero defect system	Perfection
Containment of information	Withholding of information
Combat emplacement evacuator	Shovel (military)
Aerodynamic personnel accelerator	Parachute
Mature	Fat (as in "clothes for mature women")

Watergate-ese reached its peak with Nixon's press secretary Ron Zeigler, who was responsible for the famous "all previous White House statements about the Watergate case are inoperative". Here is his reply when asked whether some Watergate tapes were still intact:

I would feel that most of the conversations that took place in those areas of the White House that did have the recording system would in almost their entirety be in existence but the special prosecutor, the court, and, I think, the American people are sufficiently familiar with the recording system to know where the recording devices existed and to know the situation in terms of the recording process but I feel, although the process has not been undertaken yet in the preparation of the material to abide by the court decision, really, what the answer to the question is.

Zeigler's remark so impressed the Committee on Public Doublespeak of the National Council of Teachers of English that they gave him their first annual Gobbledygook award for his effort. They also gave Colonel David Opfer, USAF press officer in Cambodia, an award for this gem:

You always write it's bombing, bombing, bombing. It's *not* bombing! It's air support.

Low-income	Poor
Inner city	Slum
Correctional facility	Prison
Selected out	Fired (used by U.S. State Department)
Bathroom tissue	Toilet paper
Night soil	Human excrement
Adjustment center	Solitary confinement cell
Consumer	Buyer
Investigative reporting	Muckraking
End use allocation	Rationing (specifically, in sections of the Energy Emergency Act of 1973 empowering the president to initiate gas rationing)
Director of development	Fund raiser

Supplemental relationship	Adultery
Gift	Bribe (as used to refer to political bribes paid by Nelson Rockefeller to William Ronan and others)
The final solution	Extermination of Jews

President Eisenhower's residence in Gettysburg, Pennsylvania, was usually referred to as his "farm". But newsmen once referred to it (in a fit of pique?) as his "country estate". (Richard Nixon's California estate was often referred to as his "compound". Real estate ads tout "homes", rarely houses.)

A *New York Times* page one article (October 18, 1974) quoted U.S. Commerce Department statistics as saying that the nation's total economic output declined during the July–September period for the third consecutive quarter. It then quoted Secretary of Commerce Frederick B. Dent as insisting that the United States was *not* in a recession: "He said the current state of the economy could be called 'a spasm' or 'sidewise waffling' ". Yet clearly, a nine-month continuous decline in output *is* a recession. Commerce Secretary Dent seems to have tried to "waffle" on his vocabulary.

What something is called can be extremely important. The U.S. Constitution grants the Congress the sole right to declare war. So a president who wants to engage in a military venture without getting the consent of Congress (perhaps it could be obtained at best only with great effort and expense) will be inclined to *rename* his military venture. U.S. military forces have fought in many places since World War II, our last declared war—the most prominent being Korea, Vietnam, and Cambodia.

Let's examine one more political example, this time in context, to illustrate the sneakiness of "denatured" language. Here is Admiral Isaac C. Kidd, Chief of Navy Material, explaining a Navy memo urging contractors to spend another $400 million to keep Congress from cutting Navy appropriations.[3]

We have gone with teams of competent contract people from Washington to outlying field activities to look over their books with them . . . to see in what areas there is susceptibility to improved capability to commit funds.

In other words, the Navy asked contractors to try to increase costs so the Navy could spend more money. Doublespeak masks the true import of language behind the dull mush of emotively neutral circumlocutions.

---

[3]*Washington Monthly,* May 1972, p. 40.

Fieldingese

Language is manipulated for many purposes. Temple Fielding does it to sell his famous travel guides—his gimmick is replacing the "catalogue" approach to travel guide writing with jazzier language which has "crackle", so that reading his travel guides is more fun, even if they're a little fuzzy on facts and figures. For instance, he doesn't permit his writers to call tourists "tourists"—they're "voyagers", or "nomads", or "adventurers", or. . . . His writers constantly invent new words with real crackle, like "Holiday Inn-siders", "yumptious", and "German atmosbeer". Here is an example of how it looks in context:

> Papakia (5 Iridanou St.) means 'The Duckling'—and the fowl deeds relating to its namesake are balm to the palate. Hellenic plus pan-global pannings from its versatile kitchen; somewhat costly by Athenian standards; conveniently sited 3 blocks from the Hilton, so flocks of our finely feathered American eagles and their chicks migrate here. We'd cliche it as a ducky choice.

And here is how it would look in a "catalogue" type travel guide, according to William E. Burroughs, former writer for Fielding (in his article in [More], June 1974):

> Papakia (5 Iridanou St.) means 'Duckling'. This restaurant is conveniently located three blocks from the Hilton. Although it serves no duck, it does offer a wide variety of regional and international dishes starting at $6, which is a bit higher than competitive places. The decor is stucco and timber, everything is clean, and service is prompt and friendly. Dolmades, Souvlakia, and Moussaka are the pick of the Greek specialties and are easily worth their price. Closed Mondays.

Doublespeak crops up everywhere. Superstitious people don't like living or working on the thirteenth floor. So most tall buildings have no floor *called* the thirteenth, although all tall buildings have a thirteenth floor, labeled fourteen, of course.

In New York City, corner apartments on Park Avenue have Park Avenue addresses, but on neighboring Lexington Avenue, they often have side street addresses, such as 132 E. 35th Street instead of 260 Lexington Avenue. "Lex" just isn't chic.

Governments, of course, are not exceptional in their dull use of language. So-called scholarly writing has a sleep-inducing obfuscatory quality all its own. A social science writer, Talcott Parsons, is responsible for this gem:

Skills constitute the manipulative techniques of human goal attainment and control in relation to the physical world, so far as artifacts for machines especially designed as tools do not yet supplement them. Truly human skills are guided by organized and codified *knowledge* of both the things to be manipulated and the human capacities that are used to manipulate them. Such knowledge is an aspect of cultural level symbolic processes, and . . . requires the capacities of the human central nervous system, particularly the brain. This organic system is clearly essential to all the symbolic processes . . .

This passage was cited by Stanislav Andreski,[4] who translated it into

. . . a developed brain, acquired skills, and knowledge are needed for attaining human goals.

Which sounds about right.

It is important to remember that the villain in this story is not emotive meaning, nor even its use in argument. Doublespeak shows that emotively empty language can be used just as effectively to bamboozle the public as can overcharged language. The villains are *those who use* the emotive side of language to con, and *those who permit themselves to fall for such shenanigans.*[5]

Because Christmas Eve falls on a Thursday, the day has been designated a Saturday for work purposes. Factories will close all day, with stores open a half day only. Friday, December 25, has been designated a Sunday with both factories and stores open all day. Monday, December 28, will be a Wednesday for work purposes. Wednesday, December 30, will be a business Friday. Saturday, January 2 will be a Sunday, and Sunday, January 3, will be a Monday. (From an AP report about a Prague government edict)

What's in a name? Plenty. It makes a difference what name we give to things, even days of the week, because we associate certain days (like Monday) with work, and others (like Sunday) with rest. That's why the Czechs chose to change the names of days rather than have people work on days called "Sunday" and rest on days called "Friday".

---

[4]*In Social Science as Sorcery* (London: Andre Deutsch, 1972). (Also cited in *Time,* September 25, 1972, p. 67, and in Dwight Bolinger, "Truth Is a Linguistic Question", *Language,* vol. 49, 1973.)

[5]Notice how the word "villain" sounds perfectly all right when used to refer to those "other guys" who con us via language, but perfectly dreadful when applied to *us* when *we* fall for language cons.

3. Sexism in Language[6]

George Orwell remarked that "If thought corrupts language, language can also corrupt thought." No one doubts that sexism is reflected in our language. The question today is whether the sexist features of our language tend to reinforce sexism in our thoughts. Many, perhaps most, social scientists would argue that they do, in particular in making women feel inferior or like outsiders.

Let's look at several features of the English language which make it difficult for a person to speak without making undesired references to sex or without expressing sexist attitudes one may not feel.

a. English has no neuter singular pronouns that can be used to refer to human beings. Instead, masculine singular pronouns ("he", "him", "his") must be used if singular pronouns are to be used at all. The result is often quite ludicrous, especially when attempts to avoid this sexist feature of language fail. For instance, an Ohio General Assembly House Bill (110th Assembly, Bill 302) states that "No person may require another person to perform, participate in, or undergo an abortion of pregnancy, against *his* will." Yet the person in question always is, of course, a *woman.*

b. Several key English masculine nouns also have a neuter use, which is often hard to avoid. The chief example, of course, is the word "man" itself, which may refer to men only or, in its neuter use, to the whole human race. Countless generations of logic students have encountered this use when exposed to the original syllogism: "All men are mortal. All Greeks are men. Therefore all Greeks are mortal."

In recent years, some women's liberationists have been trying to replace this neuter use of masculine nouns with truly neuter nouns. In particular, they have been trying to replace the neuter use of "man" with the word "person", and the word "mankind" with something like "humanity".

Is this attempt worth the effort? Imagine, for a moment, that you are a woman philosopher in the audience at a public lecture in which the male speaker constantly uses expressions like, "Now a *man* would suppose that. . . ." or "A *man* who felt this way. . . ." Would you feel left out, slighted, or affronted?[7] Would you feel that you are not taken as seriously as a philosopher as are men?

c. The word "man" also is the villain in many common neuter compound words.[8] Particularly vexing are position or occupational terms, such as "congress-

---

[6]Special thanks to Prof. Joan Straumanis, Denison University, for her invaluable help with this section.

[7]This happened at a public lecture given by Richard Wollheim at the City University of New York Graduate Center (May 1975). Wollheim's choice of language was particularly unfortunate because about half of his audience was female. In the question period later, Gertrude Ezorsky, philosopher and fighter for women's rights, pointedly used neuter nouns in phrasing her questions: "Suppose a *person* were to. . . ." and "If a *person's* need for. . . ."

[8]In Old English, "man" meant "human being". It did not mean "male human being". A male human being was referred to by the word "wer" (as in "were wolf"—*man* wolf), and a female human being was referred to by the word "wif" (as in "housewife"—housewoman). The sexist use of "man" is a later development.

Puzzle

A father and his son are in an auto accident. The father dies, and the son is rushed to the hospital. A doctor is called to operate, takes one look at the boy, and says, "I can't operate on him, he's my son." How is this possible?

Try this puzzle on your friends. Most people, when hearing it for the first time, automatically think of a doctor as *male,* and take some time realizing that the doctor has to be the boy's *mother.*

---

man", "salesman", "freshman", statesman", and "chairman". But other words also are loaded against women, including "manmade", "man-sized", "man-of-war", and "man power". (Ironically, a giant temporary employment agency specializing in secretarial help, that is, female office help, is called "Manpower".) It is only recently, in response to insistent demand from women's liberationists (note the emotive overtones of that expression!), that terms such as "chairperson" and "congresswoman" have come into use.

---

resource . . . 5. an action or measure to which one may have recourse in an emergency; expedient: *Woman's most frequently used resource is undoubtedly tears.* 6. capability in dealing with a situation or in meeting difficulties: *a man of limited resources. (Random House Dictionary of the English Language,* reprinted in *MS* magazine, January 1975, p. 107)

Sexism in the dictionary.

---

d. Equally bad, from the point of view of women's liberationists, are nouns that take female endings, such as "usherette", "Jewess", or "aviatrix". To see the foolishness in these endings, try forming analogous words with the male ending ". . . er", such as "usherer", or "Jewer". If that doesn't convince you, notice that feminine endings of this kind often are used to mean "small" as in "kitchen-*ette*", or "imitation" as in "leatherette". (None of this should be surprising, since the word "feminine" itself has a pejorative use in the word "effeminate" which no masculine word can match.)

e. Many common English expressions, often hard to avoid without stilted circumlocution, tend to obscure the identity of women, or reduce them to second-class status.

First, a woman loses her last name in marriage, taking on the name of her husband. Worse still, having acquired that new name, she now finds that in many cases this bow to the superiority of her spouse is not enough; she finds herself referred to as say, "Mrs. Harold Gordon", or when she and her husband are mentioned together as "the Harold Gordons", or "Mr. and Mrs. Harold Gordon". Unsympathetic males should imagine how up-tight they might be at a cocktail party after being introduced as "Mr. Alice Gordon", or with their wives as "the Alice Gordons" or "Mrs. and Mr. Alice Gordon".

In addition, it should be noted that until women's liberationists coined the word "Ms.", English forced us to provide the marital status of a woman in common greetings. "Mrs. Smith" labels a woman as married, "Miss Smith" as single, but "Mr. Smith" might be single or married.

Language and Belief

To believe that God is Father is to become aware of oneself not as a stranger, not as an outsider or an alienated person, but *as a son* who belongs or a person appointed to a marvelous destiny, which he shares with the whole community. To believe that God is Father means to be able to say "we" in regard to all men. (Gregory Baum, *Man Becoming: God in Secular Experience.* New York: Seabury Press, 1970)

Language and belief interact, one reinforcing the other. Here is a comment on the above by Mary Daly in her "New Autobiographical Preface" to *The Church and the Second Sex: With a New Postchristian Introduction* (New York: Harper & Row, 1975): "A woman whose consciousness has been aroused can say that such language makes her aware of herself, as a stranger, as an outsider, as an alienated person, not as a daughter who belongs or who is appointed to a marvelous destiny. She cannot belong to *this* without assenting to her own lobotomy."

Men are often amazed to discover how many sexist expressions there are in the English language. Here are just a few, omitting locker-room examples, with "reverse sexist" parallels to the right:

Business girl	Business boy
Man and wife	Woman and husband
Ladies and gentlemen	Gentlemen and ladies

Lady lawyer	Gentleman lawyer
Straw man fallacy	Straw woman fallacy
The fair sex	The ugly sex?
Girl Friday	Boy Friday
Man-sized job	Woman-sized job

Finally, it should be noted that feminine terms exist which have no male counterparts, even though males and females both play the relevant roles. For instance, men and women both attend colleges, yet there is no masculine counterpart to the word "coed". Sometimes, however, feminine terms come to refer to males also, one interesting example being the word "virgin". And mention of that term is perhaps as good a time as any to end our little journey into what for textbooks has been an exploration into, shall we say, *virgin* territory?

A *Wilmington Comment* on Governor Tribbitt's appointment of Irene Shadoan of the Associated Press as his press secretary at $20,000 a year. "If he wants to pay $10,000 a mammary, that's his business." (From *Delaware State News*, reprinted in *MS* magazine)

Can you imagine a similar remark about paying a man $10,000 a testicle?

Summary of Chapter Five

1. Most words have emotive meanings (in addition to cognitive meanings). Words like "oppression", "kike", and "bitch" have more or less negative (con) emotive overtones; words like "spring", "free", and "satisfaction" positive (pro) emotive overtones, and words like "socialism", "marijuana", and "God" mixed emotive overtones.

   Words that have roughly the same cognitive meaning often have radically different emotive meanings.

   Example: "bureaucrat", "government official", and "public servant".

   The point of becoming aware of the emotive side of language is not to learn to avoid such language—the emotive element gives language much of its charm, interest, and importance. Emotively neutral language is dull. The point is to learn how emotive language can trick us into accepting fallacious arguments.

Con artists use the emotive side of language (1) to mask cognitive meaning by whipping up emotions so that reason is overlooked; and (2) to dull the force of language so as to make acceptable what otherwise might not be. The latter often is accomplished by means of euphemisms (less offensive expressions used in place of more offensive ones) or a kind of doublespeak that lulls the unwary into acceptance.

2. The English language contains features which mirror sexist attitudes of our past.
   a. Masculine pronouns, such as "him", or "he", are used also as neuter pronouns, as in "Everyone should watch **his** hat or purse".
   b. Several key English masculine nouns, in particular the noun "man" itself, are used also as neuter nouns, as in **"Man** is a rational animal". Some of these are fairly easy to avoid (for instance, it's not stilted to say "Human beings are rational animals"), some not.
   c. The word "man" also causes trouble in its neuter use in many common compound words, such as "freshman" and "statesman".
   d. Special feminine endings are customary where they have no real point, unless it is pejorative. Examples are "Jewess" and "drum majorette".
   e. Many common English expressions tend to obscure or belittle the identity of women, for instance, when a woman is referred to by her husband's name, as say "Mrs. John Smith". And women are similarly demeaned by expressions like "business girl" and "girl Friday".

Exercises for Chapter Five

1. Here is a short *New York Daily News* editorial (April 5, 1972):

Any Old Jobs for Homos?

Herewith, a cheer for the U.S. Supreme Court's ruling Monday (with Justice W. O. Douglas dissenting—but you knew that) that states governments have a right to refuse employment to homosexuals.

Fairies, nances, swishes, fags, lezzes—call 'em what you please—should of course be permitted to earn honest livings in nonsensitive jobs.

But government, from federal on down, should have full freedom to bar them from jobs in which their peculiarities would make them security or other risks. It is to be hoped that this Supreme Court decision will stand for the foreseeable future.

   a. List the heavily emotive words or expressions you feel are used unfairly, explaining *why* in each case.
   b. Rewrite the editorial so that its cognitive import is the same, but the language used is as emotively neutral as possible. Compare your version with the original editorial for persuasive power.

2. Follow the instructions in question 1 for the *New York Daily News* editorial that appears in Chapter Six.

3. Here is another memo used by the *Washington Monthly* as a "Memo of the Month". Translate the body of the memo into plain English coming as close to the original meaning (so far as it can be determined) as you can.

Sacramento City-County Library

Intra-Department Correspondence

Date: October 14, 1971

To: ALL LIBRARY PERSONNEL — Shirley Louthan

From: HAROLD D. MARTELLE
CITY-COUNTY LIBRARIAN

Subject: PERSONNEL PROFILE FORM AND TELEPHONE DIRECTORY ATTACHMENT

The newly devised Personnel Profile form comprises a very necessary and integral function in the intellection of personnel services to this library system by providing data not currently available, by synthesizing employee qualifications and by projecting the basis for a comprehensive codification of all library staff experience and talent.

Although some of you have questioned the requirement for such a form by referring to application forms or Civil Service records, retrospection reveals that when the library's administrative offices were relocated to 930 T Street in February 1967, a significant portion of extant personnel files accidentally was eliminated and has never been replaced. Therefore, institution of the Personnel Profile will eliminate the paucity of available data while expending a minimum of time and expense. This form also will assist in the efficacious programming of manpower skills to related positions and/or need. In addition, the form will facilitate the immediate retrieval and expeditious articulation of available skills and personnel through an extensive codification of data.

In order to implement this form as soon as possible, please complete and return both the Profile and the attached sheet relating to the projected telephone directory of library personnel to the Personnel Office by Wednesday, October 27, 1971.

Thank you for your cooperation and immediate attention.

Harold D. Martelle, Jr.
City-County Librarian

---

4. Check current newspapers, magazines, or books and find at least two passages containing sexist language devices of the kind discussed in this chapter. Do you think that continual exposure to such language might affect your attitudes toward women? Explain.

5. Here are several ordinary English words or phrases. For each one find another having roughly the same cognitive meaning (or roughly the same reference) but different emotive meaning. (Example: The word "horse" is more or less emotively neutral. The words "steed" and "charger" are emotively pro, and the word "nag" con.)

1. Job	*7. Usury
*2. Intelligence	8. Smell
3. Unmarried young woman	9. Movie
4. Policeman	10. Dead relative
5. Caucasian	*11. Add to
6. Cemetery	12. Sign

"*If the coach and horses and the footmen and the beauti-ful clothes all turned back into the pumpkin and the mice and the rags, then how come the glass slipper didn't turn back, too?*"

Two key factors in critical or creative thinking are (1) the ability to bring relevant background information to bear on a problem; and (2) the ability to carry through the relevant implications of an argument or position to determine whether they hang together. The above cartoon illustrates the latter. The child carries through the reasoning in the Cinderella story and finds it wanting. A child who brings relevant background information to bear on the Santa Claus story (for instance, wonders how Santa could get down millions of chimneys in one night) illustrates the former.

Chapter Six

Analyzing Extended Arguments

The prejudice against careful analytic procedure is part of the human impatience with technique which arises from the fact that men are interested in results and would like to attain them without the painful toil which is the essence of our moral finitude.

Morris R. Cohen

People want answers, but they don't want to do the hard thinking it takes to get them.

Harold Gordon

So far we have considered relatively short arguments, and these only to illustrate fallacious reasoning. But in daily life we often encounter much longer passages, which in effect comprise arguments or series of related arguments. It takes more than just the ability to spot fallacies to deal with such extended passages.

There are many methods for analyzing extended passages, and each person will have his own preference. The margin note-summary method used here in analyzing an editorial and a political column is one which many people find congenial, at least as a model to be more or less approached in daily life, as time permits and interest dictates.

The first step is simply to mark each important passage and, perhaps, place an indication of its content next to it in the margin. The second step is to use the margin notes to construct a summary of the article, which can then be used in turn to evaluate the original work.

1. Editorials

Newspaper, magazine, radio, and television editorials constitute an important and interesting part of the political scene. Let's examine an editorial from the *New York Times,* often said to be the best and most influential newspaper in the United States. The flavor of their editorials reflects this august position.

Here is the *Times* editorial[1] with margin notes attached.

Astoria Compromise

As an interim answer to a difficult problem requiring immediate resolution, Mayor Lindsay's compromise decision on the proposed generating plant in Astoria has much to rec-

(1) Conclusion: Lindsay compromise is good.

---

(2) Permits Con Ed what it thinks is needed capacity.

ommend it. Consolidated Edison has won permission to go ahead and build what it regards as urgently needed capacity to meet this community's electricity needs. But

(3) But it's a true compromise: Con Ed permitted only one-half the requested increase.

those who opposed the project because of understandable fear of additional pollution can console themselves that the expansion will be only half that originally requested.

Unfortunately, before the Mayor settled the issue, he fostered a bitter public debate that not only pitted some of his key subordinates against each other, but also inflamed the passions and fears of many. The angry reactions of some Astoria residents to the Lindsay compromise raise the unhappy possibility that the dispute has not ended, and that new and difficult roadblocks may appear to hamper those trying to build even the smaller generating plant the Mayor has approved.[2]

(4) Real import of L's decision: it voices idea that air is limited & all pollution sources must be considered.

The future may show, however, that the real importance of Mayor Lindsay's decision was its enunciation of an important principle fundamental to a rational anti-pollution policy. In effect, Mr. Lindsay has recognized that the city's supply of clean air is a limited resource whose availability must be protected by a comprehensive policy that takes account of all sources of pollution, rather than merely

(5) He advocates electric power over auto pollution when choice required.

dealing with individual sources in isolation. "If some pollution is inevitable and the choice is between sufficient electrical power or streets congested with automobiles," the Mayor said, "I would choose electrical power."

(6) Believing tradeoffs necessary, he's appointed committee to plan.

Having articulated his correct understanding that tradeoffs must be calculated and choices made, Mayor Lindsay has already appointed a five-member committee to work out a plan for limiting motor vehicle pollution here. The

(7) Lindsay asked to ban private cars from Manhattan at certain times & places.

organization called Citizens for Clean Air has gone a step further and asked the Mayor to ban private automobile traffic from Manhattan south of 59th Street during business hours. This is the direction in which the city must move

(8) This will eventually have to be done.

to protect its most precious possession, the air its citizens breathe.

And here is an itemized summary of what one person takes to be the main points of the editorial:

1. Mayor Lindsay's compromise on Con Ed's Astoria plant expansion has much to recommend it.

2. It permits them to build what they believe is urgently needed capacity.

---

[2]No margin notes are needed for this paragraph because it contains no material pertinent to the main point at issue.

3. But it compromises with the other side, since Con Ed is permitted only half of the increase it asked for.

4. The real import of Lindsay's decision may rest in his voicing of the rational antipollution idea that clean air is limited and must be protected by policies that consider all sources of pollution.

5. Lindsay (rightly?) advocates choosing electric power over auto pollution when a choice is required.

6. Understanding that "tradeoffs must be calculated" and "choices made", Lindsay has appointed a committee to plan for limited auto pollution in New York.

7. Citizens for Clean Air has asked Lindsay to ban private autos from parts of Manhattan during business hours.

8. This is the direction New York must move in to obtain clean air.

At this point, two things should be said by way of caution in using the margin note-summary method. First, when you skip part of a passage, you make a value judgment that the skipped material is not important. It takes practice and skill to know what to include and what to omit, and "experts" will differ on such matters.

Second, margin notes and summaries are shorthand devices, and should be briefer than the passage analyzed (otherwise, why use them?). But any shortening runs the risk of falsification. When using margin notes or summaries to aid in reasoning, remember that you don't want to draw conclusions from the shortened version that would not be valid for the original.

Notice that the *Times* editorial contains very few, if any, unnecessary emotive or value-tinged terms, and was constructed in a fairly orderly way. (Compare this with the *Daily News* editorial used as an exercise at the end of the chapter.) Nevertheless, it is not a paragon of rationality. Let's take the important statements in the editorial one by one, and then append a general comment.

Assertion 1 simply presents the claim to be defended in the editorial, namely that Lindsay's compromise was, on the whole, good. Assertion 2 tells us what Con Ed believed, namely that the increase was needed. Was Con Ed right? A very technical question; the layman is forced to bow to Con Ed's view unless someone presents pertinent evidence to the contrary. Expert testimony of this kind frequently is refuted by other evidence. But in this case, apparently, it was not; Con Ed did seem to need increased capacity to cover increases that were likely if unrestrained use of power continued to be permitted. (Whether they needed to *double* the Astoria plant capacity is another matter.)

Assertion 3 in effect comes close to saying that Lindsay's Solomon-like decision was right *because* it was a fifty-fifty compromise. The *Times* editorial thus seems to have committed what is often called the fallacy of the *golden mean*, since it nowhere *defends* Lindsay's decision *qua* its being a halfway measure. For instance, it doesn't argue that granting only one-quarter the requested increase would not be sufficient, or that granting it all would be too much. Assertion 4 is noncontroversial. Almost everyone pays lip service to it. (Living up to it is another matter.)

Assertion 5, while controversial, was not at issue between antipollutionists, Con Ed, and the mayor. We have here a genuine value judgment of great importance concerning which all of us must make up our minds. If the need to reduce air pollution forces us to choose between restricting private auto travel or restricting electric power use (for example, of air conditioners), which should we prefer? There are facts pertinent to the choice, such as the possibility of alternative modes of transportation. But they don't automatically determine the choice. It is human beings, using these facts, who must decide. Notice that the *Times* editorial neither presents these facts nor reasons from them. It simply presents its conclusion.

But assertion 6 is the crux. (Let's skip 7 and 8 to shorten the discussion.) There are two important comments to make about 6:

a. Some opponents of Mayor Lindsay claimed that for a while at least, we could have both less power plant pollution and less auto pollution without restricting the use of either, by (1) putting new power plants out of town in low-pollution areas; (2) requiring electric power producers such as Con Ed to use more expensive but also more efficient antipollution devices;[3] and (3) requiring more expensive but also more efficient auto pollution devices, ultimately requiring replacement of internal-combustion engines by something else, such as the gas-turbine engine.

b. Talk of "tradeoffs" and "compromises" masks the fact that while Con Ed was granted something tangible by Lindsay's decision (an increase in productive capacity), the other side was given talk and promises (a commission set up to *plan* for limiting pollution).

In other words, as opponents of Mayor Lindsay argued with some justification, he granted an increase to Con Ed, which inevitably would increase air pollution, but only paid lip service to one of the antipollutionist arguments (that ultimately we must choose between power and autos, and power should on the whole win). In addition, Lindsay ignored the other major antipollutionist proposals to expand power facilities out of town and to require more expensive but also more efficient emission devices and equipment.

The *New York Times,* it should be pointed out, seems to have been guilty along with Mayor Lindsay. In particular, the *Times* was guilty of suppressing evidence contrary to the conclusion it wanted to draw. This is one of the *Times'* chief devices for making its editorials seem plausible to its readers. Its position of prestige and authority does not permit open appeals to emotion or prejudice of the kind many other newspapers employ. (Again, see the *New York Daily News* editorial in the exercise section at the end of the chapter.) Omissions are much less obvious than the use of emotively charged phrases. They also are probably more effective with an educated but inadequately informed audience.

---

[3]For example, Anna Mayo, in the Village Voice, August 13, 1970, states: "George Spitz, Upper East Side (of Manhattan) candidate for state senator and member of the IMREC environmental research firm, has discovered that controls exist but maintains that Con Ed does not want to pay for them. He recently informed the company's Robert O. Lehrman that the state of Kansas has sulfur controls, to which Lehrman retorted that Kansas had coal rather than oil-fired plants. Spitz says he fired back that Boston is using such controls in oil-fired plants."

2. *Political Columns and Articles*

Let's get some more practice with the margin note-summary method of analysis. Here is a political column by the widely syndicated columnist Mary McGrory,[4] again with margin notes attached.[5]

Washington—Charles Reich's book, "The Greening of America," which caused a great stir in "radic-lib" circles since excerpts appeared in the *New Yorker* magazine, has nothing to do with the campaign—and everything.

Long after the last word has been mercifully spoken from the stump—and forgotten—it will be pondered and argued. For it is a study of what is wrong with America and what the new generation is doing to make it right.

Focus: A book on what's wrong with America & how the young will right it.

Young Are An Issue

The young are an issue in this election, largely due to the exertions of the Vice President.

It also is a handbook of revolution, but before the Vice President dives for his dictionary, he should know it advocates a revolution by peaceful means, by the infectious sight of young Americans who love life and take literally the pursuit of happiness.

Reich, a professor of law at Yale, dismisses politics as a way of changing the system. It is not because the only political spokesman his generation has had, Senator Eugene McCarthy, was routed, or even because his young followers were beaten into the ground.

(4)[1] Politics won't change the system. . . .

Reich thinks that political and legal reforms merely perpetuate a tyrannous corporate state, whose principal products are repression, dehumanization, war, pollution, injustice and pre-mixed peanut butter and jelly.

(4)[2] Because internal reform just perpetuates the evils of the system.

Change can be brought about only when the young revolutionaries can persuade their parents and the blue-collars to share their shattering assumption: "It doesn't have to be that way."

(6) System change requires young to convince others that change is possible.

Consciousness III

This bold thesis sets Consciousness III people—Reich's designation for those smitten by the difference between the American Dream and its reality—apart from previous gen-

(3)[1] Type III: Smitten by difference between American ideals & actual practice.

[4]© 1970 Washington Star Syndicate, Inc. Reprinted by permission.

[5]The numbers in the margin notes indicate where statements occur in the summary which follows.

(1) Type I: Believe in our system; are rigid, repressive, & think Communists, blacks, & hippies threaten them.
(2) Type II: Parents, strivers, status-seekers, failed idealists who strive for internal reform of system.
(5) Young who risk bodily harm are better than liberals who spend money in support of causes.

erations. Consciousness I worshippers of free enterprise and the "American way" are rigid and repressive, see themselves threatened by Communists, blacks and hippies.

Consciousness II, the bewildered parents of today, are the strivers, the status-seekers, failed idealists who accept the institutions and strive to reform the structure.

Reich coldly compares yesterday's stricken liberal giving a check or his name to a cause with today's youth who puts his body on the line to resist the draft, to shield the black or stay the bulldozer.

New Champions

The new generation has had other champions and defenders—George Wald and the authors of the Scranton Report, for example. Reich is the first to present the defiant in full profile, the whole culture with acid, rock, bell-bottoms, and an unshakable belief that "man . . . is not a creature to be controlled, regulated, administered, trained, clipped, coated and anesthetized."

The Vietnam war, "a monster incarnated out of the madness of the state," gave them unity and an audience. In a reversal of roles still not assimilated, they led their elders in resistance to that madness. If it ever ends, they should be given a major share of the credit.

(3)[2] Type III: Bright, brave, idealists, revere life & accept each other more than have previous generations.
(3)[3] Type III: Can run a revolution because of above [(3)[2]].

To Reich, they are bright, brave, questing, white-hot idealists, with a reverence for life and an acceptance of themselves and each other unprecedented in history. We must assume, in the light of that exploit, they can run a revolution.

While it is hard in this dark season to envision the world they might make in which affection and tolerance and individual worth will be the law, it is pleasant to contemplate.

Since Reich has gone so far to make them both admirable and lovable, and has done so much to enlighten their nervous elders about their nature and their goals, it is a pity that he did not express some reservations about the most unnerving aspect of their life style, their drug habits.

(3)[4] Type III: Con: They use drugs.

He is so evangelical about the awareness-sharpening qualities of marijuana, he almost forgets to indicate that their whole beautiful dream could go up in smoke.

Subsidized by Parents

(3)[5] Type III: Con: Financially dependent on parents.

He also neglects to mention that they are the first revolutionaries to be subsidized by Mom and Dad, who pay the bills while they float about looking for their "thing."

These are lapses which will be pounced upon by the people who would most profit from his provocative and potentially healing book—an eloquent plea for reconciliation at a moment when division is being pursued as a positive good by those in charge of our society.

(7) We need reconciliation, but those in power pursue division.

Having made margin notes on the copy, the next step is to construct a summary of the main ideas in McGrory's column:

1. Reich distinguishes three types of people. Type I believe in the American system, are rigid and repressive, and think they're threatened by communists, blacks, and hippies.

2. Type II, parents (yesterday's liberals?), are strivers, status-seekers, idealists; they strive for internal reform.

3. Type III (the young? peaceful revolutionaries? hippies?) are disturbed by the difference between American ideals and actual practice. They use drugs (bad) and are financially dependent on their parents (bad), but they can run a (peaceful) revolution because they're bright, brave idealists who accept themselves and each other more than did any past generation.

4. Politics won't change the system, because reform from within just perpetuates the (in practice bad) system.

5. The young who risk bodily harm for their causes are better than yesterday's liberals who spend money in support of theirs.

6. To change the system, the young idealists must convince others that it can be changed ("doesn't have to be as it is").

7. We need reconciliation (which the young will bring?), but those in power pursue division.

After a summary of this kind is made, we're in a better position to evaluate the structure of the original, and to see how literary devices get in the way of clarity. Particularly loose is the variety of descriptions given for people of type II ("bewildered parents of today", "yesterday's stricken liberal") and type III ("today's youth", "young revolutionaries") . . . "smitten by the difference between the American dream and its reality").

Of course, good literary devices need not reduce clarity. On the contrary, when properly used in the right context (what is right for a novel may not be right for political prose), they contribute to clarity. Anyone who has ever graded term papers knows that clarity and quality of style tend to go hand in hand. We must chalk up the lack of clarity and cogency in this case to the writer (or perhaps to two writers—Mary McGrory and Charles Reich).

Let's now turn to an evaluation of the McGrory column, and of Reich's position as it is given there.[6]

---

[6]One of the problems with political columns in newspapers is that they must be short, making adequate treatment of most issues quite difficult. For a better (and longer) account of Reich's theory, see his own account in the *New Yorker*, September 26, 1970, or " 'Greening of America'—Only on Weekends," by Joel Kramer, the *Village Voice*, November 19, 1970, or read Reich's book, *The Greening of America*, Random House, New York, 1970.

There seem to be two major defects in the column. First, the three-fold classification of political types is not a very good one. Many people, perhaps most, fall into two and sometimes all three of the categories described in this column. Aren't many who believe in the American system (type I) also parents, strivers, and status seekers (type II)? Aren't many of yesterday's (type II) stricken liberals also smitten (as are type IIIs) by the difference between the American dream and its reality? Don't some type Is and IIs also put their bodies on the line as do type III people?

In addition, the classification suffers from extreme vagueness, making it often difficult, or impossible, to know what criteria to use in specific cases. What is it, after all, to be "worshippers of free enterprise and the American way"? How do we tell when people have a "reverence for life and an acceptance of themselves and each other"? How aware must we be of the disparity between ideals and practice before we can be said to be "smitten" with this knowledge? We all have some idea what these phrases mean; they aren't empty of meaning. So we can tell whether or not they apply in a few clear-cut cases. But in all too many cases their meaning is too murky to allow their application with any confidence.

One wonders, also, whether youth really is a cogent requirement for class III membership, since merely having passed thirty, or even forty, seems to be no insurmountable bar to membership in the radical or hippie communities, which presumably contain mostly type III people.

The three-fold classification suffers also from failure to cover all political types. In technical terms, it is not *exhaustive*. A great many people, from true conservatives (who aren't repressive) to socialists and communists (who aren't status seekers and who do want to change the system), are not members of any of the three classes.

But the main defect in this article is that it begs all the interesting questions. To see how large a defect this is, let's use the technique of bringing to bear opinions from other viewpoints. Since the column was written from the viewpoint of type III people, let's look at it from the viewpoints of typical members of the other two categories.

A typical type I person would challenge being characterized as repressive, claiming rather that he is in favor of all the freedom and tolerance for a given person that is consistent with law and order and with freedom for everyone else. He would claim that the charge of repression results from his favoring harsh responses to those who refuse to work within the system, those who foment protests, riots, and violence, which take freedom away from others.

He also would be inclined to wonder if perhaps the young radicals are not too impatient, expecting and demanding quick solutions to old problems, and failing to appreciate the slow improvements our system has yielded, particularly in material wealth. He would wonder if the young realize the great risks involved even in peaceful revolutions (although he would doubt that revolutions are likely to be peaceful).

Finally, he would ask whether the young, having lived their whole lives during the Cold War, have perhaps become so used to the threat from the Soviet Union and China that they treat it much too lightly.

These "right wing" conservative ideas may be wrong. But the McGrory column gave no indication that Reich seriously argued that they are wrong.

Most liberals (type II) would be inclined to agree with conservatives about the risks of working outside the system to effect change. While aware of the disparity between ideals and reality in our country, they would be more inclined than type IIIs to appreciate the progress that has been made on some of our basic problems since World War II. They would also be more aware of the repressive reaction that ill-prepared action (bodies on the line) is likely to bring about.

In addition, they would doubt that all the brightness, self-awareness, good will, and ideals in the world are sufficient to bring about major and lasting improvements without careful planning, organization, knowledge of history and sociological theory, long hard work, and cold cash—all of which they see lacking in what to them are the otherwise admirable young people of today. (Lack of knowledge of the past is perhaps the most frequently voiced liberal complaint against type III members of the younger generation.)

Finally, many liberals would be inclined to react strongly against the sentiment embodied in the fourth assertion (that you can't reform the system effectively from within by political means), on the grounds that meaningful, although slow, reform has occurred from time to time from within, especially in recent years.

It may be argued that, after all, one political column can't do everything, and that this one merely attempts to outline an important and current book. But this won't wash, because the column did not merely report; it sided with Mr. Reich and Consciousness III. And it never justified that choice. (The space limitations of a syndicated political column are cruel. But a writer who agrees to that limitation cannot then use that as an excuse for distortion or error.)

It should be obvious after consideration of the McGrory column and the *Times* editorial that analysis of political argument requires much more than cogent reasoning. The most brilliant logician in the world cannot deal adequately with typical political discussion if his mind is empty of thought on political matters. Political argument generally deals with broad topics which are the center of much controversy and which cannot all be argued about every time they are appealed to. To handle these broad topics we must bring to bear all sorts of previously accepted beliefs developed by prior thought on these matters. That's why careless thought is so deadly—it contaminates later attempts to think more carefully.

3. Political Speeches

Political speeches generally are listened to rather than read. This makes critical analysis much more difficult, and margin notes impossible except on written versions. Let's analyze twelve short passages from a rather long speech (too long to be studied here in its entirety) which President Nixon delivered at Kansas State University on September 16, 1970. Here is the first excerpt:[7]

---

[7]The interested reader may want to consult the more extensive *New York Times* excerpts, which appear on p. 28 of the September 17, 1970 edition.

1. There are those who protest that if the verdict of democracy goes against them, democracy itself is at fault, the system is at fault; who say that if they don't get their own way, the answer is to burn or bomb a building.

This occurs near the beginning of the speech, and sets the tone for the rest. It attacks the tiniest sliver of his opponents who (right or wrong) were extremely vulnerable, while ignoring those with more plausible objections and less extreme behavior. This is a typical device used by politicians of all sorts and parties. Nevertheless, it constitutes shoddy argument, and indeed amounts to a version of the fallacy of the *straw man.* It is true that a few people held the position described and attacked by President Nixon. But it is almost always possible to find a few opponents who conveniently hold vulnerable positions. If you always (or usually) attack your weaker opponents, while ignoring those who have stronger objections, you are guilty of the fallacy of the *straw man,* because ultimately you convey the impression that you are attacking your strongest opponents.

The hope of politicians who employ this kind of *straw man* is that many people with meager information will conclude falsely that there are only two serious alternatives, the one espoused by those the politician attacks and the one held by the politician himself. In other words, they employ *straw man* in order to invite commission of the fallacy of *false dilemma.*

"Blockbuster" terms such as "radical liberal" also serve to persuade the uninformed that there are only two alternatives. For the politician need only attack a few of the group, for instance, the few radical liberals (whatever that means) who believe in violence, in order to tar all the others with belief in violence. And what is worse, in so doing, the politician can expect, or at least hope, that many will unwittingly widen membership in the radical liberal camp to include not-so-radical liberals as well.

Here is a second excerpt from Nixon's speech:

2. When Palestinian guerrillas hijacked four airliners in flight, [and] . . . held their hundreds of passengers hostage under threat of murder, they sent shock waves of alarm around the world at the spreading disease of violence and terror and its use as a political tactic.

That same cancerous disease has been spreading over the world and here in the United States.

We saw it three weeks ago in the vicious bombing at the University of Wisconsin. . . . We have seen it in other bombings and burnings on our campuses and our cities, in the wanton shootings of policemen, in the attacks on school buses, in the destruction of offices, the seizure and harassment of college officials, the use of force and coercion to bar students and teachers from classrooms and even to close down whole campuses.

Consider just a few items in the news. A courtroom spectator pulls out a gun. He halts the trial, gives arms to the defendants, takes the judge and four other hostages, moves to a waiting getaway van, and in the gunfight that follows four die, including the judge.

A man walks into the guardhouse of a city park, pumps five bullets into a police sergeant sitting quietly at his desk. . . .

The chief fallacy here is that of *suppressed evidence,* or *biased selection of facts,* always an easy one to be guilty of in political arguments, because there must be *some* evidence in favor of your position. (Even the worst politicians rarely hold positions for which no evidence whatever exists.) It's always easy to cite the evidence favorable to your position, while ignoring that which runs contrary to it.

In this case, Mr. Nixon provided instances of *nongovernmental* violence, much of which could plausibly be attributed to the violent radical liberals. But he overlooked governmental violence, in particular violence by police, which his opponents with some justification believed to be both unlawful and unnecessary in defending true law and order.

The mark of such a one-sided presentation of evidence is the ease with which opponents can construct arguments similarly biased in their choice of facts. For instance, "radical liberals" easily could have constructed the following paraphrase of the above section of Nixon's speech:

> When U.S. soldiers murdered women and children at My Lai in Vietnam, they sent shock waves of alarm around the world at the spreading disease of violence and terror and its use as a political tactic.
>
> That same cancerous disease has been spreading over the world and here in the United States.
>
> We saw it in the vicious police attack on Chicago Black Panthers asleep in their own homes. We have seen it in other police attacks in Chicago, in the wanton shooting of other Panthers in Oakland and elsewhere, in the overturning of school buses by racists condoned by onlooking police, in the destruction in private homes by police in New Jersey (mentioned in the Kerner Commission report), in the harassment of college officials at the State University of New York at Buffalo, in the use of force and coercion to bar students and teachers from the Ohio State University campus, as well as others.
>
> Consider just a few items in the news. Policemen at Jackson State University pull out guns. They fire at students without provocation, killing two.
>
> A student walks across the campus at Kent State University. National guardsmen, firing wildly at demonstrators, kill that student and three others, none of whom participated in any of the disorders at Kent State at the time.

The game is too easy. To the list could be added police violence at Orangeburg, South Carolina; Lawrence, Kansas; Augusta, Georgia; and hundreds of other places. With good research, it would be easy to construct a dossier with thousands of cases in which reasonable men might conclude that police had used violence beyond that necessary to preserve law and order.

But it, too, would be a biased list. The proverbial man from Mars, coming down to earth and hearing only this recitation of police violence would not have a true picture of the situation in the United States, nor any understanding of the causes or cures of its problems. But he would get an equally biased picture if subjected only to President Nixon's Kansas State address. Yet, Nixon's remarks were typical of the level of political rhetoric in the United States.

3. The time has come for us to recognize that violence and terror have no place in a free society, whatever the purported cause or the perpetrators may be. And this is the fundamental lesson for us to remember: In a system like ours, which provides the means for peaceful change, no cause justifies violence in the name of change.

This time the chief fallacy is a variation of the general category called the *all–some* fallacy. This fallacy takes what is sometimes or even usually true and elevates it to a universal.[8]

In this case, one wonders if Nixon, or anyone else reared in the spirit of the American Revolution and the Declaration of Independence, really believes that *no conceivable* cause could justify violence.

But once it is admitted that some causes might justify violence, evasion of the true issue is more difficult. For the true issue was that those few who espoused violence, both on the right and the left, did so in the belief that the situation in 1970 was in fact one of those unusual cases in which violence was justified. The President of the United States would have done better to explain why 1970 was not one of those times, rather than mouthing universals that few other than complete pacifists really believe.

This passage also contains a subtle dual ambiguity, specifically in Mr. Nixon's phrase, "In a system like ours, which provides the means for peaceful change. . . ." the first ambiguity concerns the existence of means for peaceful change. Does he mean *formal* means? If so, he obviously is correct. Or does he, rather, mean *effective* means for peaceful change? In that case, the question is debatable, as many of his opponents would contend.

The second ambiguity concerns the fact that peaceful change can be for better or for worse. Did the President mean *mere* peaceful change, or peaceful change for the better? The point is important. Since the Civil War, there have been means for peaceful change in the status of the Negro, but only occasionally (and recently) has change for the better been possible. In the 1870s and 1880s, for instance, peaceful change was all for the worse, leading to the legalization of segregation, *Plessy* v. *Ferguson,*[9] and all the rest.

4. What corrodes a society even more deeply than violence itself is the acceptance of violence, the condoning of terror, excusing of inhuman acts in a misguided effort to accommodate the community's standards to those of the violent few.

---

[8]Some versions of this fallacy rest on the ambiguity resulting from the *omission* of quantifying phrases such as "all" and "some". In English, we can often omit these terms as understood; for example, we can say, "Police do engage in unjustified violence", omitting the word "some". If we get someone to agree to a statement like this because he construes it to mean *some* policemen are unnecessarily violent, but later use this sentence to assert that *all* policemen engage in unjustified violence, then we are guilty of the *all–some* fallacy, as are those taken in by our ploy. Commission of this fallacy is made easier by the fact that the word "all" often is used when "almost all" is meant, as in the sentence "Negroes all voted against Max Rafferty in the 1970 California election".

[9]*Plessy* v. *Ferguson* is the Supreme Court decision declaring "separate but equal" schools constitutional.

Again, we have a rhetorical device just as easily used by the other side:

> What corrodes a society even more deeply than police violence itself is the acceptance of police violence, the condoning of police terror, excusing of inhuman police actions in a misguided effort to keep those with legitimate grievances from airing their views.

> 5. Yet we all know that at some of the great universities small bands of destructionists have been allowed to impose their own rule of arbitrary force.

> Because of this, we today face the greatest crisis in the history of American education. In times past we've had crises in education. . . . We faced shortages of classrooms, shortages of teachers; shortages that could always be made up, however, by appropriating more money.

> These material shortages are nothing compared to the crisis of the spirit which rocks hundreds of campuses across the country today.

It is difficult to know where to start when confronted with a passage like this one. In the first place, there is the suppression of "facts" similar to those presented which, however, would tend to move the hearer in the other direction. Mr. Nixon mentioned classroom and teacher shortages as examples of past crises, all of which could be made up by spending more money. But he neglected one of the worst evils ever in our schools, namely racial segregation, which could *not* be made up by spending more money.

He then refers to the "crisis of the spirit" on campuses today as a much greater problem than those we faced in the past. This has some plausibility to it, *if* we consider only the problems Mr. Nixon considered. But once we mention segregated schools, which effectively denied decent education to over 10 percent of our population for several generations, then the college crisis which started in the late 1960s has to take a back seat.

In addition, President Nixon begged the question as to the *cause* of this crisis of spirit (greatly exaggerated anyway). He assumed, but did not attempt to prove, that the cause of the crisis was campus violence and "a small band of destructionists" who were "allowed to impose their own rule of arbitrary force" on these campuses. He may have been right. But many at the time contended that it was Vietnam and internal failure to live up to our ideals that caused students to have their faith in America shaken, and caused them to turn away from the traditional theoretical disciplines to more "relevant" topics. Others felt it was the failure of students to accomplish quick changes in America during the 1960s which caused many young people to turn to drugs and a few to turn to violence. It isn't that Nixon was right or wrong, but rather that he didn't *argue* for his conclusions.

Finally, Mr. Nixon took advantage (as we all do) of the ambiguity of the English word "some", as well as the quirk in English which permits omission of *quantifiers*. The word "some" can mean anything from "just a few" to "all but one". It was true that (some) students took over some universities, because they took over a very few, not because they took over many.

And by omitting a *time quantifier,* the President gave the impression that destructionists at some universities were frequently or constantly allowed to impose their own rule of force, whereas this was never more than a very isolated happening at even the most troubled schools.

> 6. And it is time for the responsible university and college administrators, faculty and student leaders to stand up and be counted, because we must remember only they can save higher education in America. It cannot be by government.

This time it's platitudes plus a begged question. Most generations see themselves as in a time of crisis or important events. It is almost always "time to stand up and be counted". The question is what specifically is to be done to solve the problem. In addition, Mr. Nixon told college administrators it was their job and not to count on government. But he neglected to argue for that view. If the problems of higher education stemmed from something internal to the system of higher education, he may have been right. But if the problem stemmed from external pressures (Vietnam, racial strife), then he was probably wrong. However, in either case, the President begged the question.

> 7. The destructive activists at our universities and colleges are a small minority, but their voices have been allowed to drown out—my text at this point reads, "The voices of the small minority have been allowed to drown out the responsible majority." That may be true in some places, but not at Kansas State!

This is just playing to the crowd, whipping up emotions, appealing to prejudice, appealing to loyalty, the fallacy of *provincialism.* It's on a par with Nixon's wearing a purple and white tie at a school where the football coach wanted the football turf dyed purple.

> 8. Automatic conformity with the older generation . . . is wrong. At the same time, it is just as wrong to fall into a **slavish conformity** with those who **falsely** claim to be leaders of a new generation, out of fear to be unpopular or considered square not to follow their lead. It would be a great tragedy for the . . . new generation to become simply parrots for the slogans of protests, uniformly chanting the same few phrases and often the same four-letter words.

In the first place, the use of the phrase "slavish conformity" is unjustified, as is the word "falsely". These are value expressions which require argument. For instance, if he believes others are the true leaders of the younger generation, he should say who they are and explain why he thinks so.

But in addition, this is one of those pat passages which are so easy to turn in the other direction. Could we not just as easily accuse Mr. Nixon's "silent majority" of slavish conformity, for instance in their pasting flags on car windows and radio antennas. Couldn't we just as easily accuse them of the fear of being unpopular? (Who isn't afraid of being unpopular?)

9. We see a natural environment. True, it's been damaged by careless nuisances and misuses of technology. But we also see that that same technology gives us the ability to clean up that environment, to restore the clean air, the clean water, the open spaces that are our rightful heritage. And I pledge we shall do that and can do it in America.

Mr. Nixon pledges, like his predecessor, to reduce pollution. What politician would say otherwise? The question is whether his *actions* mirrored or contradicted his words, and the answer is clear from the tiny amount of money requested by the president for pollution control and in the fact that pollution increased during his administration just as it had under previous presidents.

10. Look at our nation. We are rich, and sometimes that is condemned because wealth can sometimes be used improperly. But because of our wealth, it means that today we in America cannot just talk about, but can plan for a program in which everyone in this nation, willing and able to work, can earn a decent living and so that we can care for those who are not able to do so on some basis.

There is only one word for what it took to utter this remark—*chutzpah!* Or to put it more academically, this remark was inconsistent with the actions taken by the president to reduce inflation, which also were expected to, and did, cause an increase in unemployment—in fact, the highest level of unemployment in many years. The point is that a president who deliberately increases unemployment (even to reduce inflation) cannot consistently pose as a champion of the unemployed.

11. It requires that the members of the academic community rise firmly in defense of the free pursuit of truth, that they defend it as zealously today against threats from without. . . . the final test of idealism lies in the respect each shows for the rights of others.

Again, empty platitudes. Everyone is for the free pursuit of truth *in the abstract.* What counts is how they line up on the nitty gritty details. This paragraph could be inserted intact into a speech by any one of the presidents of a number of state universities harassed by state legislators, or in the case of Kent State, SUNY at Buffalo, Jackson State University, and many others, harassed by local governmental officials.

But any paragraph that can be used so widely *in toto* obviously hasn't gotten down to the details that make all the difference.

12. I speak here today on the campus of a great university, and I recall one of the great sons of Kansas, Dwight David Eisenhower. I recall the eloquent address he made at London's famous Guildhall immediately after victory in Europe.

And on that day the huge assemblage of all the leading dignitaries of Britain were there to honor him.

And in his few remarks, one of the most eloquent speeches in the history of English eloquence, he said very simply, "I come from the heart of America."

Now, 25 years later, as I speak in the heart of America, I can truly say to you here today: You are the heart of America—and the heart of America is strong. The heart of America is good. The heart of America is sound.

This passage came very close to the end of Mr. Nixon's speech, and its intent is obvious. He appealed to the loyalty of the students as Kansans, who would be proud of a U.S. president who came from Kansas, who in particular was a military hero. The appeal was a *provincial* one. And he flattered them further by playing on the ambiguity of the word "heart", since Kansas *is* the heart of America in the sense that it is the geographic center of the United States (minus Hawaii and Alaska).

Notice how foolish it all sounds when the word "heart" is replaced by "geographic center": "I speak in the geographic center of America. I can truly say to you here today: You are the geographic center of America." And so on.

A typical political speech: selection of facts favorable to your side; distortion of the position of their side; suppression of facts favorable to their position; and a bit of provincial appeal to whip up the crowd. But no carefully reasoned argument about the details that make all the difference.

Summary of Chapter Six

Chapter Six dealt with the analysis of lengthier arguments—an editorial, a political column, and a political speech. The margin note-summary method was introduced for use in analyzing extended passages. This method consists in making notes (in the margins or elsewhere) as an aid in the construction of an itemized summary of the main points in the passage to be analyzed. The passage then is analyzed through an analysis of the summary. In constructing a summary, care should be taken not to misrepresent the passage.

Exercises for Chapter Six

1. Here is a fairly typical editorial of the *New York Daily News*,[10] by far the largest selling newspaper in the United States. Using the margin note-summary method (or a similar method of your own), analyze and evaluate this editorial. (What can you tell about the underlying assumptions of the author? Do you agree with them, or disagree? Explain.)

The "White Flag Amendment"

—which masquerades as the "amendment to end the war" comes before the Senate tomorrow for a showdown vote.

---

[10]© 1970, by the *New York Daily News*. Reprinted by permission.

This bugout scheme is co-sponsored by Sens. George McGovern (D-S.D.) and Mark Hatfield (R-Ore.). And despite some last-minute chopping and changing to sucker fence-sitting senators, the proposal remains what it has always been, a blueprint for a U.S. surrender in Vietnam.

It would force a pell-mell pullout of American forces there by cutting off all funds for the Vietnam war as of Dec. 31, 1971. It represents the kind of simple—and simple-minded—solution to Vietnam for which arch-doves and pacifists (as well as the defeatists and Reds who lurk behind them) have long clamored.

This amendment wears the phony tag of a "peace" plan. More accurately, it constitutes a first step toward whittling Uncle Sam down to pygmy size in the world power scales; it would fill our enemies with glee and our friends with dismay.

McGovern-Hatfield might appear a cheap out from Vietnam. But we would pay for it dearly later in other challenges and confrontations as the Communists probe, as they inevitably do at any sign of weakness, to determine the exact jelly content of America's spine.

The McGoverns, Hatfields, Fulbrights, Goodells and their ilk would have the nation believe that its only choice lies between their skedaddle scheme and an endless war. That is a lie.

President Richard M. Nixon has a program for ending America's commitment in Vietnam, and it is now underway. It involves an orderly cutback in U.S. forces.

The White House method assures the South Vietnamese at least a fighting chance to stand on their own feet and determine their own future after we leave.

Equally important, it tells the world the U.S. is not about to pull the covers over its head and duck out on its responsibilities as leader of the free world.

We urge the Senate to slap down the McGovern-Hatfield amendment, and scuttle with it any notion that America is willing to buy off noisy dissidents at the price of its honor.

*2. Here is a political column by Jeffrey St. John, which appeared in the *Columbus* (Ohio) *Dispatch* (May 9, 1972).[11] Using the margin note-summary method (or a similar method of your own), analyze and evaluate this column:

Could Swamp Courts
Women's Lib Amendment
Not Simple Legal Formula

By Jeffrey St. John

(Copley News Service)—"The legal position of women," observed the late Supreme Court Justice Felix Frankfurter, "cannot be stated in a simple

[11]© 1972 by Copley News Service. Reprinted by permission.

formula, especially under a constitutional system, because her life cannot be expressed in a single simple relation." A procession of contemporary legal scholars made much the same argument prior to congressional passage of the Women's Equal Rights Amendment now before various state legislatures for ratification.

Political pressures in this presidential year have given a militant minority of women powerful leverage for enactment. However, the respective state of the Union may come to regret ratification, if the two-thirds majority approves.

North Carolina Democratic Senator Sam Ervin has argued, along with legal scholars from the University of Chicago, Yale, and Harvard, that while the amendment would have no effect upon discrimination, it would "nullify every existing federal and state law making any distinction whatever between men and women, no matter how reasonable the distinction may be, and rob Congress and the 50 states of the legislative power to enact any future laws making any distinction between men and women, no matter how reasonable the distinction may be."

In the wake of any ratification, moreover, a legal avalanche would be unleashed that is likely to overwhelm the already overcrowded courts of the country.

In reality, the aim of a minority of militant women's liberationists is to bring about just such a state of legal and social anarchy. Like the disciples of Lenin in the early part of the century, Women's Lib seeks to use the law to destroy both existing law and the social structure.

In abolishing a legal distinction between men and women, the way is paved for sociological anarchy which militants can exploit for their own purposes of achieving political power.

The profound effect the Equal Rights Amendment would have on marriage contracts, the home and children is precisely what Women's Lib wants; to sweep such established social units away as a prelude to pushing the country headlong into a life-style not unlike that now practiced in hippie communes.

Philosophically, at the root of women's liberation movement is an attempt to destroy the family structure as a means of bringing down the whole of society.

The form of "discrimination" upon which the Women's Lib movement bases much of its false, misleading, and dangerous campaign is less in law than in custom and social attitudes, especially in the fields of career and employment.

Like the civil rights movement, Women's Lib is seeking, by using the power of the state, to forbid individual discrimination as opposed to discrimination legally enforced.

This crucial distinction has not been made by most in Congress who approved the Equal Rights Amendment for Women. Nor has it been made by the few state houses that have already ratified the amendment.

One can predict the same chaos will follow passage of this amendment as that which followed the 1964 Civil Rights Act.

Legal scholars like the late dean of the Harvard Law School, Roscoe Pound, have argued that the guarantee of "due process" in the Fifth Amendment and "equal protection" clause in the 14th Amendment provide the necessary legal instruments for reform now demanded by women's liberationists.

But like some elements of the civil rights movement, militant feminists are not really interested in reform, but rather in revolution and destruction of the existing social fabric of the society.

*3. The following is part of a political column by the nationally syndicated columnist Jenkin Lloyd Jones on "law and order".[12] Analyze and evaluate this political column:

In his recent speech to the American Bar Assn., an authentic card-carrying "liberal," Hubert Humphrey, said it is high time his fellow liberals got over on the side of law and order.

Four days later, as if to illustrate his point, the federal office building in his home town, Minneapolis, was rocked by a blast that shattered windows blocks away. This building which contained a military induction center has been a favorite target of antiwar demonstrators.

The former Vice President warned that attempts to describe as "well-meaning" all authors of violence and disruption are creating a credibility gap from which political liberals are suffering.

"Police brutality"—which has come, in the fevered imaginations of some, to mean any attempt by police to resist snipers and rioters—degenerates into unreal polemics as the arsenals of the Black Panthers and the Weathermen are revealed and the bodies of policemen pile up.

There has been no public recantation from those free-swinging libertarians who had been crying out to heaven that the painful and only barely successful effort to pry the communist professor, Angela Davis, loose from the state university payroll in California was a violation of academic freedom. But since her guns were allegedly used in the murder of four persons at the Marin County Courthouse we haven't heard a peep from the apologists.

The incredible presidential Commission on Pornography, appointed by Lyndon Johnson, has spent $2 million and come in with a preliminary report, written by the staff, which concludes that wide-open, anything-goes pornography has no relation to sex crimes.

This ignores the latest FBI report that states that in 1969 over 1968 rapes rose 17 percent, the biggest increase in any major crime category except larceny. Dr. Victor B. Cline, professor of clinical psychology at the University of Utah, has damned the report as "an almost Alice in Wonderland distortion of the evidence." . . .

Hubert Humphrey is right. Anarchy leads inevitably to repression. There is neither freedom nor social progress outside of law and order.

---

[12]By Jenkin Lloyd Jones, 1970, General Features Corp., Los Angeles Times Syndicate. Reprinted by permission.

4. Analyze and evaluate the following political column by Bill Anderson *(Chicago Tribune,* January 31, 1974):[13]

A Word of Praise for Rose Mary

By Bill Anderson

Washington—While waiting to listen to the State of the Union message, I would like to nominate Miss Rose Mary Woods as secretary of the year.

My main reason for doing this is because Rose is a heck of a nice person. There is no reason to pick on her just because she works for Richard M. Nixon.

It is true that in the cocktail talk around town, Rose is often accused of erasing tapes and of stretching beyond her capacity. So what? A lot of those same people like Alger Hiss never worry about another President who came to Washington with $25,000 [as a congressman] and left with $33 million.

The people who pick on Miss Woods really don't know anything about good secretaries. I always thought a good secretary was supposed to take care of the boss, come hell or high water. In fact, a goodly number of the secretaries I know are smarter than their bosses.

None of them, however, works any harder than Rose. If you don't believe me, just ask her brother, Joe, a former sheriff of Cook County. Rose is Joe's baby sister, and I'd bet good money he would punch anybody in the nose for saying anything bad about her.

Actually, how could you blame Joe? Just exactly what has Rose Mary done except go to court and say she may have accidentally erased a tape she was monitoring? I use a tape recorder and to this day can't figure out how I got Spiro T. Agnew and Gov. George Wallace of Alabama on the same reel.

If Judge John J. Sirica persists in picking on Rose, I'm going to start a rumor he can't stand Italian food.

When and if the House Judiciary Committee gets off the mark, why doesn't a congressman from Missouri, William L. Hungate, a Democrat, please explain how he can approach the subject of impeachment without egg on his face. Hungate thought he was cute last year when he personally made a record called, "Meet Me Down at the Old Watergate." Lawyer Hungate sounded as impartial as Johnny Carson in the 45 rpm hit in Georgetown, anti-Rose town.

Also, did you realize that the studio lights used to luminate the grey in Carson's hair would take care of the after-midnight needs of any town the size of Pinedale, Wyo.?

5. Analyze and evaluate the following passage by Dr. M. H. Nickerson, *Christian Science Monitor,* used as an editorial by the *Hartford Courant* (28 July 1972).[14]

On Tax Loopholes

The reader of this and other editorial pages has certainly seen the outraged exponents of tax revision decrying the inequities of the income tax system. Allegedly it lays an oppressive burden on the poor while allowing the rich to escape through gaping loopholes in our tax structure. A figure which may be cited in support is that in 1968, by valid government figures, 222 income tax returns showed incomes in excess of $200,000 and yet paid no tax.

Sort of shakes you up a bit, and that was certainly the intention. The writer won't tell you to view this against a background of 72 million tax returns. It's difficult to build a credible case for "gaping loopholes" which allow only 3 in a million to escape.

But these are the rich and the sin is more heinous. Is that a fact? Not really. The writer didn't tell you, dear reader, that in 1968 there were 12,400,000 tax returns with reportable income which also did not pay any tax. To do that would destroy the carefully contrived illusion that deductions are only for the rich. Obviously all these people aren't rich, and a glance at the statistics provided by the IRS confirms that over 12 million of these escapees had under $5,000 of adjusted gross income.

In the scathing indictment of the 222 rich escapees, it is never mentioned that in this same wealthy category (over $200,000 income) there were 19,001 returns which did not find a loophole. As a group they contributed nearly $4 billion in income taxes. Numerically they represent far less than 1 percent of all the returns, but they nevertheless contributed 4.9 percent of all the income tax dollars. If you want to argue that this already heavy tax burden is not heavy enough, at least do it on the basis of *all* the above data. The figure of 222 has no meaning when taken out of context.

In a similarly emotional and illogical manner, the disparity in income between the various strata of our society is used to create a self-serving rationale. References are cited showing that the top quintile (20 percent) garner in 46 percent of all the income while the lower quintile receives only 3.2 percent. That's not particularly new or earthshaking. It has been noted since the beginning of recorded history that there are those who are much more wealthy than others.

An ancient Greek philosopher allegedly observed that if all the wealth of the world were gathered in one place and then redistributed equally among the people, it would be only a short time before the original disparities returned unchanged. In the face of such a long-standing and fundamental stratification, it is a little presumptuous to suggest that our present layering of society is the result of a faulty economic or governmental system and should be corrected forthwith. The implication that we are doing little or nothing to equalize the wealth is absurd. The writers of such nonsense have again carefully omitted important relevant data which would destroy their case.

The upper 20 percent do get 46 percent of the income but they also pay 65 percent of all the income taxes. The tax burden clearly gets disproportionately heavier as you move up the income scale.

The lower 20 percent do receive only 3.2 percent of the national income BUT they are called upon to pay only 0.5 percent of the income taxes. If that isn't tax relief, what is it?

The reader, at this point, can choose to cluck over the 15–to–1 disparity in income between the two groups, or he can choke over the 130–to–1 ratio of relative tax burdens. It's a free choice, but let's make it without having most of the data hidden.

In case you are wondering just how rich this upper 20 percent is, take a look at your own financial status. If you earn more than $12,000 per year, you have joined the group. That rich guy you're planning to soak with more taxes just might be yourself.

6. Analyze and evaluate the following political column by William F. Buckley, Jr.:[15]

The Victory of Cesar Chavez

The Cesar Chavez people appear to have won their fight to unionize the grape-pickers in Southern California, and it is worth a moment to meditate on the means through which they succeeded in winning, and the consequences of their victory.

1. It is easy enough to say simply that it cannot be other than glad tidings that the grape-pickers in Southern California will be earning 20 percent more than they earned before. But of course there are those who will remind themselves that economics doesn't work that way, else—for instance—we would send Cesar Chavez to India, to call for a general strike because, over there, the hourly pay of a Ph.D. is less than the hourly pay of a grape-picker in Southern California.

The emotional difficulty with any discussion in this area is obvious. If it is established that the hourly pay of the grape-picker in Southern California is, say $1.67, the temptation is to say that so insufficient a wage ought not to be condoned.

But the free market does not dispose of moral judgments. The question has been whether (a) you permit migrant workers, many of whom come in from Mexico, to continue to work at a price which is acceptable to employer and employees; or (b) you simply forbid said workers to come in to work at wages we consider to be too low.

---

[15]*On the Right,* © 1970, Washington Star Syndicate, Inc. Reprinted by permission.

The trouble with siding automatically with the apparently benevolent side of this argument is simply this: if the price of labor is raised, by political pressures, say by 50 percent, then of course the extra cost is passed along to the grape buyers. Since the desire for grapes is not inflexible, it follows that there will be those who reject the new price; and their rejection will mean, according to the terms of the economic argument, very simply: fewer grapes sold, fewer migratory workers hired.

2. But even if in the long run the grape-pickers lose, you have to hand it to Cesar Chavez, who succeeded in intimidating everybody you ever heard of not to buy California grapes. Indeed, non-California grape-eating was indisputably the single most important thing that a lot of people, primarily eastern seaboard blue bloods, were able to manage during 1969–1970.

Mr. Chavez's campaign was effective, reaching even to the airlines, although their boycott was less than candid.

TWA—for instance—reported through a vice president to one inquirer last May that although it theoretically isn't proper for an airline to take sides on a political controversy, "We were well aware that this is a case where, in effect, one can take sides by inaction as well as action." The solution? ". . . We had decided to remove fruit baskets from our domestic flights on June 15. We will substitute a so-called Fruit Bowl au Kirsch; grapes will not be utilized in this concoction."

A few weeks later another vice president of TWA wrote to a different inquirer, "I . . . appreciate this opportunity to discuss the reports which appeared in the press to the effect that TWA was 'boycotting' grapes. The change which apparently gave rise to this erroneous and unfortunate report involved, among other things, the substitution of a so-called Fruit Bowl au Kirsch for a fresh fruit tray which we had been offering under the previous menu. The recipe for this fruit bowl was developed in an effort to make the dish taste good; that was the only criterion used in its development. The fruit tray for which it substituted included, in addition to grapes, things like oranges, apples, pears and bananas."

So that, depending on what you want to hear, official A says: We're cutting down on grapes, because if we use grapes we are in effect siding with the pro-grape people; and official B of the same company says: You're crazy if you think our nongrape position has anything to do with Cesar Chavez.

3. Will Mr. Chavez now rest? Or will he move on to unionize farm workers in general? If he calls for a more general boycott, the poor people in Southampton—and in TWA—may find that they are reduced to a diet of Fruit Bowl au Kirsch made up exclusively of grapes.

7. Analyze and evaluate a current political column, newspaper, magazine or television editorial, press conference, or political speech. Determine which fallacious arguments (if any) it contains, and check for illegitimate uses of emotive language (including the use of emotively neutral language designed to dull impact).

David Levine is one of America's foremost caricaturists. In this drawing, he pictures the television viewing audience as contented sheep being fleeced. Do you agree?

Chapter Seven

Advertising: Selling the Product

Would you persuade, speak of interest, not of reason.

Ben Franklin

You can tell the ideals of a nation by its advertisements.

Norman Douglas

Advertising persuades people to buy things they don't need with money they ain't got.

Will Rogers

Advertising is the most exciting, the most arduous literary form of all, the most difficult to master, the most pregnant with curious possibilities.

Aldous Huxley

1. Pro Advertising

A profession seemingly without a product needs to justify its existence. If advertising makes sense, it has to benefit three groups: those in the advertising profession; those who advertise; and those to whom advertisements are directed (consumers). There is no doubt that it benefits the first two groups—the first receive relatively high salaries, the second increased sales and thus increased profits. But advertising also is of great benefit to consumers, which means all of us at one time or another:

(1) Advertising tells us which products are available and where.

(2) Advertising gives us information about those products.

(3) Advertising sometimes gives us something free (usually entertainment—for example, a television program) in exchange for our attention.

(4) Advertising plays a part in providing us with the variety, quality, and lower prices that result from mass production (for without advertising, the rapid sale of many mass-produced items would be next to impossible).

We could easily do without the third of these advertising benefits (pay television could replace advertising-supported television). But the first two, at least, are essential in any but the tiniest societies (as even the Soviet Union, which has a socialist economy, has discovered). We are constantly buying things—whether goods or services—and in almost every case we learn of and about the things we buy through advertising.

2. Con Advertising

Advertising is objected to primarily for three reasons:

(1) Ads raise prices by increasing the costs of selling an item. The claim is that advertising expenses, like any others, are passed on to the consumer in the form of higher prices.

But this frequently made claim has never been proved. Indeed, there is good reason to believe it is false. Take heavily advertised products, such as ball point pens or hair shampoo, where a fifth (20 percent) or more of the retail price of an item may stem from advertising costs. Without advertising, these items would not be mass produced (because they could not be mass merchandized). But if produced on a small scale, their unit costs would be greatly increased, surely by more than 20 percent. So advertising almost certainly reduces the prices of these products instead of raising them.

(2) Ads create irrational demand for products. Literally thousands of new products come on the market every year, ranging from new model automobiles to new political candidates to vaginal sprays. Most of these products, it is argued, serve little or no useful purpose, and may even be harmful. And few could be marketed without heavy ad campaigns.

The problem is that this is an objection against some ads, but not others. Yet how are we to decide which ads to allow (because the products they tout are useful) and which to forbid (because the products they tout are useless or harmful)? One person's useless product may be another's favorite (cosmetics, vitamin C tablets, electric can openers). In a socialist country, such as the Soviet Union, government officials decide which products are useful and which not. But if we believe in a free system, in particular if we believe in free speech and a free marketplace of ideas, we don't want governments to make such decisions.[1]

We surely don't want to forbid all advertising (for the reasons discussed above). So it may be best to forbid none (with the usual provisions against libel and fraud).

(3) Ads appeal chiefly to emotions, not to reason. They typically make false, misleading, or irrelevant claims, or contain fallacious arguments.

There can be little doubt that this claim against advertising is true. (One of the main tasks of this chapter is to illustrate this fact.) The question is what to do about it. Perhaps the best thing we can do, all things considered, is to learn to guard against ad con artistry in general. If we can't do as well without advertisements, perhaps we can learn to use them with intelligence and profit.

3.   Three Basic Advertising Principles

When you cut through all the malarky about advertising, you find that most successful ads follow two (or perhaps three) basic principles.[2] The first is that most successful ads are directed towards *selfish* human desires and motives.

Claude Hopkins, one of the great advertising geniuses, explained the reason for the first rule as follows:

> The people you address are selfish, as we all are. They care nothing about your interest or your profit. They seek service for themselves. Ignoring this

---

[1]This question is exactly as complicated as is the general free speech question. Free speech doesn't mean freedom to libel or yell "fire" in a theatre. Similarly, freedom to advertise useless products doesn't mean freedom to write fraudulent copy.

[2]Omitting technical principles of composition, type face, and page placement.

fact is a common mistake and a costly mistake in advertising. Ads say in effect, "Buy my brand. Give me the trade you give to others. Let me have the money." That is not a popular appeal. Whatever people do they do to please themselves.

Although Hopkins' psychology is not quite correct (people sometimes act from unselfish motives), almost every successful ad does appeal somehow or other to human selfishness.[3]

The second basic advertising principle is that successful ads appeal to the emotions, not just (or even) to reason.

One would suppose that the best ads would make rational appeals to selfish interests. A few successful ads do just that. And most ads, after all, do contain some useful information. Still, the chief appeal in almost all successful ads is emotional.

Consider the recent highly successful Schlitz ads, which shouted at listeners to grab all the gusto in life they could, because "you only get one go around in life". The appeal was selfish, following rule one. (Imagine them saying instead that you only get one go around in life, so do all the good things that you can for others—give Schlitz to poor beer drinking friends now.) But it also was an emotional appeal, empty of reasons for drinking Schlitz rather than a competing brand, following rule two. Examine a hundred successful ads and you'll find that the vast majority follow these two principles.

One of the classics of advertising history is built around a headline which for a time became a part of the language:

> *They laughed when I sat Down at the Piano*
> *But when I Started to Play! . . .*

The appeal of this ad was to the desire to shine at parties. In the fine print, having put the prospective customer in the proper emotional frame, the ad promises to teach piano playing quickly and with "no laborious scales—no heartless exercises—no tiresome practicing". Reason would caution the reader. How, after all, is it possible to learn to play the piano without lots of practicing? But no matter; emotions sufficiently aroused will override rationality—in a sufficient number of cases. This famous ad was a tremendous money maker.[4]

Ads for deodorants and mouthwashes play on our fear of offending when we get close to others. Yet they rarely provide rational grounds for choosing the

---

[3]One of the greatest ads ever, in the opinion of this writer, was the one that began, "If you have to kill children, it's nicer to let them starve than to put them into a gas oven. This is about the war on page 12 of your newspapers . . . ," and then told about the war in Biafra. This ad drew as many letters and donations as other ads on the Biafra war, but did not produce the hoped-for result—a flood of letters to the President of the United States.

[4]The headline on the ad became so well known, and remained so, that Frank Rowsome, Jr., used its opening phrase as the title of his delightful book on advertising, *They Laughed When I Sat Down* (New York: Bonanza Books, 1959). Some of the other examples used in this chapter also appear in Rowsome's book.

brand advertised. The same is true of cigarette and beer ads. Very few cigarette smokers can tell "their" brand from its chief competitors (easily proved by conducting blindfold taste tests). So cigarette ads have to appeal to emotions, since there aren't any rational grounds for smoking one standard brand of cigarettes rather than another of the same type.

Early ads for automobiles stressed mechanical qualities of the cars advertised. But by the 1920s, auto ads had by and large switched to the emotional appeal that still is used. One of the first great auto ads was run by a small company, the Jordan Motor Car Co., which put out a car called the Playboy. The ad pictures a young woman in a Playboy, mountains in the distance, and a cowboy on horseback being overtaken and passed. The copy reads, "Somewhere west of Laramie, there's a broncho-busting, steer-roping girl who knows what I'm talking about. She can tell what a sassy pony. . . ." And on and on. A tremendous emotional appeal totally empty of reasons for buying a Playboy rather than some other car. Jordan made millions.

Critics of advertising often claim that *competitive* advertising, designed to switch people from one brand to another, is wasteful and undesirable, although *informative* advertising is legitimate. Defenders of advertising generally reply by claiming that good advertising is truly informative. Advertising genius David Ogilvy, for instance,[5] claims that uninformative competitive advertising is poor advertising and won't sell the product anyway.

This sounds fine until you begin to look at Mr. Ogilvy's own ads. What information is imparted by the black eye patch in the famous Hathaway Shirt ads? Did Mr. Ogilvy really believe Hathaway shirts were superior to those made by Arrow or Van Heusen? Weren't his great ads for Shell gasoline and Schweppes soft drinks uninformative competitive ads designed to switch readers from one brand to another? How, for instance, could an ad for Shell gasoline show why Shell is better than its competitor if it isn't better?

The fact is that in spite of advertising industry claims to the contrary, most successful ads have not been truly informative. Bayer aspirin is not better than other aspirin; it only costs more. There isn't any reason "when you're having more than one", to have Schaeffer beer instead of Schlitz, Budweiser, or dozens of others. There is no detergent that gets clothes noticeably whiter than all of its competitors. You're not more likely to get the job if you use Listerine, because Listerine doesn't cure bad breath, much of which originates in the lungs and stomach anyway. If Avis tries harder than Hertz, it doesn't seem to make a noticeable difference when you rent an automobile. And whatever Winstons taste like (or as?), they don't taste better than all of their competitors; even experts would have difficulty distinguishing Winstons from competing brands. (The Winston ads built around the theme of good-looking young smokers who smoke for taste, and so smoke Winstons, were unusually silly since most smokers are hooked primarily by the *drugs* in cigarettes, chiefly nicotine. Taste is relatively unimportant. The same is true of most hard liquor. Almost no one would drink gin, vodka, rum, or even scotch or bourbon if liquor had no physiological (and hence mental) effects on us.

---

[5]See David Ogilvy, *Confessions of an Advertising Man* (New York: Atheneum, 1963).

Somewhere West of Laramie

SOMEWHERE west of Laramie there's a broncho-busting, steer-roping girl who knows what I'm talking about.

She can tell what a sassy pony, that's a cross between greased lightning and the place where it hits, can do with eleven hundred pounds of steel and action when he's going high, wide and handsome.

The truth is—the Playboy was built for her.

Built for the lass whose face is brown with the sun when the day is done of revel and romp and race.

She loves the cross of the wild and the tame.

There's a savor of links about that car—of laughter and lilt and light—a hint of old loves—and saddle and quirt. It's a brawny thing—yet a graceful thing for the sweep o' the Avenue.

Step into the Playboy when the hour grows dull with things gone dead and stale.

Then start for the land of real living with the spirit of the lass who rides, lean and rangy, into the red horizon of a Wyoming twilight.

JORDAN

JORDAN MOTOR CAR COMPANY, *Inc.*, *Cleveland*, *Ohio*

Appeals to emotions sell products. Reason gets left behind.

This brings us to a very disputed third rule of successful advertising, which is simply to *repeat the message ad nauseum.*[6] The late George Washington Hill of

---

[6]Much formal education also seems to follow this rule. For instance, students in American public schools are subjected to U.S. history four, five, or even more times—much more than all other histories combined. And they do know more about American history than all other histories combined.

the then American Tobacco Company was the champion of this idea, with the result that for years on radio and in newspapers and magazines the nation was bombarded with the message that "L.S.M.F.T.—Lucky Strike means fine tobacco". (Track coaches throughout the nation changed that one to read "Less smoking means finer trackmen", which at least had the virtue of being true.)

But whether or not endless repetition is effective, there does seem to be some value in limited repetition. This is true not merely in promoting belief in the message, but more importantly, in promoting belief that results in action. It is repetitive advertising, for instance, that is responsible for our instant recognition of most brand names in supermarkets and department stores—a crucial fact since most of us choose familiar brands over unknown ones almost every time. (Check that for yourself next time you shop for, say, toothpaste, cigarettes, a television set, or a box of cereal.)

4.   How Advertisements Con

If we are to use ads intelligently and avoid being taken in, we should become familiar with a few of the basic devices and gimmicks used by advertisers to con the unwary into reasoning fallaciously about advertised products.

(a.) Ads never tell what is wrong with a product. No product is perfect. Hence the completely informative ad would mention at least some drawbacks of the product. But no one has yet seen an ad which deliberately says anything negative about a product.[7] As David Ogilvy stated in his best seller, *Confessions of an Advertising Man* (p. 158), "Surely it is asking too much to expect the advertiser to describe the shortcomings of his product." And that's exactly the point, for this means that practically every ad is guilty of the fallacy of *suppressed evidence* by concealing negative information about the product.

This is a good deal more important than it sounds when you consider that the information suppressed may be about serious side effects of a drug (for example, birth control pills), or the relatively poor food value of commercial breads and breakfast foods (for example, Wonder Bread, Pop Tarts, or Kellogg's Corn Flakes).

Movie and theater ads routinely quote the few nice words in a negative review, while omitting all the critical ones. Here is a quote from an ad for a porno flick, *Sometime Sweet Susan,* which appeared in the *New York Post,* February 21, 1975:

Shawn Harris is pretty . . . the lusty doings, of course, get the most screen time.—Judith Crist, *New York* magazine

And here's the entire Judith Crist review:[8]

---

[7]Except when employing "reverse twist", that is, trying to make a virtue out of an apparent defect. The Avis Rent-A-Car campaign—"We try harder (because we're only number two)"—is an example. Another is the Volkswagen "think small" ad campaign.

[8]*New York* Magazine, February 24, 1975, p. 66. Copyright Judith Crist. Reprinted by permission.

Sometime Sweet Susan's press agent boasts that it is "the *first* hard-core film *ever* made with Screen Actors Guild approval." Lord knows there's little else to boast about in this dreary little film that tries to rise above its genre with superior performances, auspices, and production values. It succeeds only in being less ugly than some and as boring as most. Co-produced by Craig Baumgarten and Joel Scott, with a screenplay by Scott and Fred Donaldson, who directed and edited the film, it's a two-thirds rip-off of *The Three Faces of Eve,* with Susan a schizophrenic as a result of her inability to reconcile her lusty doings with her moral upbringing. It's *the lusty doings, of course,* that *get the most screen time,* with all the porn rituals (hetero- and homosexual twosomes, threesomes, and a dash of sadism) observed.

Union membership does not guarantee quality of performance. As Susan, *Shawn Harris is pretty* and uninteresting, and Harry Reems, the biggie of *Deep Throat* and *The Devil in Miss Jones,* proves, as Susan's psychiatrist and sex-fantasy lover, that acting with clothes on is not his forte. Neil Flanagan, a professional nonporn actor, tries unsuccessfully to beat his low-comedy dialogue as the head of the mental hospital. And Baumgarten, an ex-Lindsay aide, shows small promise as an actor in his role as Susan's first lover, although a male critic thought he "makes a rather impressive debut as a hard-core performer." To each his impressions.

(b.) Some ads say things about the product that are simply false, and thus invite commission of the fallacy of the *questionable premise.* Whatever "tired blood" was, Geritol was not good for it. Toothpastes on the market before the age of fluorides advertised reductions in tooth decay, but they didn't deliver. Ads for hair restorers "guarantee" to restore lost hair, but nothing yet discovered can do that. Diet pills advertise weight loss without cutting down on favorite foods (impossible—if you consume too many calories, you get fat—pills or no pills). Thousands of commercials have shown celebrities "using" products they wouldn't ordinarily touch with a ten-foot pole.

Sometimes an advertising claim is not only false, but absurd. An ad from a Washington, D.C. television channel stated that "On Channel 9 (news) we ask [experts, and those in the news] what you'd ask." But that's impossible since different television viewers would ask different questions. Anyone who was persuaded by this ad to watch Channel 9 news committed the fallacy of the *questionable premise.*

Of course, those persuaded by ads with false claims do not necessarily commit the fallacy of *questionable premise.* It depends on whether they should have realized that the ad's claim is probably false. As usual, the basically uninformed person is likely to have no way to sort the reasonable from the questionable and thus commits no fallacy in accepting questionable claims. Such a person is just an innocent, unknowing victim of advertising con artistry.

To avoid being such a victim, we have to acquire a bit of relevant background information,[9] or at least become aware of the widespread use in advertising of

---

[9]That is one reason basic science courses are so important. No one who has taken and understood a good physiology or biology course is likely to be taken in by a scientifically unsupported claim, say, to regrow hair on a balding head.

false or exaggerated claims ("lowest price", "highest quality", "miraculous cure", "absolutely free", "completely guaranteed").

(c.) Ads often play on our fears or desires without providing reasons why we should believe using the advertised product will satisfy them. In other words, ads often invite us to commit the fallacy of *irrelevant reason.*

More precisely, the gimmick is this: Stress a problem lots of us would like to solve (getting a job, or perhaps a mate) while misdirecting attention away from the fact that the product won't help significantly to solve that problem—or solve it better than competing products. We all have countless needs and desires, many of which cannot be satisfied by any product yet on the market. Most of us want a better job, a nice marriage partner or lover, good health, good looks, and loving children. But, in general, ads for products claiming to help satisfy these desires fail to provide *reasons why* these products will satisfy them. (They fail to do so either because the products are not in fact significantly useful in satisfying these desires, or else because they don't satisfy them *better* than competing products. For instance, the famous Ban deodorant ads, which advertised the use of Ban to "take the fear out of being close", gave no reasons for supposing Ban is any better than many other deodorants—because it isn't any better.)

Schoolchildren might examine . . . the meaning of *free gifts* offered by savings banks in return for new deposits. Strictly speaking, if a gift is not free, it is not a gift. The bank's gifts, however, are not really free: If the deposit is withdrawn before a minimum period, the gift, or an equivalent amount of money, is taken back. The free gift turns out to be a conditional gift all along. (Fred M. Heckinger in *Saturday Review/World,* March 9, 1974)

(d.) Ads often trade on the fuzziness (ambiguity or vagueness) of language, thus inviting commission of the fallacy of *ambiguity.* Natural languages are very flexible—they can be used to state precise ideas or fuzzy ones. There are good purposes for fuzzy language (for instance, to soften the blow of bad news). Unfortunately, there also are nasty ones and ads contain more than their share of the latter.

A cold tablet ad began, "At the first sign of a cold or flu—Coricidin". Does this imply that if you take Coricidin at the first sign of a cold or flu that it will cure your illness? Or does it imply that it will relieve symptoms? The ad writers hope (and expect) that most readers will assume it says Coricidin cures, although, in fact, at best it relieves symptoms. (There is no generally accepted cure for colds or flu, although various remedies, for example, vitamin C, have their champions.) Incidentally, notice that this ad also employs the gimmick just discussed. It plays on our desire to get rid of a cold without giving any reasons for thinking Coricidin will help do this.

An interesting variation on the ambiguity theme is the *ambiguous comparison.* A Colgate fluoride toothpaste ad claimed that "Most Colgate kids get fewer cavities", but failed to state fewer than who. Again, the hope was that readers

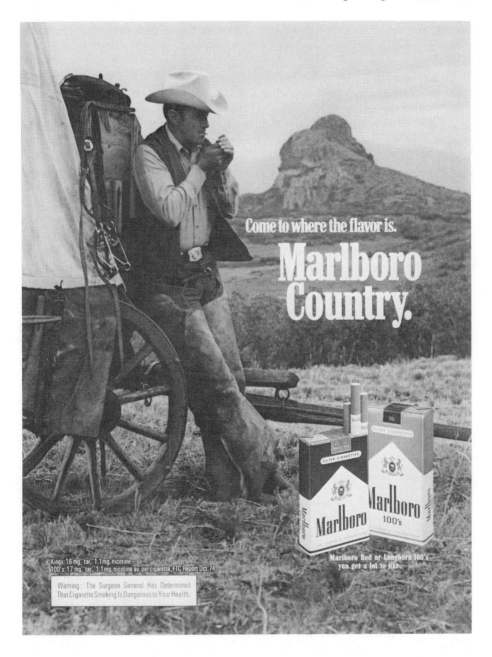

The new advertising. Robert Glatzer, in *The Great Ad Campaigns from Avis to Volkswagen* (New York: Citadel Press, 1970), called the Marlboro campaign the "campaign of the century". This is a typical ad from that campaign. Notice that it gives no reason why anyone should smoke Marlboros rather than another filter cigarette of similar flavor. The warning note appearing in the lefthand corner is required by law and did not appear in earlier ads of the campaign.

would take the ad to claim that Colgate kids get fewer cavities than those using other fluoride toothpastes, such as Crest, by far the best seller at that time. But the *true* claim was that Colgate fluoride kids got fewer cavities on the average than they did before using Colgate, when, of course, some of them used a non-fluoride toothpaste, or perhaps didn't brush their teeth at all.

(e.) Ads often contain relatively meaningless jargon. As language is used with less and less precision, it comes closer and closer to being meaningless noise or jargon (jargon fools us because it so often sounds sensible). Ads, of course, contain lots of examples (in some of which there is a kernel of sense to mask their general mindlessness). On the whole, jargon is used more in ads for products that either don't do the job well at all (cosmetics, hair restorers, weight reducers), or don't do it better than competing products (cigarettes, detergents, beer). But what does it *mean*, really, to say that a brand of detergent gets clothes "whiter than white", or "beyond white"? What does an ad ask you to do when it advises you to "recreate yourself"? When should you go to Bermuda to enjoy their "rendezvous season"? What is the "spring elegance" of a Denice original? All of these use language more or less in a jargony, almost meaningless way, a way designed not to *inform* but to misdirect. (Notice that most of these jargon expressions are loaded with highly positive, emotionally charged words.)

(f.) Many ads are literally true but imply falsehoods. They trade on the fact that thoughts implied (but not literally asserted) by a statement often are ambiguous in that implication. That is, they are ambiguous as to whether or not they make the implication.[10]

A cigarette ad which claims that Brand X is lowest in tar and nicotine implies that the difference between Brand X and the next brand is a significant one. (Otherwise, why bother mentioning it?) Old Gold touched bottom in this false implication game when it used a *Reader's Digest* report indicating it was lowest in nicotine without mentioning that the difference was a completely negligible 1/177,187 of an ounce per cigarette!

The Armour Star frank ads, which correctly stated that one pound of Armour franks and one pound of steak are equal in nourishment, implied that a hot dog meal is just as nourishing as a steak meal. But did you ever try eating ten Armour franks at one sitting?

A Bayer Aspirin television commercial pictured an announcer holding a bottle of Bayer aspirin while stating that doctors recommend aspirin for pain relief. He didn't say that doctors recommend Bayer's, but the implication was there.[11]

Claude Hopkins was the first person in advertising to understand and use a beautiful variation on the false implication gambit. Hopkins believed it was

---

[10]This is slightly different from the *ambiguous comparison* case where there is definitely an implication, but what is implied is ambiguous. The reason for treating false implications separately is simply the frequency of the use of this ploy.

[11]Purists, of course, argue that truth in advertising need extend only to that which is literally asserted. The trouble is that in daily life we often say things by implication rather than directly; yet it would be wrong to claim we haven't said them. If Smith, for example, when asked if he wants a cup of coffee, says "I won't say no", he says "yes" by implication. You would be justified in getting angry if he then refused the coffee on the grounds he's never said he wanted any.

SCENES OF TALMAN FAMILY IN VARIOUS PHASES OF ACTIVITY AROUND THE HOME.	This is the house we live in. That's Billy, he's pretty handy to have around; Steve, home from college; Barbie, looking after her brother Timmy; Debbie, who'll soon graduate from high school; Susan, who has captured all our hearts; and my wife Peggy, who looks after all of us.
CLOSEUP OF PHOTOGRAPH WITH TALMAN AND RAYMOND BURR.	And that's me--Bill Talman, with a friend of mine you might recognize. He used to beat my brains out on TV every week for about ten years.
MEDIUM CLOSEUP OF TALMAN IN DEN.	You know, I didn't really mind losing those courtroom battles. But I'm in a battle right now I don't want to lose at all because, if I lose it, it means losing my wife and those kids you just met.
CLOSEUP OF BILL TALMAN.	I've got lung cancer. So take some advice about smoking and losing from someone who's been doing both for years. If you haven't smoked, don't start. If you do smoke, quit. Don't be a loser.
AMERICAN CANCER SOCIETY LOGOTYPE BOTTOM SUPER-IMPOSED OVER TALMAN.	

William Talman, who appeared as the district attorney on the TV "Perry Mason" show, knew that he had incurable lung cancer before he died on August 30, 1968, and he arranged a special legacy—a personal TV message then released by the American Cancer Society. This commercial presented the other side to cigarette smoking—the link between it and lung cancer—that cigarette advertisements suppress. Of course, in presenting its side, the ACS commercial adheres to the usual advertising rules: it is long on emotion and short on facts. (Compare this ad with the Marlboro ad reproduced on p. 147.)

a waste of money to claim your product is the best, or pure, or anything so general. He tried to understand his product sufficiently to be able to provide more specific "reasons why" a person should buy that product. (This may sound as though his ads really did inform the public about the product, and Hopkins himself may have believed this. But it didn't work that way.)

One of Hopkins' early and famous ad campaigns illustrates this well. When he was put to work on Schlitz Beer ads, he discovered that each Schlitz bottle was sterilized with live steam. So he built his campaign around headlines such as "Washed with Live Steam!" omitting the fact that all breweries used live steam. He knew that competitors could not then advertise that they too used live steam—that claim had been preempted for Schlitz. And he knew most readers would *assume* that only Schlitz washed their bottles with live steam. (Apparently, he was right; Schlitz sales went from fifth to first in short order.)

Most ads which claim a certain quality for their product without explicitly asserting its uniqueness to that product are designed to make you *assume* that only their product has that quality. If you make that assumption, you reason fallaciously.

(g.) *Ads often use humor (especially plays on words—puns) to mask a weak or ambiguous appeal.* A full page Eastern Airlines ad centered around a headline statement that "It is now within your means to live beyond your means. At least for a weekend." Stripped of ambiguity and humor, the ad's claim fizzles down to simply "Fly now-pay later."[12] But they want you to act as though Eastern will somehow enable you to live beyond what, were it not for Eastern, would be your maximum means. If the ad cons you into taking a trip it would be financially unwise to take (given, perhaps, other ways to spend your money), then you are guilty of fallacy.

Here are a few more examples of humor in advertising designed to put you in the mood to spend money on the product:

"Have you ever done it the French way?"[13] (French Lines); "Like money in the bank: the shoe that takes you everywhere, building interest all the way" (Saks Fifth Avenue); "Why anyone would want to fly beyond us is beyond us" (Jamaica Tourist).

Of course, humor has a legitimate use in advertising—to present significant claims in a more enjoyable, more palatable manner. For over twenty years Volkswagen ads have humorously played on the fact that Volkswagens are much smaller than most American cars, and thus better by and large in gas mileage and ease of parking. This has been a legitimate use of humor because Volkswagens do get better gas mileage than large American cars and are easier to park. It's the humor designed to con you into false beliefs or into reacting irrationally to emotional appeals that has to be looked out for.

(h.) *Ads often exaggerate to make their point,* inviting the fallacy of *exaggeration.* This is perhaps the most common of all ad ploys. Here are a few relatively mild

---

[12]In other words, Eastern will extend you credit—if you're a reasonable risk, of course. If it were really beyond your means, Eastern obviously wouldn't extend credit.

[13]Sexual double entendre is common.

examples (all from ads for Broadway plays), culled at random from just one section of one newspaper.[14]

"Best musical show of the year" *(The Rocky Horror Show)*
"In Praise of Love is Magic" *(In Praise of Love)*
"A mind boggling bawdy romp" *(The Madhouse Co. of London)*
"I haven't laughed as often or as heartily in years . . . Audiences will howl with laughter for years . . ." *(The Ritz)*
"Yes, Yes, a thousand times yes!" *(Diamond Studs)*
"The most foot-stompin', hand clappin' fun musical . . .
in a dog's age" *(Diamond Studs)*
"Irresistible" *(An Evening With H. L. Mencken)*
"Tremendous! Engrossing! Devastating! Fantastical!" *(Black Picture Show)*
"The best I have seen in the American Theatre in 25 years" *(Sizwe Banzi is Dead)*
"A comic masterpiece" *(God's Favorite)*
"Best mini-musical in town" *(I'll Die if I Can't Live Forever)*

These are advertisements for Broadway productions all of which were box office flops.

Seven movie ads in the same paper claimed their film was either the best or one of the ten best movies of 1974 (extremely unlikely given that only a few end-of-the-year 1974 films were playing in town at the time). (In an average year, about fifty films will advertise in New York as one of the year's ten best.)

In the same newspaper there were hundreds, perhaps thousands, of ads for all sorts of products, which contained gross exaggerations. Products were advertised as: "A touch of the past, at yesterday's prices"; ". . . the most unique darkroom offer ever made"; ". . . incredibly warm and glamorous"; "the king of comfort chairs"; "Fifteen very special tours for a very special year"; ". . . still one great big beautiful bargain"; "offers you one incomparable ship . . . [and] a rare exciting transatlantic crossing"; "Unrivalled for quality service"; "The sale nobody can afford to miss"; "The world's most appreciated home spa"; "The event that fur connoisseurs wait for"; "The most creative furniture ever made for kids".

All of these almost surely were exaggerated: there is no "king" of comfort chairs; who could know in January 1975 that 1975 would be a "very special year"; what is so rare about a "rare exciting transatlantic crossing"; hardly anyone's "quality service" is "unrivalled"; and there is no sale "nobody can afford to miss".

Ads which exaggerate in this way seem so obvious when we stop and *think* about them. The trouble is that most of us rarely stop and think about them. We have become so used to this bloated verbiage that we forget how effective it is in getting *us* to buy, buy, buy. *Exaggeration is effective.* Like all successful ad ploys, it touches something basic in human nature. It tends to work on everybody (although more intelligent, experienced, or discerning people usually fall for subtler examples).

---

[14]*New York Times,* January 26, 1975.

Here's one last example of *exaggeration* (a more subtle specimen for the discerning). Back in 1972, when Detroit was striking back at foreign small car imports, they attached a "Buy American" flavor to their campaigns to woo back small car buyers. So Volkswagen launched their own "Buy American" campaign, centered around an ad which, after the "Buy American" headline (note the use of reverse twist humor) over a picture of a Volkswagen, launched into lengthy copy whose message was that Volkswagens have so many American-made parts, and Volkswagen pays so many American salaries, that buying a Volkswagen is almost like buying an American car. The copy starts out: "Just because you're determined to sit behind an American steering wheel, don't think you can't drive a Volkswagen. Do you know who we buy steering wheels from? The Crucible Steel Company. In Detroit. Michigan."[15]

The trouble is that the ad never tells you (even approximately) what *portion* of a Volkswagen sold in America is made in America. It doesn't because Volkswagens are made primarily in Germany, which is also where most of the profits go. So the ad's "Buy American" slogan and theme amounts to nothing but an exaggeration of the truth that Volkswagen autos contain a few American-made parts and are sold in the United States by dealers who employ American workers.

A complete list of the psychological ploys used in advertising, if such a list were possible (no one has ever compiled one), would be very long indeed, perhaps exactly as long as a complete list of fallacies (no one has ever compiled that sort of list either). Let's very briefly discuss just a few more to illustrate variety and subtlety.

(i.) Ads often compare apples with oranges, inviting commission of the fallacy of *faulty comparison.* A Plymouth Duster ad[16] compared the Duster to a Datsun 610: "Our small car is $754.50 less than their small car." It stated that the Duster is larger inside and has a longer wheel base along with that lower price.

But it compared apples with oranges. For the 610 was at the top of the Datsun line, while the Duster was at the bottom of the Plymouth line. A better comparison would have been between the Datsun B210, the cheapest Datsun, and the Plymouth Duster, the cheapest Plymouth. And, in fact, the B210 had a slightly lower list price than the Duster.[17]

(j.) Ads often use deceptive "sight or sound" techniques. Some of these are simply fraudulent, for instance the Colgate Rapid Shave Cream commercial, which showed "sandpaper" being shaved. The "sandpaper" was, in fact, a sheet of plexiglass with sand on it.[18] Another example is the television vacuum cleaner ad that shows "one swipe" cleaning a "filthy" floor—but the "filth" is just powdered graphite, and thus child's play for *any* vacuum cleaner.

---

[15]Notice they don't say how many, or what percentage of the total. The statement would be true if they bought one, a thousand, or a million.

[16]*New York Post,* March 13, 1974.

[17]The choice between the B210 and the Duster was one of a slightly larger, roomier car with "American style" handling, compared to a smaller car with better mileage and operation economy, easier parking, and more "road feel".

[18]For more on this and other fraudulent ads, see Samm Sinclair Baker's excellent book, *The Permissible Lie* (New York: World Publishing Co., 1968).

But most deceptive devices are not out-and-out frauds. For instance, it's common practice to use higher sound volume for television commercials than for television programs, in order to jog your attention back to the tube for the sales pitch. Similarly, there is nothing fraudulent in the Dristan schematic diagrams that "illustrate" how Dristan works in the system, or in "before and after" photos which use photographic techniques to exaggerate the difference between the "before" and the "after". But this sort of thing *is* deceptive—it may work even though, in general, we're aware of the practice. So we have to be on our guard against it.

(k.) Let's conclude by noting that *some ads appeal covertly to selfish desires while appealing overtly to unselfish ones.* (Some, of course, appeal overtly to both—selfish desires are thus reinforced by unselfish ones.) Few parents, for instance, want to think that they are selfish when it comes to their children. So adult-directed ads for children's products often contain a double appeal, on one level to the benefits the product will bring to children (good health through the high nutrition of Battle Creek's *Snicker Snacks*), while on the other to product benefits for the parents ("Snicker Snacks will solve *your* child-feeding problem"; "Camp Winnebago, a rewarding experience for your child this summer . . . while you relax, CARE-FREE, on that trip to Paris you've dreamed of for so long").

5. *Selling the Candidate: The Candidate as Product*

By now, just about everyone knows that political candidates are marketed pretty much like breakfast foods or laundry detergents. And that might be all right if the appeals in breakfast food and detergent advertising were rational. But they aren't, a fact we have been taking pains to illustrate.

Let's briefly discuss two of the major devices used by political "image makers" to sell their product, the political candidate—namely (a) lawn signs and billboards; and (b) television and radio ads.[19]

a. *Lawn signs and billboards* In some areas of the country, lawn signs, bumper stickers, and billboards are an important part of political campaigns (although this is true less and less, especially for national elections). In general, lawn signs carry only the name of the candidate and (sometimes) party affiliation. Billboards and bumper stickers rarely have room for more, but when they do, the extra material is usually a slogan. And yet, a man's name never constitutes a good reason for voting for him. And only occasionally is his party affiliation a good reason (it almost never is a *sufficient* reason).

At work in these cases is the psychological mechanism that lies behind the commission of the fallacy of *popularity,* namely familiarity and the desire to be one of the crowd. Psychologically, voting for a familiar name is little different

---

[19]Two other aspects of political campaigns, political speeches and free time on radio and television news programs, as well as free space in newspapers, are discussed at least by implication in other chapters.

from buying a product because advertising has made it familiar and because so many other people are buying it.[20]

Billboard ads come in for particularly heavy use during political campaigns and generally consist of the candidate's name, party affiliation, picture (sometimes), and a slogan. Here are a few slogans used on billboards in the 1970 elections in just one state (Connecticut):

> Keep a Strong Voice in Congress (Kilbourne, running for U.S. Congress)
> Because you care . . . (Uccelo, running for U.S. Congress)
> Ella Grasso Cares (Grasso, running for U.S. Congress)
> One man can make a difference (Duffey, running for the Democratic nomination for the U.S. Senate)
> Put your confidence in a man with guts (Weicker, running for U.S. Senate)
> All the people must be heard (Daddario, running for Governor)

None of these provided the slightest reason for voting for the touted candidate. One man sometimes *can* make a difference. But was Duffey that man? A slogan can't tell us that. All the people *ought* to be heard. But would they get heard if Daddario were elected? Again a slogan can't tell us that. All of these slogans trade on our desires—for a strong voice in Congress, someone who cares—without giving "reasons why" the candidate in question will satisfy them.

In Tennessee in 1970, Senator Albert Gore ran against William Brock, III, the Brock candy heir. One of Gore's more effective lines was that "I came up here with Tennessee dirt on my hands, not chocolate." True, and Gore may have been the better man, but dirt rather than chocolate didn't prove it.

In the 1960 presidential campaign, John Kennedy projected the image of youthful vigor, and repeated over and over the slogan that he wanted to "get the country moving again". In all fairness, he did explain to some small degree *how* he would get it moving again, but by and large he won by projecting the *image* of a young, virile man who would get us moving again. His slogan mirrored that image and thus contributed to his election.[21]

b.   Television (and radio) advertisements   It is television on which most advertising money and effort has been lavished in major political campaigns in recent years. In the 1970 New York State Senatorial campaign, Congressman Richard Ottinger, not well known in the state outside of his own territory, won the Democratic nomination by making himself well known via television. He then came very close to victory in the November elections even though he was one of two liberals running against one conservative. In both the primary and general elections, he spent millions on television advertising.

---

[20]The advertising principle at work here is *repeat the message ad nauseum.* It works in this case because of the psychological fact which makes us fall for the fallacy of *popularity.*

[21]Of course, he ran in a year when a Democrat had a good chance to win. In 1964, when Senator Goldwater ran as a conservative Republican, the liberal tide was strong. His silly slogan, "In your heart you know he's right" was countered by the even sillier back room liberal response, "In your guts you know he's nuts."

In the 1970 New York race for Governor (which he won quite handily), Nelson Rockefeller used by far the most massive television campaign in New York history (in fact, in any nonnational election in history). And yet, there is extremely little that is informative in television ads for political candidates.

The chief political ad device on television is the spot commercial, which generally runs from thirty to sixty seconds. It is almost impossible to say anything that is truly informative on any controversial topic in sixty seconds or less. Senator Philip Hart of Michigan, who used television ads in his successful 1970 campaign, put it perfectly, "How the hell can you describe in thirty seconds why you think a volunteer army is necessary?"[22]

In the 1968 campaign, the democratic presidential candidate Hubert Humphrey made the spot commercial his chief television venture. Humphrey was advised to stop talking about his Marshall Plan for cities and start talking about law and order. So one of his spots showed a mother holding a baby, and musing to herself, "I wonder what he'll be like when he's older. I hope he won't be afraid the way we are." Then an announcer's voice said, "Hubert Humphrey has said that every American has a right to a safe neighborhood. . . ."

Of course, Humphrey was not ahead of Richard Nixon on this issue. One of Nixon's commercials showed scenes of violence and fear, followed by Nixon stating:

It is time for some honest talk about the problem of order in the United States. Dissent is a necessary ingredient for change. But in a system that provides for peaceful change—there is no cause that justifies resort to violence. There is no cause that justifies rule by mob instead of reason.

The commercial ended with an announcer saying, "This time vote like your whole world depended on it", while the name "Nixon" appeared on screen.

If both candidates say just about the same thing, and that amounts to little more than platitudes playing on the public's fears, then how can an intelligent voter make a decision between them?

Still, these spot commercials were better than the ones created for the 1952 Eisenhower campaign, the first presidential campaign in which television ads played an important role. In that campaign, General Eisenhower would read from letters received from "citizens" asking questions that Eisenhower then "answered". Here is an example:

Citizen: Mr. Eisenhower, what about the high cost of living?
General Eisenhower: My wife Mamie worries about the same thing. I tell her it's our job to change that on November 14th.[23]

---

[22]Quoted in *Time,* September 21, 1970.

[23]Quoted by David Ogilvy in *Confessions of an Advertising Man,* p. 159. Ogilvy quotes Eisenhower as moaning between television takes, "To think an old soldier should come to this." Notice again that the ploy used is to bring up a strong desire (for lower prices) and tie the product (candidate) to the satisfaction of that desire *without* giving a single "reason why" the product will satisfy the desire.

The appeal here is to Eisenhower the father figure who will set things right just as daddy used to. (Appeal to a father figure may well be the most effective version of *appeal to authority.*) You don't have to know *how* papa fixes things, and you didn't have to know how Eisenhower was going to reduce prices. (He didn't, of course, but that's hindsight.) All you had to know was that if you voted for him, he would be on the job after the election doing something about the high cost of living.

Perhaps the most effective Nixon spot (in 1968) was his first, which ran often while the Humphrey campaign was bogged down. The video portion of the spot consisted of shots from Vietnam cleverly dovetailed with Mr. Nixon's voice:

> Never has so much military, economic, and diplomatic power been used as ineffectively as in Vietnam. And if, after all of this time and all of this support, there is still no end in sight, then I say the time has come for the American people to turn to new leadership, not tied to the policies and mistakes of the past. I pledge to you: we will have an honorable end to the war in Vietnam.

(An ironic commercial, given what transpired in Vietnam after Nixon took office.) Notice, however, that the punch line, the promise to get us out of Vietnam, is extremely *vague.* In particular, he doesn't tell us *when* or *how* he will get us out, only that it will be honorable. Yet the tone of the commercial gives the viewer the impression that Nixon will get us out *quickly.*

The ambiguity here tends to work this way: You are moved to vote for Nixon because you think he is pledging an honorable end to the war *quickly*—but when he doesn't end it quickly you can defend your vote (to yourself, the person you often ultimately have to con), and thus defend Nixon, by pointing out that Nixon didn't *literally* say he would end the war quickly, and after all, he did finally get our combat troops out of Vietnam four-and-a-half years later.

Many of Humphrey's 1968 spot commercials were directed against his opponents, Nixon and Wallace. One series of commercials had pictures of bubbles as their main video prop. As the announcer burst a political bubble, a visual bubble also would burst. For instance, Wallace stressed law and order, so one bubble commercial presented the following:

Fact:
Alabama:
Highest
Murder Rate

thus exploding another bubble (that Alabama Governor Wallace would reduce crime in the United States if elected president). Another hit Nixon on the health issue:

Nixon:
Opposes Medicare

Another burst bubble (that Nixon would improve health care in the United States if elected).

These ads were very simple and very effective. But they tell the television viewer almost nothing about what a vote for Humphrey would amount to. And they were misleading. To be sure, Nixon opposed Medicare; but he did have a program to improve medical care in America. The question was whether his plan or Humphrey's was better, and whether either program was likely to be carried out. (Nixon, of course, never carried his out.) Humphrey's television spots never went into such details.

The same is true of Humphrey's commercial that played on the fact that Nixon had chosen as his running mate a man who was almost unknown outside of his home state of Maryland, a man who happened to have the unusual name "Agnew". Democrats at the time often bucked up their sagging spirits by asking each other, *"Spiro who?"* So Humphrey's television advertising geniuses concocted a television spot consisting of almost a minute of laughter, with a voice saying, "Agnew for Vice President?" and at the end of the video reading, "This would be funny if it weren't so serious. . . ." All of which amounts to nothing other than a vicious *ad hominem* argument directed against Spiro Agnew.

One of Lyndon Johnson's television spots in 1964 emphasized the claim that Johnson was a peace candidate, while the Republican candidate Barry Goldwater was a violent hawk. (Lyndon Johnson as peace candidate seems foolish now, but, again, that's hindsight.) The commercial shows a cute little girl plucking the petals from a flower one by one while on the sound track we hear, "Ten, nine, eight, seven, six, five, four, three, two, one", at which point an atomic fireball flashes on the screen. A very informative commercial.

In addition to thirty- and sixty-second spots, political candidates also buy longer periods of time on television. In the 1968 campaign, the Republicans made hay on television with several hour-long question-answer panel shows. The format was pretty uniform: a "balanced" panel of voters, typically composed of a house-wife, *one* Negro (generally light skinned), a "senior citizen", a Jewish professional man, and a working man, asking questions of Mr. Nixon.

For him, it amounted to a press conference with two important and comforting differences: the audiences were hand-picked and guaranteed to applaud his every word; and the panelists were "safe", or in any event inexperienced (except for occasional newsmen), and tended to be as overawed by Mr. Nixon as most of us would have been. In addition, the format was designed to gain sympathy for Mr. Nixon. He stood alone on a platform, without props, facing the six or seven panelists who surrounded him. The program was live; he had no way of knowing what questions would be asked. The result was that the viewer tended to sympathize with Nixon and hope he would not be trapped or flub an answer.

Of course, there was no need for anxiety. Predictable questions were asked (with one exception out of the hundreds of questions on the many shows). The first question on the first panel show was typical. It was asked by a Jewish attorney on this balanced panel:[24]

> *Question:* Would you comment on the accusation which was made from time to time that your views have shifted and that they are based on expediencies? *Nixon:* I suppose what you are referring to is: Is there a new Nixon or is there an old Nixon? I suppose I could counter by saying, "Which Humphrey shall we listen to today?" [applause] I do want to say this: There certainly is a new Nixon. I realize too that as a man gets older he learns something. If I haven't learned something, I am not worth anything in public life.
>
> We live in a new world. Half the nations in the world were born since World War II. Half the people living in the world today were born since World War II. The problems are different, and I think I have had the good sense—I trust the intelligence—to travel the world since I left the office of Vice President and to bring my views up to date to deal with the new world. I think my principles are consistent. I believe very deeply in the American system. I think I have some ideas as to how we can promote peace, ideas that are different from what they were eight years ago; not because I have changed, but because the problems have changed. . . .

The question was about the frequently heard charge of expediency—that Nixon's views "blew with the winds of popularity". Much of his answer was irrelevant to that question, and what was relevant said what he could be expected to say, namely that his underlying principles remained the same, changes in his opinions resulting from changes in the situation (and from Nixon's greater experience).

So we did not get the crucial details. The format ruled against that for at least three reasons. The first was lack of time; every panelist had to ask two or three questions, and answers had to be short. The second was that the panelists were not professionals, and lacked knowledge of the details that make all the difference. Instead of this first question, we needed one giving *details* of Nixon's switches which could reasonably be construed as motivated by expediency. But it wouldn't have mattered in any case. For the third impediment to a truly informative session was that Nixon's answers tended to be vague and general, floating above any specific probe, and the questioners were psychologically not ready to press for a better answer. (It takes a very strong character to push forward in such an intimidating situation. Only one panelist—Jack McKinney—had what it takes to try it, and he was a person with a great deal of airtime experience.)

Let's include one more example of political campaigning on television, to illustrate the evils of the "no-comeback" feature of political campaigning by advertising. It concerns a television spot for Nelson Rockefeller in his successful 1966 race for Governor of New York. Rockefeller, as usual, outspent his opponent

---

[24]For a much more complete and revealing account of the Nixon television campaign and in particular the panel shows and spot commercials, see Joe McGinniss, *The Selling of the President 1968* (New York: Trident Press, 1969) (also in Pocket Book paperback, 1970).

by a wide margin. During the last ten days of that campaign, Rockefeller "saturated the air waves"[25] with the following spot:

> Frank O'Connor, the man who led the fight against the New York State Thruway, is running for Governor [against Rockefeller, of course]. Get in your car and drive down to the polls and vote.

O'Connor did *not* lead the fight against the New York State Thruway: he did not even oppose its construction. But he did oppose *Rockefeller* on the Thruway; O'Connor wanted it to be free, while Rockefeller insisted on a toll. So the concealment and distortion is that O'Connor opposed *Rockefeller's* thruway proposal. (The distorted position constituted, of course, a *straw man.*)

The main evil of such political advertisement is that the other side rarely can strike back and effectively explain the facts. In this case, the television spots ran near the end of the campaign, so that the other side had little time to prepare a professional reply based on effective advertising techniques. And in any event such denials would have been drowned out by the sheer volume of the Rockefeller barrage. Rockefeller had tremendous *repetition* going for him, just as did Lucky Strike cigarettes at an earlier time. "M.C.M.R.C.: More commercials mean richer candidates."

Summary of Chapter Seven

Chapter Seven dealt with advertising as a form of argument.

1. We first discussed reasons in favor of advertising (for example, that it gives us useful information about products and services), which show that advertising has a useful social role.

2. We then discussed arguments against advertising (for example, that it creates irrational demand for products or appeals primarily to emotions) and concluded that some of these objections are legitimate. The moral is that advertising is useful, but we must learn how to cope with it, that is, learn how to avoid being conned by it.

3. We then discussed three basic advertising procedures or principles: (1) Successful ads generally appeal to selfish human desires and motives; (2) they appeal to those selfish desires through the *emotions*, not reason; and (3) the message, if possible, should be repeated over and over again.

4. Next, we discussed devices used in ads to con the unwary: (1) Ads almost never mention the drawbacks of a product; (2) often say false things about the product; (3) play on our fears or desires without giving reasons for believing

---

[25]To borrow a phrase used by Jack Newfield in his *Village Voice* article "Nelson Rockefeller: The Chutzpah King", October 8, 1970.

the product will satisfy them; (4) trade on the fuzziness of language to confuse us; (5) use relatively meaningless jargon; (6) often state literal truths that *imply* falsehoods; (7) use humor to mask weak or ambiguous arguments; (8) exaggerate to make their point; (9) compare apples with oranges; (10) use deceptive or even fraudulent "sight or sound" techniques; and (11) appeal covertly to selfish desires while appealing overtly to unselfish ones.

5. Finally, we discussed a particular kind of advertising (political advertising) and its product (the political candidate running for office). We discussed chiefly two areas: (1) lawn signs and billboards (almost never good sources of information); and (2) television and radio ads (in general, not a good source of product [candidate] information—for instance, we noted that television spot commercials are not a good source of product information.)

Exercise I for Chapter Seven

Here are several ad snippets (usually including the main ad ploy). In each case, state: (1) whether the ad, if true, would provide a good reason for buying the product; (2) whether the ad contains questionable claims, and if so which claims are doubtful *and why;* (3) which, if any, of the devices employed were discussed in this chapter (explain); and (4) which, if any, of the ads use emotive language unfairly (that is, designed to con).

*1. *Ad for Senator McGovern in 1972 presidential campaign:* Nixon has a secret plan for ending the war. He is going to vote for McGovern.

 2. *Rolaids television commercial, showing a Rolaids user rejecting another brand:* Rolaids active ingredient—medically recognized safe and effective.

*3. CHEMICAL BANK has an answer to all your borrowing needs. The answer is "Yes". ("Yes" is a chemical reaction.)

 4. *Bloomingdales Department Store ad, January 1975:* Our very finest sofas, now at our lowest prices in years.

 5. *The Night Porter*—most controversial film of all time.

 6. *Ad for James Buckley, conservative senatorial candidate from New York:* Isn't it time *we* had a senator?

 7. Take my "Hundred Dollar Knife", yours for only $4.99.

 8. The shaver that went to the moon! Just wind it and enjoy an out-of-this-world shave!

*9. Martha West's exclusive dress frames the face, and flatters the figure.

10. There's only one King David, and there's only one King David Manor.

11. Take the big skirt route from Paris.

12. *British Airways ad:* "If I didn't live in Britain, I'd take these tours myself."—Robert Morley

13. *Ad for Toronto Dominion Bank:* We have a new way to lend you money.

14. *Sign on Highland Park, Illinois, retail establishment:* 100% PRE-DRIVEN CARS.

15. *Datsun advertisement (in* Money, *July 1973):* L.A. to N.Y.—$29.85—37.9 miles per gallon. We drove a new Datsun from L.A. to N.Y. . . . we averaged 37.9 miles per gallon. Just $29.85 coast to coast. The average car in America gets around 13½ miles per gallon. It would cost nearly three times as much for the same trip!

16. Try our 7-day "Linger Longer" cruises.

17. Send for our free master catalogue of exciting new bargains.

18. San Diego is: Golf! Tennis! Swimming!

19. The best Island buy since Manhattan.

20. We do everything a bank should do. And then some.

21. *Ad for the new Olympic Towers Apartments:* A landmark ahead of its time.

22. *Ad for Michael's Jewelers:* Give the world's oldest love symbol.

23. *Fur sale ad:* Some styles sold by prestige furriers for $495 to $6000!

*24. *Ad against smoking:* [Large type]: 100,000 doctors have quit smoking cigarettes. [Small type]: (Maybe they know something you don't.)

25. *Western Union Mailgram, dated October 30, 1972, sent by Senator George McGovern, asking for funds for his 1972 Presidential campaign:* Getting astounding reports from everywhere. Massive shift away from Nixon toward our ticket. Due in large part to impact of television talks you helped finance. . . .

26. *Winston cigarette ad (showing picture of beautiful woman):* If it wasn't for Winston, I wouldn't smoke. Taste isn't everything. It's the only thing. I smoke for pleasure. That's spelled T-A-S-T-E. That means Winston. Winston won't give you a new image. All Winston will ever give me is taste. A taste that's very real. If a cigarette isn't real, it isn't anything. Winston is for real.

Exercise II for Chapter Seven

1. Watch television for two continuous hours, noting the main ploys of at least three or four commercials. Then analyze for fallacies, use of emotive language, and other advertising gimmicks discussed in this chapter.

2. Rewrite an advertisement containing highly charged emotive language and fallacies (in other words, a particularly gimmicky ad). Once you have discovered its true informational content, compare your version with the original ad, and then critically evaluate the original ad.

"Attention out there! We now bring you an opposing viewpoint to a CBS editorial!"

Drawing by Richter. © 1975 The New Yorker Magazine, Inc.

Humor is often the best way to make a point. This cartoon effectively makes the point that the power of freedom of speech is relative. If you set policy for CBS news, your views will be widely heard and very influential, but if you're just one of the rest of us, you have no *effective* way to compete with the giants in the marketplace of ideas. You might just as well let off steam by shouting from the rooftops.

Chapter Eight

Managing the News

When a dog bites a man, that is not news, because it happens so often. But if a man bites a dog, that is news.

John B. Bogart

When covering the Capitol, the first thing to remember is that every government is run by liars.

I. F. Stone

Reasoning about political and social issues requires factual knowledge. That is why the success of a democratic form of government depends on a *well-informed* electorate. The American mass media (newspapers, television, mass magazines, and radio) do not adequately or accurately inform their readers or listeners. In particular, they fail to inform them of the great gulf between the way our society is supposed to work (the ideal—the "official story") and the way it actually works.[1]

Yet, we all have to rely on the mass media for news. Hopefully, the person who understands the workings of the mass media will be better able to use them as a source of information, or at least not be taken in by their manipulation of the news. (It is also hoped that some who read this chapter will be motivated to look elsewhere, for instance, to non-mass media journals and magazines, for vital information on how our society really functions, and why.)

1. Why News Reporting Is Poor

Mass media news reporting is poor for several reasons: (1) the theories of news reporting most widely held by those working in the media are incorrect; (2) poor procedures, which save time or money, tend to become standard practice; (3) workers in the media tend to be biased, just like the rest of us; and (4) those who own newspapers, and television stations want to protect their investments in these valuable properties and perhaps make a good deal of money.

a. The theories of news reporting most widely held by those working in the media are incorrect. In the first place, *the unusual is considered to be news, the usual is not.* Yet what happens every day is generally more important than the unusual occurrence. Prison uprisings get big play, but the poor treatment prisoners receive every day, which leads to the uprisings, goes relatively unreported. Big court cases such as the Watergate trials receive much attention, but thousands of everyday cases in which justice is flouted tend to be ignored. (A whole disgraceful area of courtroom

---

[1]Chapter Nine deals with the same theme and another branch of the mass media establishment, public school textbooks.

practice, plea bargaining, was pretty much ignored in the media until Vice President Spiro Agnew "copped a plea".)[2]

Most workers in the media also subscribe to the view that *objectivity requires reporters to present the facts, not draw conclusions or make value judgments.* Facts are objective; conclusions or value judgments are subjective. The media are supposed to be objective. (Even J. Edgar Hoover subscribed to this view although he didn't practice it. His motto was that the F.B.I. does not draw conclusions, it only reports the facts.)

But this theory of objective reporting is mistaken. *All* reports of facts depend on someone's *judgment* that they are facts. The reporter must *conclude* that they are facts. Take the following excerpts from an Associated Press story carried in the *Lawrence Daily Journal World* (October 30, 1970) on an alleged riot in San Jose, California, before the November 1970 elections:

> President Nixon, the target of rocks, bricks, bottles, eggs, red flags and other missiles hurled by antiwar demonstrators. . . .
>
> The San Jose violence was the most serious aimed at any president in this country since the assassination of President John Kennedy. . . .
>
> [Nixon's] limousine and other vehicles in the cavalcade were hit repeatedly by large rocks and other objects.

Clearly, the reporter did not *see* that the alleged attack on President Nixon was the worst attack on a president since the assassination of President Kennedy. He had to *conclude* to the fact—if it *is* a fact—by using judgment as well as eyesight.

But often we overlook the fact that judgment and conclusion-drawing are required even in reporting more immediate facts. Did the AP reporter—or any AP reporter—actually *see* rocks hit the president's limousine? If not, who did? Are those who think they did sure no visual distortion was at work? Did they hear a crunch as the rocks hit the car? These questions are not academic; it is well known that honest reports by onlookers frequently differ seriously about what took place. In this case, many eyewitnesses, including television and newspaper reporters, said that *nothing* was thrown at the presidential limousine, although objects were thrown at the press corps bus.[3]

A great deal of reporting is of this kind. If the reporter is not an eyewitness, he must draw a *conclusion* about what happened from what he is told by others. If he is an eyewitness, what he thinks he has seen needs to be checked with what others have seen and with later evidence (for example, if he thinks he saw

---

[2]An exception is the excellent article by Leonard Downie, Jr., "Crime in the Courts: Assembly Line Justice", *Washington Monthly,* May 1970. Another is a *New York Times* article, December 13, 1970, p. 26.

[3]See, for instance, the *Village Voice* article by Tom Devries, November 5, 1970, in which Mike Mills, a television reporter, when asked why his films of the event show no flying objects, stated, "That is because nothing was thrown." The article quoted several other reporters who supported this statement. And the San Jose police chief confirmed reporters' claims.

rocks thrown, there should be rock fragments on the pavement at the correct location[4]).

So the idea that reporters must stick to facts and not draw conclusions is a myth. One must *reason to the facts* just as one reasons to anything else.

The Tearful Mystery Resolved[5]

Did Muskie cry or not? It's not a question which has troubled many breasts since that fateful day on February 26, 1972 when an alleged trickle down Muskie's cheeks amid the New Hampshire snows turned into a mighty river of defeat. But it has been worrying Joe Zellner and John Milne. Zellner and Milne were, respectively, the AP and UPI wire-service reporters covering Muskie's fateful press conference in which he denounced Bill Loeb, publisher of the *Manchester Union Leader.*

Both Zellner and Milne discuss the matter in an article by Stan Friedman in *Wireport,* the paper of the Wire Service Guild. They were the nearest to Muskie as he spoke and were the only ones out of 60 who did not have tears in their leads. Everyone else, from the *New York Times* and the *Los Angeles Times,* to the *Washington Post,* did. David Broder had Muskie's face streaming with tears. The result was that although early UPI and AP stories had no tears, the wire-service editors began to panic when they saw all the other tear stories, joined the pack, and had Muskie blubbering themselves.

Zellner says, "At one point he put his hand to his forehead and eyes and sort of looked down . . . the snow was blowing and water was just trickling down his hairline, just like it was on most of us, down Muskie's cheeks and down mine, too. I was very careful for accuracy's sake, and I never saw wet eyes." Milne agrees, and says that the most Muskie did was to "choke up." So how did all the other papers have Muskie crying? Zellner says, "I was told by a couple of correspondents that they asked a Muskie aide if he was crying and they were told yes. It was going to be a plus to show him human in that way."

It's only a footnote to history, I suppose, but it shows you need not believe everything you see in the papers.

The common belief that then presidential candidate Edmund Muskie cried during the 1972 New Hampshire primary is thought by many to have destroyed his chances to win the Democratic party nomination. But did he cry? Did the "media" botch the job again?

---

[4]Mr. Devries, the *Village Voice* reporter, wrote that he later checked the area for loose rocks and broken glass and found none. This does not mean that we can conclude he is right that rocks were not thrown at the president's auto, for he had to *conclude* no rocks were thrown, and he too could be wrong. But his failure to find such debris is evidence that no rocks were thrown at the president's vehicle.

[5]Alex Cockburn, *Village Voice,* December 30, 1974. Copyright © 1974 The Village Voice, Inc. Reprinted by permission.

Similarly, the idea that newspapers should not make value judgments is incorrect. When we read of the death of a famous movie star on page one of our morning newspaper, but read nothing of the death of the eminent philosopher Rudolf Carnap (reported in the obituary section of the *New York Times* but ignored in most papers), it becomes obvious that newspapers have to make *value judgments* to determine what is important and what is not. The same is true when a hurricane on the Gulf Coast, which kills two dozen people, gets more space than reports of the My Lai 4 massacre in Vietnam, or when the George Foreman–Muhammad Ali fight in Zaire gets more space than mass starvation in Africa.

In other words, *editing,* one of the chief tasks of any newspaper, requires value judgments about the relative importance of events. And *moral* value judgments are required as well as others. It should be news that thousands of children die each year in the United States from lack of proper food precisely because it is so horribly *wrong* and *ought* to be corrected.

An Offering of Bullets[6]

By Russell Baker

While President Ford and Professor Kissinger were whooping it up for more war in Cambodia the other day, Sydney Schanberg was writing for the *New York Times* from Phnom Penh. If we juxtapose excerpts from Schanberg, Ford, and Kissinger, we begin to understand how American policy relates to Cambodian reality.

Thus, Schanberg: *Cambodia before the war was a country so rich in her food produce that even the very poor were never hungry. Everyone had a piece of land and there were always bananas and other fruit growing wild and a river or stream nearby where fish could be easily caught.*

"I wish to convey to the House of Representatives my deep concern over the present critical situation in Cambodia. An independent Cambodia cannot survive unless the Congress acts very soon to provide supplemental military and economic assistance."—President Ford.

Now it is a country of landless nomads with empty stomachs—human flotsam living amid damp and filth in the flimsiest of shanties, thatch shacks and sidewalk lean-to's. The countryside is charred wasteland that either belongs to the Cambodian insurgents or is insecure, so the population huddles in the cities and towns, doing marginal work that never pays enough to feed a family adequately. Growing numbers of children and adults are taking to begging.

"Unless such assistance is provided [by the Congress] the Cambodian Army will run out of ammunition in less than a month."—President Ford.

In a World Vision clinic, Ah Srey, a 2-month-old girl, grossly dehydrated from

---

starvation, has just been brought in by her grandmother. Ten days before, they were caught in the maelstrom of a battle a few miles from Phnom Penh. In the panic, the family became separated and the grandmother found herself alone with the child. For ten days they had been surviving on handouts and scraps of garbage. The child had been malnourished before. Now she is a skeletal horror, little more than bulging eyes and a protruding rib cage. Every few seconds she produces a wail that racks her body. In three hours she is dead.

"If a supplemental is not voted within the next few weeks, it is certain that Cambodia must fall because it will run out of ammunition."—Professor Kissinger.

Waves of mothers carrying gravely ill children—swollen children, children with stick-like concentration-camp bodies, children with parchment skin hanging in flaccid folds, coughing children, weeping children, silent children too weak to respond anymore—press forward every day against the doors of the relief agency clinics, desperate to get in. But there are not enough doctors or nurses or medicine or food for them all, so for every 500 who come, only 200 or so can be treated.

"Therefore, the decision before us is whether the United States will withhold ammunition from a country which has been associated with us and which, clearly, wishes to defend itself."—Professor Kissinger.

On the table next to Ah Srey is an older child—19 months—who is dying right now. His name is Nuth Saroeun. From his mouth comes a steady whimper and rattle. His father was killed by a rocket three months ago. His 25-year-old mother, also suffering from malnutrition (she has beri-beri and her feet are going numb), stands at his side sobbing. A doctor tries to force a tube down the child's throat to get out the mucus that is blocking his breathing. Suddenly the child utters a tiny cry that sounds like "Mak" ("Mother") and then his head slumps and he is gone.

"If the Congress does not provide for continued deliveries of rice and other essential supplies, millions of innocent people will suffer—people who depend on us for their bare survival."—President Ford.

Americans have stepped up an emergency airlift of supplies from Thailand because the insurgents have blockaded Cambodia's main supply line, the Mekong River, but until now the cargo these planes have brought is all military aid, mostly ammunition. There has been no food.

"Our national security and the integrity of our alliances depend upon our reputation as a reliable partner. Countries around the world who depend on us for support—as well as our foes—will judge our performance."—President Ford.

At least every other person in this country of seven million is a refugee from war.

Russell Baker's *New York Times* column (March 8, 1975) presents two different accounts of the situation in Cambodia in early 1975. It is reprinted here to illustrate the view that *value judgments* are required in selecting "facts" to be printed in newspapers or heard on television. A value-free "objectivity" is impossible.

Television reporting requires the same selection of "facts". During a bomb scare break in proceedings of the House Judiciary Committee considerations of the Nixon impeachment question, most television stations filled in with interviews of members of Congress and other politicians. But WNET, Channel 13, New York, chose to interview a literary-political figure, Barbara Tuchman, instead. Tuchman's comments differed greatly from those heard on other channels. (For instance, while listeners on other channels heard congressmen say it would be improper to impeach Nixon for his Cambodia activities, listeners on WNET heard Tuchman state that that was precisely the most important charge to impeach him on.) Officials at WNET clearly made a *value judgment* that Tuchman's remarks were more important than those of others they might have interviewed. Ditto for the other channels.

Another belief widely subscribed to by those in the media is that *"in-depth", or background, reporting should be separated from straight news reporting.* (The idea is that straight news reporting should be as "objective" as possible.) The trouble is that this view leads to much less useful news reporting than otherwise. It's true that facts are indispensable in making decisions. But the unordered acquisition of facts leaves one a long way from intelligent opinion. Facts need working on, and in particular comparison with related facts. In general, because reporting of current news lacks *depth*, it is rendered much less useful than it could be in forming opinions.

An Associated Press photo captioned "Lawmen and Indians Fight", showing policemen apparently beating Indians, appeared on page one of the *Hartford Courant*, (October 29, 1970). Below the caption was a brief story about the fight between lawmen and Pit River Indian tribesmen, started, lawmen said, when the Indians tried to publicize their claim to the land by building on it "illegally". The story identified the police units and where the fight had occurred. It also stated the Indians claimed that the land was taken from them back in the Gold Rush days.

But we weren't told enough for us to deal intelligently with this news. Did the Indians resist arrest? Was police force necessary? Is there anything to the Indian land claim? Have they tried to gain redress via the courts? The picture seems to show a policeman beating someone with a long nightstick. Is he? If so, was this force necessary to subdue the person? The caption says lawmen and *Indians* fight. Did the Indians do any fighting? We aren't given the answers to any of these questions.

And yet it is impossible to form an intelligent opinion on the events described if we don't know at least some of these facts. Not that this deterred most readers. Some no doubt shrugged and muttered about drunken Indians acting up again, while others commented about more pig brutality. The story as presented justifies neither of these conclusions. In fact, it doesn't justify any conclusion at all. But it does give readers an opportunity to vent their prejudices and thus become further polarized.

Inadequately reported news stories appear in the media every day, increasing misunderstanding and polarization. Reports that Georgia Governor Lester Maddox's son was sentenced to six months of weekends in jail plus a $500 fine for burglary of a service station omitted the crucial information about the same judge's normal penalty for similar crimes, as well as the sentence of another man convicted with Mr. Maddox's son for the same crime.

Yet one thing that splits this nation into factions is the question of equal treatment before the law. Millions of Americans believe that, by and large, justice in America is fair, while other millions believe it is not. At least one side must be wrong; but the matter will never be settled by appeal to the contents of daily newspapers or, for that matter, television.

The *Boston Herald Traveler* (November 14, 1970) contained a story on charges by the Massachusetts Bar Association that Massachusetts' no-fault auto insurance law would result in "legal chaos" if allowed to go into effect. The story cited a paper in the *Massachusetts Law Quarterly* which stated that the law is "both inconsistent and incomprehensible". But the newspaper article failed to quote a single relevant reason *why* legal chaos would result, or in what way the law was inconsistent and incomprehensible. Instead, it quoted the claim of the president of the Massachusetts Bar Association that legal chaos would result if the law went into effect: It cited an authority's opinion on a controversial matter, but failed to provide any of his reasons. It thus invited the reader to commit the fallacy of *appeal to authority*.

To make matters worse, the newspaper article failed to point out that lawyers had a special interest in fighting this law, namely to maintain one of their most lucrative sources of income: auto accident litigation. Instead, it quoted the charge of M.B.A. President Donahue that the law would "result in both increasing claims and increasing rates", again without furnishing any evidence pro or con. Nowhere in the article is there any mention of the frequently cited statistic that lawyers get as large a slice of auto insurance premiums as do those suffering losses in accidents, a slice of the pie that no-fault insurance laws greatly reduce. Yet, how can anyone get any benefit from a story on the Massachusetts "no fault" insurance law without at least some of these facts?

Even when newspapers attempt to give greater depth to the news, we still generally are not told all in one place what we need to know. A story on law and order, entitled "The Cops—Victims of Ghetto Ambush"[7], contained a long tally of police deaths attributed to "black and white revolutionaries", and provided evidence that underground newspapers encourage such violent acts.

But the story was hopelessly inadequate to help us understand anything. In the first place, it was a completely one-sided story. It gave interesting and important statistics on police deaths (sixteen in the first 8 months of 1970 against 4.3 per year in the sixties), but not the equally important statistics on "black and white revolutionaries" killed by police. It described one cause—left-wing encouragement—for police killings, but not what motivates the radical left to be against police (for example, alleged police brutality and prejudice).

---

[7]*The Hartford Times,* September 6, 1970, by Richard Lemon, Newsweek Service.

In other words, the story divorced police killings from their settings, leaving the reader with no idea *why* anyone would want to risk his life to kill policemen. Could the average newspaper reader tell us, for instance, why so many more policemen are killed in the United States than in England?

An interesting postscript is that the newspaper which published this one-sided account had previously published several news stories on police brutality—for instance, at the Chicago Democratic Convention in 1968, as well as the later Chicago Black Panther shootings. But all this relevant information on the subject was never put together in one place.

Occasionally, newspapers do intersperse a current news story with pertinent background information. An example is a *New Britain Herald* (October 27, 1970) AP story about a Boeing 747 jumbo jet, one of whose engines burst into flames in flight. The story also contained information about the running battle between the Federal Aviation Administration and the National Transportation Board over the latter's claim that 747 engines dangerously overheat, thus giving the reader some inkling of the import of the event reported on. There is no *good* reason why newspapers could not always provide such background information.

Some workers in the media believe that *good citizenship requires self-censorship.* A *Washington Post* reporter learned that two Army intelligence officers claimed the C.I.A. and Army Intelligence were training men in torture and assassination techniques to be used against National Liberation Front members in Vietnam.[8] But his story never appeared in the *Washington Post,* an apparent victim of self-censorship by that newspaper.

Though unusual, self-censorship is not rare. The nation's major newspapers, which have large investigative staffs, tend to engage in self-censorship more often than other newspapers, no doubt because they have access to more sensitive information. Perhaps the most famous example of this kind is the *New York Times'* decision to go easy on the Bay of Pigs story during the Kennedy administration.[9]

Another revealing example is the 1970 U.S. invasion of Cambodia. Associated Press reporters covering this invasion wrote that U.S. troops engaged in much looting during the venture.[10] But newspapers on the AP wire never received this portion of the report from Cambodia, which apparently was edited out partly because the AP wanted their men during that troubled period to report news that is "down the middle and subdues emotion", and because "in present context this report of looting can be inflammatory".

---

[8]George Wilson, "The Fourth Estate as the Fourth Branch", *Village Voice,* January 1, 1970.

[9]President Kennedy is alleged later to have had the "chutzpah" to take the *Times* to task for this censorship on grounds that publication of the story by the *Times* might have resulted in calling off that ill-fated venture! The June 1971 publication by the *New York Times* of excerpts from a classified Pentagon report, which describes behind-the-scenes planning for the Vietnam war, was an exception to the usual self-censorship of newspapers; but we can hope that it represents a permanent policy change.

[10]According to a story in the September 1970 issue of the *AP Review.*

Self-censorship

The *New York Times* quotes two aides to Sen. Robert F. Kennedy as saying Kennedy told them he stopped a CIA plan to use the Mafia to assassinate Cuban Premier Fidel Castro. . . . The *Times* said the alleged CIA-Mafia plot was first disclosed to the newspaper off the record in 1973 by Adam Walinsky and Peter Edelman, the former Kennedy aides, and that last week they gave permission to the *Times* to attribute the story to them. (From an article in the *New York Post,* March 10, 1975, p. 5)

An even better example is the *New York Times* killing of a story by veteran reporter Tad Szulc stating that the United States and South Vietnam were about to invade Cambodia. According to Roger Morris, Henry Kissinger asked that the story be killed for national security reasons (for we *were* about to invade Cambodia).[11] Self-censorship due to respect for social conventions is usually relatively unimportant in each particular case, but quite important in the aggregate. Unfortunately, it often is hard to know when censorship is being practiced. All that can be determined in most cases is the lack of certain kinds of news.

One unfortunate aspect of this kind of self-censorship is that no strict ground rules exist for what should be printed and what should not. The result, for example, is that newspapers all over the country printed and even headlined a story about the alleged homosexuality of an aide to President Johnson, but rarely report on the alcoholism of local and state officials, or of members of Congress. Yet, homosexuality does not render one less able to perform public duties, while alcoholism does.[12]

The problem of self-censorship is made particularly difficult by the counter tug of the right to privacy. A person in the public eye is still, after all, entitled to a private life. And yet it is difficult to know what bears on a person's public life (and thus can be exposed) and what does not (and thus ought to be censored). It was well known to newspeople, for instance, that as a Congressman and then as a Senator, John F. Kennedy was quite a lady's man (both before and after his marriage). The media, on the whole, chose not to report this feature of Kennedy's private life, and were generally applauded for their restraint (after all, stories on Kennedy's sex life would have found an eager audience).

---

[11]Roger Morris, *Columbia Journalism Review,* May–June 1974. Also see John D. Marks' "The Story That Never Was" [*MORE*], June 1974, p. 20. (Incidentally, the *New York Times* editor, A. M. Rosenthal, denies Szulc ever submitted the story to the *Times.*)

[12]Readers inclined to believe that the lack of reporting on this topic due to a lack of things to report should recall that most Americans were unaware of the late Senator Joseph R. McCarthy's problems with the bottle until in defeat he became fair game for everyone. Even then, many newspapers and radio and television stations never mentioned McCarthy's drinking problem. Similarly, reporters knew of Congressman Wilbur Mills' "affair" with a strip tease artist for quite a while before circumstances forced news of that affair into national headlines.

And yet, self-censorship of similar stories concerning Kennedy's brother, Edward M. (Ted) Kennedy, may well have been a mistake, given what happened at Chappaquiddick. Knowledge of a person's sexual life *may,* after all, be relevant to his character and thus to his suitability for public office. (Of course, it may be that a person's right to privacy is stronger than the public's right to knowledge about his character. The point is that the question is extremely difficult, and as yet not adequately answered.)

Similar remarks apply to a person's private wealth. What someone owns might seem to be his own affair, and yet in the case of Nelson Rockefeller, who in 1974 admitted to a personal fortune of over $200 million, it seems clear that the matter is of vital public interest. Indeed, in Rockefeller's case, the personal wealth of at least his four brothers, even if not that of the other seventy or so members of the Rockefeller family, may have been something the public had a right to know. For it meant that as a public servant Nelson Rockefeller could hardly make a move without affecting either his own fortune or that of his brothers.[13]

Self-censorship of socially sensitive topics extends even to advertisements. Ads for items related to homosexuality are routinely rejected by the mass media. For instance, the *Boston Globe,* relatively liberal about ads, rejected the following copy:

Read about Father Paul Stanley, Priest to 100,000 Boston homosexuals, in the *Advocate,* newspaper to America's homosexuals.

Some newspapers reject ads for X-rated movies. Even the *Village Voice* refused to carry an ad for the movie "Tits", unless the titillating title of that flick were removed from the copy.

Finally, in reporting news, *the opinions of authorities or experts, especially if they're powerful, are supposed to be reported before anyone else's.* The trouble with this plausible sounding theory is that politicians, government officials, and the economically powerful automatically qualify as authorities on political and social issues. Yet

---

[13]The mass media tended to accept the figure of $200 million, although the only hard evidence in its favor was the word of Rockefeller himsclf. As usual, fringe media, rather than the mass media, provided reasons for supposing this figure to be much too low. The *Village Voice,* for instance, ran an article (September 19, 1974, page 7, by Dick Roberts), when Rockefeller was being considered by the Congress for Vice President, in which it was pointed out that John D. Rockefeller, Sr. reported his income for 1917 as $60 million, and was held to be worth about $1 billion ten years earlier (according to a *New York Times* article of March 13, 1918). A billion dollars invested, say, in 1910 in just an ordinary way would have multiplied many times over; in the hands of insiders, as the Rockefellers have been since then (David Rockefeller currently is Chairman of the Chase Manhattan Bank, the third largest in the country), anything less than a fifty-fold increase in principal would indicate gross mismanagement. While there are over seventy current Rockefeller family members, most of the Rockefeller fortune is believed held by the five brothers, including Nelson and David. It is possible that Nelson Rockefeller's statement concerning his wealth is correct, but in the absence of concrete proof, accepting it constitutes commission of a fallacy. For there isn't any reason to suppose either that the Rockefeller fortune has been mismanaged or that Nelson Rockefeller's share is a great deal less than that of his brothers.

Last year, 300,000 Americans were arrested for smoking an herb that Queen Victoria used regularly for menstrual cramps.

It's a fact.

The herb, of course, is *cannabis sativa*. Otherwise known as marijuana, pot, grass, hemp, boo, mary-jane, ganja—the nicknames are legion.

So are the people who smoke it.

By all reckoning, it's fast becoming the new national pastime. Twenty-six million smokers, by some accounts—lots more by others. Whatever the estimate, a staggeringly high percentage of the population become potential criminals simply by being in possession of it. And the numbers are increasing.

For years, we've been told that marijuana leads to madness, sex-crimes, hard-drug usage and even occasional warts.

Pure Victorian poppycock.

In 1894, The Indian Hemp Commission reported marijuana to be relatively harmless. A fact that has been substantiated time and again in study after study.

Including, most recently, by the President's own Commission. This report stands as an indictment of the pot laws themselves.

And that's why more and more legislators are turning on to the fact that the present marijuana laws are as archaic as dear old Victoria's code of morality. And that they must be changed. Recently, the state of Oregon did, in fact, de-criminalize marijuana. Successfully.

Other states are beginning to move in that direction. They must be encouraged.

NORML has been and is educating the legislators, working in the courts and with the lawmakers to change the laws. We're doing our best but still, we need help. Yours.

Ad censorship: NORML marijuana ad rejected by *Time* and *Newsweek,* accepted by *Playboy.*

they frequently are a far cry from being experts on these issues, and almost always have an axe to grind.

The reason for this reverence for authoritative opinion is quite simple. A reporter who sticks his neck out and includes his own judgment of the facts on an issue may turn out to be wrong, and in a serious case may risk being fired. But if he reports the opinion of an "expert", he runs much less risk. For it is a fact that the expert did state that opinion. So by reporting what an expert says, a reporter plays it as safe as possible, although at the same time playing into the tendency of his readers to commit the fallacy of *appeal to authority*.[14]

The *New York Post,* which runs news stories on alcoholism no more often than most other papers, on February 18, 1972 gave its page one headline to a government report stating that alcohol is the nation's most abused drug. That statement became news not because it is true, since it was true the day, the week, the month, even the year before the *Post's* headline. No, it became news because *government experts* held a press conference and issued a report claiming it is true.

b. Poor procedures that save time or money tend to become standard practice. Procedures and customs do not develop in a vacuum. They are the result of all kinds of pressures and forces, even though these forces do not dictate practice in any absolute fashion. The chief force at work in the development of news gathering practices is the ease with which certain kinds of news can be obtained. The result is what may well be the greatest bar of all to adequate news reporting—*most news is given to reporters, not discovered by them.* Check the front page of almost any newspaper and you will find as often as not that the vast majority of items on that page were acquired by that newspaper (or by the wire services—AP and UPI) from someone-or-other's press release, press conference, or speech. Thus, most news stories report what someone, usually someone powerful, has said about the news, rather than what reporters have discovered for themselves. Even stories in which news is *assembled* usually turn out to be just a collection of statements by the powerful on some topic of interest.

Here is a front page sampling from two large metropolitan newspapers, the *Baltimore Sun* and the *Miami Herald,* both considered better than average newspapers. Two recent *Baltimore Sun* front pages chosen at random (August 21 and 22, 1974) contained seventeen front page stories: four were reports of speeches, statements, announcements, or handouts of local government officials (for example, headline story on the transfer of 1250 local teachers); four of federal government officials (President Ford was considering running again in 1976); four of United Nations or foreign government officials (the Turks ordered the United Nations out of a key district in Cyprus); two of big business spokesmen (General Motors would cut its auto prices); one of a standard news item (Congress passed a pension bill); one of news leaked by an "informed source" in the government (Ford was eyeing a 10¢ gas tax boost—this trial balloon didn't fly; no gas tax increase was imposed); and one news item from the police/fire beat (a headline story on a local fire).

---

[14]Another reason the opinions of whoever has power are reported most is that those in the media themselves tend to know very little about what they report on. See the Walter Cronkite television example later in the chapter.

Only one story (the local fire) required much legwork, although a few others showed evidence that they were at least *assembled* from several (establishment) sources. (The coverage of the bill passed by Congress was routine. They tell you it is going to happen, and you send someone to record it.)

Most of the news, then, was given to the *Sun* (or to a wire service the Sun subscribes to). And in every case except one, it was the news, words, or announcements of political or big business figures or organizations. Not one item concerned the "news behind the news".

Now let's look at two front pages (August 21 and 22, 1974) of a better, but surely not the best, newspaper, the *Miami Herald.* Of their fifteen front page stories, six were taken from speeches (handouts or announcements) of federal government officials (for example, a speech by Henry Kissinger); one from a big business announcement (General Motors was going to lower auto prices); one from a speech by an expert (on the subject of nutrition and obstetrics presented before the Western Hemisphere Nutrition Conference); two from "informed sources" leaks (Dan Rather and another CBS reporter were expected to be demoted out of cushy jobs); and five from routinely covered sources (Dow Jones closing averages and bills passed by Congress).

None resulted from any serious *investigative* reporting by the *Miami Herald,* and only the two informed source leaks from investigative reporting (very mild) of wire service personnel.[15] *News is usually given to reporters, they don't often dig for it.* Of course, checking four front pages, while evidence, does not constitute proof. But the proof is all around us. Check almost any edition of any newspaper—the exact figures will differ, but the general result will be the same almost every time.

It wouldn't be so bad having our daily news constructed for us out of press releases, political speeches, press conferences, and the like, if all opinions had equal access to these megaphones. But clearly they don't. It is the economically or politically powerful who can afford news conferences and publicity agents, and who tend to be invited to speak at important events and conferences. So the powerful, the establishment, have their views heard nationwide, day after day, while the voice of the rest of us is muted.[16]

Take the story described earlier about the Massachusetts no-fault auto insurance law. The story was written around the words of a person with power and authority, the president of the Massachusetts Bar Association. He gave his opinion but not (presumably) his reasons for holding them—that is, not his defense of those opinions. So that is what the *Boston Herald Traveler* printed as news.

One would have supposed that the real news was not these undefended opinions, but what the no-fault auto insurance law said, as well as a description of its likely operation (or at least a comparison of reasonable arguments pro and con). But no. Since it is safer and easier to print handouts, that is what the *Herald Traveler* gave its readers, just as all papers do most of the time.

---

[15]There is more investigative reporting on the inside of both these newspapers. But it tends to get buried back on page 49.

[16]Business news is perhaps the worst case. Business pages probably contain more "plants" than any other section—auto items at new model time are a notorious example.

The result is that the news is *used* for all sorts of private gain. A president of the United States who wonders how voters will respond to an impending action need only try it out in the press and assess the results. Whether he will choose to use the "informed White House source" routine, have an underling make the proposal, or risk coming out with it himself depends on particular circumstances. But in any case, he is assured that newspapers all over the country will play up his trial balloon as news, even though nothing much of anything has happened.

Similarly, a labor leader, big business executive, or the president of the Massachusetts Bar Association can sound off with his own opinions, however self-serving, confident that they will be reported as news, however much they may be designed to fog an issue. These men also can be confident that no matter how far from the truth their statements may be, they need not worry that this will be pointed out to readers. For that would constitute opinion, not objective news, no matter how correct, whereas the opinions of the powerful are news, no matter how foolish or false they may be.

Radicals of both the right and left have long complained about the lack of newspaper coverage of their views, and in particular of the slanting of news towards establishment middle ground. But it would be wrong to assign this bias primarily to malice or prejudice on the part of news editors. Editors no doubt do exhibit a certain amount of prejudice against far-out opinions; people holding extreme views, no matter how right they may ultimately turn out to be, seldom become editors. But that does not begin to account for the facts. We also need to consider the *method* newspapers employ in gathering the news. For it is those with power or authority in the nation who comprise the establishment (if that concept is to have any meaning at all), and it is exactly these people whose opinions automatically are news according to the theory and practice of news reporting. If (however impossible) the president of the United States (or of General Motors) were to propound the views of Norman Thomas, then the socialist position would be heard. And if the vice president of General Motors or the president of Stanford University started voicing the views of the John Birch Society, then that right-wing position would become news. Remember, it is exactly those people (the very rich or powerful) who are able to hold the press conferences at which instant news items are handed out free of charge. It takes a great deal of idealism to dig for stories when the powerful hand them to you on a silver platter (even forgetting the many risks involved in digging for news that the powerful do not want the masses to hear).

News stories on the medical industry (generally referred to as the medical *profession*) illustrate all this very nicely. Most such stories are, of course, simply rewrites of handouts either from government officials or eminent members of the industry. The result is that serious charges of malfunction in the medical industry tend to go unreported, or buried on page 49.

A typical example was the charge that Blue Cross is dominated by hospital administrators and officials of the American Hospital Association.[17] The charge,

---

[17]See Sylvia A. Law and the Health Law Project, University of Pennsylvania, *Blue Cross: What Went Wrong* (New Haven, Conn.: Yale University Press, 1974). The book *was* reviewed, however, in the *New York Times Book Review*, June 23, 1974.

more specifically, was that 42 percent of the members of the various Blue Cross boards are hospital representatives, 14 percent are physicians, and most of the rest bankers and business representatives, including many from hospital supply companies and the like.

The charge is serious because, for one thing, a government contract makes Blue Cross the intermediary in Medicare payments between hospitals and the government—the Department of Health, Education, and Welfare pays Blue Cross when a claim is made and Blue Cross then pays the hospital. But at the same time, Blue Cross has the public responsibility to see that hospital charges are reasonable, services really needed, and quality care provided. If Blue Cross boards are dominated by medical industry representatives, then the medical industry in effect has been made its own watchdog.

Yet, most Americans have never heard these charges against Blue Cross. Nor are they likely to unless and until an important government official or medical industry expert trumpets them in a news handout or at a press conference.

c. Reporters tend to be biased just like the rest of us. Injustices that conform to accepted social practices generally go unreported (in part) because those in the media tend to share the same biases as the rest of us. Thus, the busing of blacks to inferior segregated schools received little notice before, say, 1954, because reporters, like most other white Americans hardly gave a second thought to the education of blacks.[18]

For the same reason, news items that mention women, members of minority groups, or other peoples or governments often contain emotively loaded words or prejudicial locutions. Women tend to be referred to as "Miss Jones", "Mrs. Smith", or perhaps by their full names, men by their last names alone (after their first reference). Typical is a *New Republic* article (May 27, 1972, p. 16). After the first full reference the writer refers to Mayor Daley as "Daley" and Daniel Walker as "Walker", but to Illinois political analyst Paula Wolf as "Paula Wolf" throughout.

Consider the choice of terminology in the *New York Daily News* lead headlines (May 29, 1974):

2 CAREER GIRLS ARE MURDERED
Librarian strangled on E. Side;
Time, Inc. Girl Shot in W'chester

Imagine reading the analogous headline in your local newspaper.

2 CAREER BOYS ARE MURDERED
Librarian strangled on E. Side;
Time, Inc. Boy shot in W'chester

During the time when American troops were fighting in Vietnam, reports from that country often referred to American victories as "battles", while referring

---

[18]Almost all reporters, editorial employees, and owners of the major news outlets in the United States at that time were white. The vast majority still are.

to those of the North Vietnamese as "massacres" (except for My Lai, which finally came to be referred to as a massacre when the true nature of that slaughter became clear).

d. Owners of newspapers, radio and television stations want to protect their investments in these valuable properties and perhaps even make money. Truly philanthropic media owners are rare. A newspaper owner may want to print the truth, but sometimes it is just too financially risky for him to do so. In the first place, there is the threat of legal suits *(The Saturday Evening Post, Fact,* and *Look* magazines all went under while involved in or threatened by costly libel suits.)

But more importantly, media owners are beholden to three very powerful groups: advertisers, their listeners or readers, and the politically or economically powerful. So they occasionally twist or withhold the truth so as not to annoy these groups and harm their own economic interests.

The Fortune Book Club (Time, Inc.) chose the book *DuPont: Behind the Nylon Curtain* as a future selection, but changed its mind after a complaint from a DuPont executive. (Reported in *Washington Monthly,* April 1975)

Self-censorship

Recall the advertisement for a homosexual newspaper which was rejected by the *Boston Globe.* Ads of this kind typically are rejected not so much because they offend those in the media as that they offend some (usually quite vocal) readers. For this reason, the *Boston Herald Traveler* refuses ads for X-rated movies, as do many other newspapers, magazines, and television stations. Very few newspapers will run an ad for a female willing to share bed and board with a male (although circumlocution sometimes is permitted to accomplish the same result). The *New York Times* generally (but not always) rejects ads for sex manuals; for instance it rejected one for *The Sex Book: A Modern Pictorial Encyclopedia.*[19]

But the most important reason ads are rejected is *fear of offending other (larger) advertisers.* A firm called Car/Puter sells a computer printout for $5, which will list the dealer price and sticker price for any auto with all combinations of accessories. The allied firm, United Auto Brokers, will arrange for you to buy almost any standard automobile for $125 over the dealer price.

Yet, it is unlikely that you have heard of these firms, one reason being the great difficulty they have placing ads. In 1971, their ads were rejected by most big city papers including the *Miami Herald, St. Louis Post Dispatch, Los Angeles Times, Philadelphia Daily News,* and *Houston Chronicle.* (The *Cleveland Plain Dealer* did run the ad.)

When the *Washington Post* ran a story by Nicholas von Hoffman on Car/Puter's problems, auto dealers withheld ads from the *Post* for several days as a way of applying pressure where it hurts. After the *Reader's Digest* rejected a Car/Puter

---

[19]*The Sex Book: A Modern Pictorial Encyclopedia* (New York: Herder & Herder, 1971).

ad, a *Digest* representative stated, "I know you will understand that manufacturers do not like to advertise in media which (auto) dealers do not heartily endorse."

In other words, the *Digest* was not about to risk losing all those lucrative Detroit auto ads by printing an ad for tiny Car/Puter.[20]

The power of advertisers extends beyond ad censorship into news pages and feature stories. The business sections of major papers rarely contain articles critical of the business community, although many of their articles, in particular automotive articles, are nothing but handouts from large corporations. Similar remarks apply, of course to magazines and television.

The *New York Times* ran an article in their Sunday Real Estate section (March 5, 1972) titled "We Tried to Sell the House with No Broker" in which we learn that the author failed to sell on her own but did succeed after calling in a real estate agent. But how often do you read a story titled "We Sold Our Home *Without* a Broker and Saved the Agent's Commission"? Real estate agent ads are extremely lucrative—newspapers don't often rub the real estate business the wrong way.

Finally, let's mention Abbie Hoffman's problems with his book titled *Steal This Book*. He had the usual problems trying to place ads. But in addition, the mass media generally would not even review his book, until finally, the *New York Times* did so (on July 18, 1971).[21]

Just as reader prejudices nudge the media into refusing sex advertisements, so also they inevitably force the slanting or censoring of news stories, columns, and editorials. Indeed, the desire not to annoy their audience is an important reason why opinions that stray from the center of political climate are not often heard in the mass media. The media court their audience by trying to give them what they want and by offending them as little as possible. So they tend to run the safe pablum of establishment opinions and viewpoints.

"In-depth" reporting on the drug scene in America furnishes a good example of the desire of the mass media to avoid offending their audience by voicing nonestablishment opinions. By the late sixties, a whole subculture of drugs had arisen in the United States. While there was disagreement on the relative merits and dangers of LSD and speed, there was overwhelming conviction in this subculture in favor of marijuana. Yet almost no mass media stories on drugs played it that way.

Typical was the AP story titled "Ex-Pot User Anti-Drug Crusade", (carried in the *Topeka Capital-Journal,* July 5, 1970), in which newspaper objectivity was preserved by putting anti-marijuana opinions into the mouth of a reformed seventeen-year-old pot smoker. But who recalls an article built upon the opinions of even one of the hundreds of thousands of satisfied grass fans?

This push to the middle in order not to offend readers is evident in every aspect of the typical newspaper. Advice columns, such as those of Ann Landers and Abigail Van Buren, inevitably reflect the safe middle position. A typical

---

[20]See von Hoffman, "Where Not to Find Your New Car", [*MORE*], November 1971, pp. 1 and 14.

[21]The so-called underground or free press was of course another matter.

column of this kind will deal with a young man of 17 in love with a divorced woman of 35 (or perhaps a married woman of 25) who is advised to try someone his own age (or someone who is single).

Or a young reader will write in that according to his experience, marijuana, unlike heroin or LSD, is neither harmful nor habit-forming, and on the whole is great fun. The inevitable "Dear Abby" reply will be that it is inadvisable for anyone to try marijuana. Over the years there have been thousands of questions answered on these topics, always as much as possible within the established limits of opinion current at the time. Imagine, if you can, Ann Landers advising a 17-year-old teenager that love conquers all, and wishing him good luck with the 35-year-old divorcee next door; or agreeing with her young reader hipped on grass that marijuana isn't habit-forming or dangerous, is great fun, doesn't result in hangovers (unlike alcohol), and consequently is something everyone ought to try at least once in a lifetime.[22]

This is not to say that those who write advice columns are liars for hire. It may well be that their success flows from the fact that their beliefs are in tune with mass opinion. A recent Ann Landers column *(Miami Herald,* August 24, 1974) deals with a letter from a "disillusioned mother" about her son's trial living arrangement with his girl friend (living together to see if they're sufficiently compatible to get married). Ten or fifteen years ago, such an arrangement would have been denounced by Landers as utterly immoral. But by 1974 public opinion was more lenient on the matter, or at least more mixed. At any rate, Landers' reply was mixed, at worst only mildly disapproving. It could well be that her personal opinions on such matters were changing along with or perhaps slightly ahead of many of her readers.

Finally, the mass media tend to stay near safe middle ground in order not to offend the economically or the politically powerful. It surely was not lost on media moguls that the Pacifica Foundation, which runs left-wing "unconventional" radio stations in Los Angeles, Berkeley, New York, and Houston failed during the six years of the Nixon administration to obtain Federal Communication Commission approval for a station in Washington, D.C.

Nor did they overlook the fact that during the same period the pro-Nixon *New York Daily News* managed to hang on to its very valuable New York television channel in the face of extremely convincing evidence that it had failed to live up to the public service rules of the F.C.C.[23]

---

[22]The only advice column of any kind this writer has ever seen that tweaked the establishment's nose was that of Dr. William Brady, M.D. In what other advice column could we read, for instance, that "Some people are woefully ignorant and some doctors take advantage of this ignorance" *(Hartford Courant,* January 9, 1971), or "Three kinds or classes of physicians worry patients about cholesterol in the diet; . . . those who are shrewdly aware how much such dietary advice impresses customers . . . [those] who go along with the fad because they can't stand seeing their patients running from one specialist to another . . . [and those] who think there may be something in the theory . . ." *(Hartford Courant,* January 11, 1971)?

[23]The politically powerful have many ways to strike back at their opponents. The U.S. military establishment regularly makes its facilities available to movie makers who present the military in a favorable light, but denies them to those whose intent is critical. For instance, the producers of the movie "Limbo", about the wives of men missing in action in Vietnam, were denied use of a U.S. Air Force base for background shooting.

Powerful people also can withhold lesser goodies, in particular the free news handout. For reporters come to rely on the handouts of their sources, and as a consequence tend to protect their sources from bad publicity. Even Jack Anderson who (along with his assistants) does as much real digging for news as anyone, is alleged at one time to have agreed to write only "nice things" about J. Edgar Hoover in exchange for access to F.B.I. files.

Reporters at the White House are particularly vulnerable. Presidents (and their press secretaries) naturally tend to leak items to friendly reporters rather than hostile ones. Someone like Dan Rather, who asks relatively pointed questions at press conferences and then tries hard to get relevant answers, is not likely to be favored with an exclusive news leak. (Indeed, Rather's reward for annoying the White House seems to have been transfer to a less visible, less important assignment.)

But it isn't only the politically powerful who receive gentler treatment by the media. The economically powerful almost always receive better treatment than the rest of us. An example is the way David Rockefeller, Nelson's brother, is dealt with by the media. He and his family control the Chase Manhattan bank, the third largest bank in America, and David is the bank's chairman. Understandably, the press treats the Chase and David Rockefeller with special deference.

In fact, all truly large banks get special treatment from the media. Stories with a negative bank image are played down. (For example, the U.S. Senate's 419 page report, "Disclosure of Corporate Ownership", contained a great deal of information on how huge institutions like Chase Manhattan and other super banks control most of the largest corporations in America. The *New York Times* ran only eight column inches on this report.) Stories favorable to banks or bankers are played up (the *New York Times* ran a forty-column-inch plus pictures story on page one of the Sunday Business Section [February 18, 1973] on a David Rockefeller trip to Eastern Europe, entitled "An Eastern European Diary").

The powerful also manipulate the media with the carrot as well as the threat of using the stick. Media members at all levels become accustomed to their special little fringe benefits, and it *is* hard to write nasty things about someone who has just, say, wined and dined you free of charge.

In 1972, Senator Fred Harris of Oklahoma campaigned briefly for the Democratic party's nomination for president. He gave up quickly, however, because he didn't have enough money for a media blitz and reporters just did not pay much attention to him. But suppose he had been able to give a lavish party for Henry and Nancy Kissinger, celebrating their marriage. And suppose he had been able to invite all sorts of news people like television personalities John Chancellor, Barbara Walters, and Howard K. Smith, editors Hedley Donovan *(Time)*, Osborne Elliott *(Newsweek)*, A.M. Rosenthal *(New York Times)*, James Wechsler *(New York Post)*, and Mike O'Neill *(New York Daily News)*, columnists Marquis Childs, William F. Buckley Jr., Rowland Evans, and Joseph Kraft, and publishers Jack Howard (Scripps-Howard Publications), Thomas Vail *(Cleveland Plain Dealer)*, Gardner Cowles (Cowles Communications), and Dorothy Schiff *(New York Post)* to name just a few. It runs contrary to human nature to expect that coverage of his campaign would not have improved.

> ". . . if you are going to dine with these people and covet their information and access, and have them to dinner, then you have to take them and their mock world of mock information and mock reality seriously and at face value."(David Halberstam, in letter to the editor of *Washington Monthly*. The reference is to columnist Joseph Kraft socializing with the great people he gets his information from.)

Yet that is exactly the party Nelson Rockefeller threw at his immense and lavish Pocantico Hills estate in June 1974, two months before President Ford chose Rockefeller to be his vice president. It takes an extremely strong-willed person to eat and drink someone's food one day and write a seriously critical article on that person the next.[24]

When the force of public opinion lines up with that of wealth and political power, the media almost always have to give way, even if they want to take the other side. When Gerald Ford became President Ford, a nation sick of Nixon and Watergate was in no mood to hear anything negative about their new leader. The rich and powerful agreed on this with the man in the street. As a result, no paper or television station would have dreamed of running, say, a background story critical of Ford's voting record in the House, even though many of them attacked that record when Ford was a member of Congress.

Similarly, reporters would not have dared ask the new president difficult questions at the first few news conferences during Ford's "honeymoon" period. Nor did columnists or editorial writers feel free to write anything pessimistic about the new administration. But after the Nixon pardon tarnished Ford's image in the eyes of their readers and viewers, he became fair game for the media.

Perhaps the most serious recent case of the censorship of political humor was that of the Smothers Brothers. A hit on television, they were bounced by CBS in 1969 because their political humor was too barbed. For over five years, neither CBS nor any other network would hire them although their night club appearances were a sock success. The Smothers Brothers television act was pushed off the air and kept off for a long time by the combined pressure of the politically powerful and those television listeners who found their irreverent antiestablishment humor offensive.

---

[24]Also consider this point. It is well known that the rich tend to the status quo politically, perhaps in order to protect their wealth. And the real media powers, the owners or managers of powerful newspapers, television networks, and magazines are all reasonably wealthy.

Even cartoon strips are not immune from censorship. Several papers cut this *Doonesbury* strip because it showed U.S. Congressmen asleep on the job. See Mark McIntyre, "Muting Megaphone Mark", [*MORE*], July 1974, p. 5.

2. Devices Used to Distort the News

So far, we have been considering *why* the media distort the news. Now let's think of *how* they do so, that is, what devices they use to distort the news.

a. The media manage the news by *playing stories either up or down,* depending on the effect intended. The *Canton* (Ohio) *Repository* may have set some sort of record on this in its July 28, 1974 issue. Under the front page headline "Wowee. . . . What a Weekend", the *Repository* devoted most of its front page to an account of the first National Football League exhibition game of the season, plus a description of ceremonies surrounding the induction of four new members into Canton's Football Hall of Fame. The decision of the House Judiciary Committee to recommend impeachment of President Nixon, a key event in the story of the only presidential resignation in our history and one of the great news events of the year, was relegated to a bottom corner of page one.

Just before the 1972 elections, the *New York Post,* a strong McGovern supporter, chose as its lead story a report headlined "Chou Dims Hopes For Early Peace". In it, Chinese Premier Chou En-Lai is reported to have said he was in contact with both the United States and North Vietnam on a Vietnam ceasefire, and felt that prospects of a quick ceasefire were "not so good". The *New York Daily News,* a strong Nixon supporter, chose to ignore the story altogether. One up, one down.

When President Nixon went to China in 1972, he received some of the friendliest and most extensive coverage of any president in history. The pleasant side of his visit was played up, all signs of thaw in U.S.-China relations were emphasized. Only a very few who covered that event (James Michener on television, William

An American film producer who is also a professor at Harvard University had been sent to the Middle East to make a film for educational television about Arab-Israeli relations. He had a team of technicians and plenty of funds for the purpose of photographing scenes illustrating the relations between them. One scene in the film consisted of a conversation between the deputy speaker of the Knesset and one of the most prominent Arab notables of the Old City, a spokesman for his people, who had once been a government official. The discussion proceeded in a cordial way and there seemed to be complete understanding on both sides. At the end of it the professor who acted as chairman during this discussion asked the Arab dignitary what he thought should be the relationship between Israel and her Arab neighbors. He answered, seriously and politely, "There isn't a single Arab who recognizes the existence of the Jewish state." The professor told N [an Israeli], that he would "edit" this part of the conversation out of the film, because such a conclusion was not consistent with his idea of the picture he wished to give of relations between Israelis and Arabs.

Editing used to slant news the way you want it to be.

Buckley on television and in his column) mentioned the glaring absence of Chinese crowds to greet Nixon. (Buckley, for instance, compared this "slap in the face" to the huge crowds the Chinese turned out to greet Ethiopean leader Haile Selassie.)

b. News also is distorted by *misleading or unfair headlines,* some deliberate, some accidental. Many more people read the headline on a story than the story itself. So even if the story is accurate, a misleading headline results in a distorted picture of the news for many readers.

Here are some typical examples:

Headline on *Hartford Courant* political column (January 11, 1972):

State Support for Nixon Low

But in the story below we learn that Connecticut's representatives in Congress voted for Nixon-backed bills less often than the average for Congress as a whole. Nothing is said about Connecticut *voters* (who continued to support Nixon in 1972), although the headline gives the impression they were deserting Nixon in significant numbers.

Headline in *New Britain Herald* (October 24, 1972):

McGovernites oppose Nixon on Crime Cuts

In the article below we learn that six Connecticut McGovernites challenged Nixon's claim that his administration had reduced crime in America. The impression created by the headline that McGovernites opposed cutting crime was, of course, false.

New York Post (February 2, 1974):

Oil Profits Dip in Last Quarter

Readers of this headline, expecting to read that last quarter profits in 1973 were lower than those for the same quarter of 1972, read instead that oil profits for the last quarter of 1973 were up 25 percent, while the previous quarter's profits *increase of profits,* not a decrease in profits themselves.

New York Daily News:

Secret Bar Study Pounds Five Judges

New York Times headline (same general story):

Bar Report Clears 3 on State Bench
of Accusations Leveled in Magazine

Hartford Times (May 21, 1972):

North Viets Repelled in Attack

Hartford Courant (same day, same general story):

S. Vietnam Repulsed in Push Toward
Beleaguered An Loc

Boston Globe (same day, same general story):

Battle See-Saws at An Loc

Hartford Times (September 18, 1970):

$500 Million U.S. Aid to Israel

But below, in the AP story, we learned that:

> *President Nixon* reportedly *was preparing today to promise Israel Premier Golda Meir* . . . officials say no final decision on exactly what the package will contain has been made.

Hartford Times (September 13, 1970), headline on story, p. 1B:

Additives Almost All Gone Now

Headline on continuation of same story, p. 2B:

Cyclamate Food Still on Shelves

Kansas City Star (June 28, 1970):

Drug Smuggler "Educated" by Reds

The story below told of a 22-year-old student caught smuggling dope into Russia who was "educated" by his two years in Russian jails. But the quick reader may well have gotten the false impression that the Soviets had educated the young man in drug smuggling.

   c. The media also manage the news by *slanting the first few paragraphs of a story.* In playing a story one way or another, the headline obviously is most important (next to its location), since it is read by many who never read further. But the first few paragraphs are more important than what follows, for the same reason—readership drops off after that point.

   A television debate between three candidates for the U.S. Senate from Connecticut was played quite differently by means of headline and lead-in paragraph distortion. Here is the story in the *Hartford Courant* (October 28, 1970):

Dodd Says Fear Grips U.S., Censure "A Grave Injustice"

New Haven—U.S. Senator Thomas J. Dodd Tuesday admitted he is running on a platform of fear.

   "Yes, I am, I'm afraid. And the vast majority of our people are afraid. . . . There never has been such violence in this country," he declared during his only debate with his two opponents during the current senatorial campaign.

Not a word in the headline or first two paragraphs (nor in the third) about the other two candidates, one of whom was an easy victor in the election itself.

   Now see how the same debate was handled by the *New York Times* (October 28, 1970):

Weicker Assails Two Rivals in Connecticut Senate-Race Debate

New Haven, Oct. 27, 1970—In the only scheduled debate for all three candidates, . . . the Republican lashed out today at both his opponents.

The Republican, Representative Lowell P. Weicker, Jr., who describes himself as a moderate, charged that Senator Thomas J. Dodd's censure by his colleagues three years ago for misuse of campaign funds had damaged his effectiveness, and he accused the Rev. Joseph D. Duffey of contributing to the division in American society.

It was not until the sixth paragraph that the *Times* reported a single word about the performance of Senator Dodd in the debate; Mr. Duffey had to wait until the ninth paragraph. (Curiously, a *Times* editorial then endorsed Duffey, while declaring that Weicker was also a good man.)

But the *New Britain Herald* story distorted the television debate even more. In the debate itself, Senator Dodd attempted several times to project himself as the main issue of the campaign, because the other two candidates had battled primarily against each other, saying little of Dodd's censure by the U.S. Senate. The television debate definitely did not center around the Dodd censure issue. Yet the *New Britain Herald* headlined their story:

Dodd's Censure a Major Issue in Debate of Senate Candidates

And they centered their story on the censure issue. Not until the tenth paragraph was any other issue mentioned. Weicker was not quoted on any other topic until the sixteenth paragraph. (Curiously, a *New Britain Herald* editorial endorsed Weicker on the same day the television debate story appeared.)

Many newspapers subscribe to both major wire services, AP and UPI. Sometimes the AP and UPI wire stories have a basically different story structure or outlook; usually they are quite similar. However, occasionally the wire services provide their subscribers with material suitable for slanting in several directions.

The *Topeka Daily Capital* (July 3, 1970) began its story on the upcoming right-wing July 4th celebration in Washington, D.C. this way:

Evangelist Urges Honoring America

Washington (AP)—The Rev. Billy Graham said Thursday the purpose of Honor America Day July 4th is to say "there are some good things about America."

Its story continued in the same vein.

On the other hand, the *Lawrence Daily Journal World* tried to be objective by running two separate stories based on AP releases. The first was headlined:

Big July 4 Events Slated

The story described the event in glowing patriotic terms. But the second account, placed right below the first, was headlined:

Event Likened to Nazism

And the AP account described the event as "the kind of thing that took place in Hitler's Germany". Same event, same wire service, radically different account. *Within certain limits,* a newspaper can portray an event just about any way it wants to. So much for the myth of objectivity.

One reason the news gets slanted is *circulation.* The *Los Angeles Times*[25] relegated a particularly shocking murder to the bottom of page one in its home-delivered morning edition, with a rather small-type headline. But its morning street edition gave the story its main headline, in extremely large type:

ZODIAC KILLS NO. 5

While not wishing to offend any of its regular readers, the *L.A. Times* evidently wanted the added sales of a sensational street edition.

News is played up for many reasons. Perhaps the most common reason is that nothing out of the ordinary happened on a particular day. Manchester Boddy, of the old *Los Angeles Daily News,* once remarked that one of his ambitions was to print a headline stating something like "No Important News Today". But he never did, and neither has anyone else. Instead, when nothing flashy is available, newspapers raise the ordinary to headline status and make it appear more important than it really is.

Newspapers also manage the news through their power to print or fail to print letters to the editor.

Here is a letter to the editor of the *New York Times* (which the *Times* chose not to print) protesting its publication of a House Internal Security Committee's list. (The *Village Voice* did print the letter—on November 19, 1970):[26]

> On October 14 the House Internal Security Committee branded 65 individuals as "radical" speakers at college campuses. On October 15, the *Times* compounded this blatant infringement of constitutional rights by publishing the list in full—the names and alleged affiliations of the 65.
>
> As Nat Hentoff, one of the victims, reported in the *Village Voice* (October 22), the *Times* did not first check the veracity of the accusations with the accused. (Mr. Hentoff notes he was falsely charged as being affiliated with three organizations.)
>
> Even more significant than these lapses in fair reporting is the fact that the *Times* published the "blacklist." As the *Times* emphasized in its editorial of October 24, the Committee's promulgation of the list violated the First

---

[25]*Los Angeles Times,* October 16, 1969. See the article by John Corry on the *Los Angeles Times* in the December 1969 issue of *Harper's Magazine.*

[26]Reprinted by permission of Jerome Weidman and the *Village Voice.* Copyrighted by the Village Voice, Inc., 1970.

Amendment freedoms of speech and press. The purpose and effect of the list are to intimidate universities into closing their doors to those on the list; to deny the accused the right to speak at educational institutions; and to deny students and faculties the right to hear them.

The blacklist is also a warning to others not to utter viewpoints inimical to the Committee's political philosophy at pain of being listed in the future. Its effect, 'as always, is to suppress freedom of expression and also, not insignificantly, to punish those listed, without trial or hearing. The *Times* owes the First Amendment more than the lip service paid in editorials. It also owes the affirmative loyalty not to serve as an instrument to suppress the rights of free speech and press. By broadcasting the Committee's blacklist, the *Times* has struck a heavy blow against those rights, and the 65 individuals who were pilloried by the Committee. The *Times* was not faced with the choice of burying the story or printing the names. It could have reported the Committee's action in violation of the District Court's temporary injunction against the publication without printing the blacklist itself.

> Jerome Weidman
> President
> Authors League of America

Here is a letter (whose author you ought to be able to guess) critical of Walter Cronkite, "objective" reporting, and (indirectly) of *Look* magazine, which *Look* chose not to print:

Oriana Fallaci ended her conversation with Walter Cronkite (What Does Walter Cronkite Really Think," *LOOK,* November 17) with the remark that Cronkite "really is a person you can respect." If there is anyone on TV this very occasional TV viewer could respect, it is Walter Cronkite.

But I wonder if the discussion did not reveal a hidden difficulty in his views on the role of a TV reporter. Perhaps his idea that the product—news—he reports on is objective is a myth:

1. The number of "facts" to report on each day is indefinitely large. Yet he can report only a very few. Could it be that the job of editing requires Mr. Cronkite to employ value judgments? Doesn't he have to decide that one fact is *more important* than another? And shouldn't it often be more important because of *moral* considerations? (Surely, the starvation of thousands of children in the U.S. each year is an important fact to report precisely because it is so immoral to permit such a thing.)

2. A careful TV viewer will notice that much of the news consists in what someone says about the world: presidential speeches on law and order, blasts by the Soviet government, Senator Phogbound, etc. TV reports an expert's attack on the food industry. But wasn't it an objective fact that breakfast cereals were nutritionally poor before the expert's pronouncement? Weren't children in the U.S. starving to death before an expert (and senators) made it known?

3. TV news reporters seem to feel that unusual evils—such as prison riots—are news, but not the day to day horror we call our prison system.

At least we rarely hear of this horror except when prisoners riot. But isn't the everyday brutal treatment of prisoners just as objective and factual as a prison riot?

I suggest Mr. Cronkite consider the possibility that objectivity can be used all too easily as a mask behind which lurks the *fact* that in editing the news value judgments must be made, and the possibility that editing the way he and his fellow TV newsmen do plays into the hands of those who would hide the great gap in America between noble ideals and much less than noble actual practice.

d. The media also manage the news through their *selection of columnists, editorials, photographs, and even comic strips.* It is well known that Republican newspapers tend to run right-wing and Democratic papers left-wing political editorials and columnists. The same is true of political cartoons, although to a lesser degree because (for reasons not at all clear to this writer) most of the first rate political cartoonists in recent years (Mauldin, Conrad, Herblock, Sorel, Feiffer, and Levine) have been left of center.

But even comic strips can be political, and thus selected according to political bias. Doonesbury, Andy Capp, the Wizard of Id, Pogo, and even Beetle Bailey at least occasionally touch raw political nerves.

Newspaper editorials usually reflect the opinions of their owners, and are pitched to the level of their readers, as is most news coverage. But they tend to be dull, and hence less important than political columns. (No editorial page in recent years has had impact equal to, say, the columns of Jack Anderson.) But political columns themselves are usually chosen so that their general political viewpoint is close to that of the newspaper editor or owner.

In fact, *any* feature of a newspaper or magazine can be, and often is, used to intrude political bias. Even photos are so used. Papers run more and better photos of candidates they support than they do of their opponents.

During the Watergate period, with the Nixon presidency collapsing around him, the *Boston Globe,* anti-Nixon all the way, ran an *extremely* unflattering photo of Nixon on a story headlined, "Nixon felt besieged by bureaucrats". Under the photo we read (the quote is from the Nixon tapes):

"Fire, demote him or send him to the Guam regional office. There's a way. Get him the hell out."—President Nixon (AP photo from files).

Few will notice that small print (AP photo from files); most readers must have believed the photo was of Nixon saying the very words quoted, instead of, as a matter of fact, having been taken at another time during a political address.

Pictures set an emotive tone for a story. The *Boston Globe* Nixon photo just mentioned is an example. But words can do the same job. For instance, John Chancellor on NBC news (July 24, 1974), in discussing a Supreme Court decision on the Nixon tapes, referred to it as ". . . today's *sledge-hammer* decision".

Of course, news reported solely with emotively neutral terms would be dull; the point is that listeners and readers should realize that *value judgments* lie behind the use of emotively charged expressions—value judgments which may or may not be supported by evidence.

The media also distort the news by failing to *follow up* on news stories.[27] When the Office of Economic Opportunity (O.E.O.) was set up to help the poor, it was played up as big news, showing that America does indeed provide opportunity for all. But when the Nixon administration effectively throttled O.E.O., this news was buried in small print on back pages.

Similarly, the Attica prison uprising and massacre (notice that emotive word) were big news, including a promise by Attica Commissioner Oswald to implement prisoners' demands for twenty-eight improvements, which Oswald agreed were "reasonable and desirable". But later reports that none of the twenty-eight improvements were made received hardly any play at all.[28]

The media covered Richard Nixon's political campaigns from 1946 through 1972. Stacked away in their files, their "morgues", were mountains of items on Nixon campaign rhetoric and performance, showing that Nixon's performance bore little relation to his campaign promises. Worse, it showed Nixon's attacks on his opponents *always* consisted primarily of *ad hominem, false dilemma,* and *straw man* arguments. Yet it was rare for a news outlet to follow through on the news and point out this great disparity between his words and subsequent actions, or between his portrayal of opponents' positions and their actual positions.

Similarly, when on October 26, 1972 Henry Kissinger announced that "peace is at hand" in Vietnam, this news appeared on page one across the country. Typical was the *Hartford Courant,* which devoted almost one-third of its October 27th front page to that happy news. But months passed and the war in Vietnam continued. Questions about Kissinger's failure to bring peace in a few days were relegated to back pages.

Follow-up stories rarely make headlines, primarily for two reasons. The first is that they are relatively difficult to obtain. It takes much less time and effort to report a prison uprising than to investigate day-to-day prison conditions. The second is that the public (and media) conception of "news" is what is *new,* and therefore different. Follow-up is reporting on "old news". But old news isn't *new;* hence it isn't *news.*

The media also distort the news by their selection of informed source leaks to be used in news articles and editorials. The *Hartford Courant* (November 9, 1970) and many other newspapers picked up a story from *Time* magazine in which President Nixon was quoted as informing his cabinet and top advisors that Republican chances in the 1972 elections would be good; the Vietnam war would be over, crime would be on the downturn, and the economy would be strong. But *Time* stated that no source could be given for these statements.

---

[27]A mild exception is the *New York Times,* which runs a weekly follow-up column. The trouble is they rarely follow up important news. Instead, they follow up on stories like the Joe Colombo shooting, reporting (June 30, 1974) that no one had yet been charged with the crime.

[28]See a letter to the editor, *New York Times,* March 9, 1972.

This is a typical use of the informed source. There is no way to know the motives of the person who "leaked" this information to *Time* magazine. But such leaks frequently are employed by political officials for all sorts of devious purposes other than informing the press of the truth. Imagine that you were president of the United States and wanted to assure loyal Republicans around the country that all would be well in 1972 without at the same time going out on a limb. You could easily have arranged to have a report to this effect leaked to the press through an anonymous informed source (that is, someone allegedly close to the president). If your predictions turned out to be true, you could then take credit for them. If they turned out to be false, you could always deny them, something it would be impossible to do if you had stated them in public. (The leaks in *Time* turned out to be false, but in 1972 no one was paying any attention.)

Informed sources can be used for many other purposes. President Johnson is said (by informed sources) to have used informed source leaks quite frequently as trial balloons. They also (according to insiders) are used to inform foreign powers about our government's position on an issue when, for one reason or another, the president cannot come right out with it. *None* of these uses has anything to do with the truth, except accidentally. Yet, newspapers eagerly print informed-source leaks, perhaps because they sound important and make newspapers appear to have a great deal more inside information than in fact is the case.

Political columnists also use informed sources as their stock in trade. Rowland Evans and Robert Novak seem to be the current informed-source champs; their column specializes in inside information (or political plants, depending on one's point of view). Here are several examples culled from a few November 1970 issues of the *Lawrence Daily Journal World:*

(November 5, 1970) Most important, *as seen by objective Republican politicians,* the President's inner circle has become almost pathological in its protection of Mr. Nixon. . . .

(November 7, 1970) With a surprising unanimity that crosses ideological and geographic lines, *Republican leaders* agree that: Mr. Nixon's ill-advised campaign has damaged his credibility. . . .

(November 12, 1970) Shortly after emerging from a rosy-hued White House post-mortem on the election, a *top Republican strategist* said out loud. . . .

(November 13, 1970) Although [Senator] Byrd is a longshot [for Sen. Kennedy's Majority Whip post], *Kennedy's most knowledgeable supporters* in the Senate believe. . . .

So frequent is their use of inside information from unnamed sources that Evans and Novak often omit even the mention of "top Republican strategists" or "Kennedy's most knowledgeable supporters". Here is an example *(Lawrence Daily Journal World,* November 2, 1970) in which the source (assuming it was not a case of mental telepathy) is never mentioned:

. . . President Nixon is now plotting a precisely opposite diplomatic course designed to force Israeli withdrawal from most of the Israeli occupied land.

Finally, the media distort the news by exuding a *false aura of authority,* which lends credence to what otherwise might be taken more skeptically.

Way back in the 1920s and 1930s *Time* magazine developed a "you are *there"* style of news reporting, which became an essential part of the *"Time*style" that all newsmagazines have copied at one time or another. *Time*style is currently less in evidence than formerly, even in *Time* itself. But it hasn't entirely disappeared, nor is it likely to, because, for one thing, it lends an *aura of authority* to news reports.

A *Newsweek* report (November 2, 1970) on the 1970 elections is typical. The story was simply that Republican Mayor Lindsay of New York had announced he would support the Democratic gubernatorial candidate Arthur Goldberg. But *Newsweek* starts its article with inside information, a call from Lindsay to Goldberg:

Hello, Arthur?
     With a single late-night phone call last week, New York's liberal Mayor John V. Lindsay paid off an old political debt. . . .
     The call, at 1 a.m., roused Democratic gubernatorial candidate Arthur Goldberg . . .

Time, incidentally, reported Lindsay's endorsement straight, omitting the 1 a.m. phone call.

Not that *Time* has given up completely on *Time*style, although sleek black Rolls Royces and Cadillacs don't drive up to No. 10 Downing Street or the White House steps as frequently as they used to. In their November 2, 1970 issue, *Time* began its article on the My Lai trials with a typical insider's irrelevant detail:

A sudden susurrus of shock ran through the Fort Hood, Texas, military courtroom. Defense Attorney Ossie Brown reacted as if someone had pinched his neck. . . .

In the same issue, *Time* ran a story whose main point was to emphasize how much of our air effort in Vietnam had been turned over to the South Vietnamese. *Time* reported that:

"The target today is a suspected enemy location near the gully behind that clump of trees," says the American Forward Air Controller (FAC) from a tiny spotter plane just above the treetops some 30 miles northwest of Saigon. . . .

Obviously, if *Time* reporters are so knowledgeable that they can quote word for word the remark of a FAC man in action, they surely must have been correct about the main point of their article (which happened to be quite controversial—

many claimed at the time that Vietnamization of our air effort was nothing but a token gesture).

But *Newsweek* is up to *Time* in *Time*style. The same issue of *Newsweek* mentioned above contained a long article on Governor Ronald Reagan, which began:

> The head at a boyish tilt, the blue eyes batting modestly, the huckleberry grin crinkling the age-resistant fan-mag face. Gosh—Ronald Reagan. He slides out of the back of a gray Lincoln hard-top and glides into the crowd. . . .

In addition to using their insider's "you are there" style, newsmagazine writers and others in the mass media often write or speak with an aura of expertness they frequently lack. The November 2, 1970 issue of *Time* contained an article on Charles Reich's book, *The Greening of America,* which started out:

> Sociology has spawned more games than Parker Brothers. But all the *divertissements* rest upon a single process—the breakup of phenomena into categories. It has been so ever since Auguste Comte invented the "science" and divided human progress into three stages, theological, metaphysical and positive. . . .

Forgetting the question whether any one man invented sociology, does the *Time* writer really understand the complex philosophy of Comte to which he so blithely refers?

Whatever the answer may be in that particular case, it seems true that experts in various fields frequently find errors when *Time* and *Newsweek* report on their own areas of knowledge. This fact casts serious doubt on the general competence of newsmagazine writers to talk so flippantly of technical matters. Here is a particularly revealing flub, which occurred in *Time*'s April 14, 1967, review of the autobiography of the great philosopher Bertrand Russell. Wrote the *Time* reviewer:[29]

> [*Russell's*] historic collaboration with Alfred North Whitehead . . . that resulted, after ten years' labor, in the publication of *Principia Mathematica,* named after Newton's great work, *which in many respects it superseded.* . . .

The writer didn't mention in *which* respects Russell's work superseded Newton's *Principia,* since there aren't any. Newton's *Principia* formed the foundation of *mechanics,* a topic on which Russell's *Principia* has nothing to say.

Has any reader even found perfect accuracy in the newspaper account of any event of which he himself had inside knowledge? —Edward Verrall Lucas

---

[29]Pointed out to me by a *knowledgeable* layman, C. W. Griffin, Denville, New Jersey.

3. Television: Tail Wags Dog

The newest of the mass media, television, is also the most important (even for straight news reporting). Americans spend much more time watching television than they spend on all the other media combined. And they get more of their news first from television.

How then does television compare with the other media? The answer is complex. In the first place, in terms of overall world view, television is a disaster. Most television programs are fictionalized adventure stories or comedies, which give us a hopelessly juvenile impression of human nature and human society. Hollywood endings are the almost universal rule—the good guys win in the end, or the foolish misunderstandings that sustained half an hour of comedy are cleared up, and everyone is happy (except for a few villains).

Marcus Welby, M.D., is as much like the average family doctor as Santa Claus is like the parents who actually give children those Christmas presents. Lawyers in *The Defenders* never worked for legal aid, or anyone else making less than half a mint per year. The West of *Gunsmoke* never existed, even in the minds of public school textbook writers. Nor does the jolly bigotry portrayed in *All in the Family* bear any resemblance to the genuine article.

It's hard, for instance, to imagine Archie Bunker killing anyone, even indirectly. He talks against blacks, but never *ever* raises his fist against them, or anyone else. He's a friendly bumbler. Real life bigots are another matter. They frequently do things that *kill,* as did U.S. State Department bigots during the Nazi period by refusing entry into the United States to thousands of Jews trying to escape from Hitler's horror.[30]

Of course some argue that fiction on television is just entertainment, and that few television viewers believe, say, that the Western frontier was anything like its television counterpart. But this view is almost certainly false. Ask children in your neighborhood about Daniel Boone, Doc Holliday, Wild Bill Hickok, Davey Crockett, Matt Dillon, Calamity Jane, Butch Cassidy, Billy the Kid, Jesse James, and all the rest. Ask them which of the characters just mentioned really existed? Ask them to describe life on the edge of the Western frontier. Our picture of the old West comes to us primarily from television, textbooks, and movies, and a true picture hardly ever is carried by these media (although textbooks do get closer to the truth).

Television is chewing gum for the eyes. —Frank Lloyd Wright

Let's concentrate for a moment on one television series, ABC's *The F.B.I.* Our source is 1972 testimony before the Senate subcommittee on Constitutional Rights by David Rintels, a television writer and Chairman of the Committee on Cen-

---

[30]Arthur D. Morse, *While Six Million Died* (New York: Random House, 1969) has the grisly details.

sorship of the Writer's Guild of America.[31] He testified before the Committee on two related issues:

> First, the right of the men and women who write for television to deal in ideas and truths and realities free from the repressive censorship and program practices under which we do, in fact, write (and) Second, the right of the American people to be exposed to something more than the *endless cycle of programs that mislead them and distort the realities of what is happening in America today.*
>
> The *F.B.I.* series . . . under the official imprimatur of J. Edgar Hoover and the F.B.I., formerly claimed that its programs were based on real F.B.I. cases, when they frequently were not, and even now [1972] claims that its programs are "inspired" by real F.B.I. cases, which they frequently are not; that although the names and places are fictitious, everything you see on the air happened, and they have even broadcast official looking file numbers on the air to prove it . . . a narrator begins each program by announcing the exact date on which the crime was committed and ends each program by announcing, documentary style, the Federal prison terms meted out by Federal courts to the criminals. They then show you the great seal of the F.B.I. and thank the bureau and Mr. Hoover for their cooperation. They strongly imply . . . that they are telling you the truth about what the F.B.I. does.
>
> But it doesn't always work this way. Sometimes the producers invent and write out . . . one page 'notions' which they then assign to writers; sometimes the shows are in fact *based* on real cases. But in many cases the story is not only not "based on" or "inspired by" real F.B.I. cases, it is invented solely by the writer and/or producer, and *inevitably the story details are fabricated from beginning to end.*

Rintels was asked to write an episode on a subject of his choice, and chose to write a fictionalized account of an actual Birmingham, Alabama, church bombing in which four black girls had been killed. He was told that he could ". . . write about a church bombing subject to these stipulations: The church must be in the North, there could be no Negroes involved, and the bombing could have nothing at all to do with civil rights." Rintels continued:

> Then I asked to do a show on police brutality, also in the news at that time. Certainly, the answer came back, as long as the charge was trumped up, the policemen vindicated, and the man who brought the specious charge persecuted . . . in the seven years up to 1972 in which the series has been on the air, . . . the producers have never—not once—done a program about any aspect of the violation of the civil rights of a minority. . . . On the series, no F.B.I. agent has ever bugged a house or tapped a phone or hired

---

[31]See the *New York Times,* March 5 and 12, 1972, for a slightly shortened transcript of the Rintels testimony.

a paid informant . . . Should a writer want to write, say, about violations of anti-trust laws, he is told to go elsewhere . . . not one episode has been allowed on this subject. . . . nobody who depends on television for his knowledge of the world will ever know that crime in the real world is sometimes committed by respectable white collar types. . . . again, although the F.B.I. explicitly teaches its agents never to shoot except to kill, on the series nobody has been killed for years now—wounded by the carload certainly, but never killed.

Rintels also claimed that no women or blacks were ever hired to write for the show, and that ". . . producers acknowledge privately what has long been an open secret in the industry—that all actors, writers, and directors are screened by the F.B.I. and only those who are 'politically acceptable' to the F.B.I. are hired to work on the show."

So that's the inside story about a television series that may well have shaped its viewer's opinions on the F.B.I. and crime in America as much as any other single source. Nor is there some other source powerful enough to counteract the propaganda disseminated by television series like the *F.B.I.* (Incidentally, similar testimony was given on *Marcus Welby, M.D.*)

What about television news programs? How do they compare with other news sources? While there is no consensus on television news quality, even within political groups on the right, center, or left, the opinion of one writer on the matter is this: "The network evening news shows are in some ways the best mass source of news in the United States today. This doesn't mean they're doing a good job, just a better one in some ways than most newspaper, radio, and mass magazines."

Television does a better job than the other mass media in *assembling* stories and in *making the news meaningful,* helping average viewers to better understand what is happening. CBS' 1972 coverage of Watergate[32] and in particular the Russian wheat deal are two of the best examples. In the latter case, CBS used Madison Avenue techniques to explain the all important economic details that most Americans find either boring or too difficult to bother with. They showed *graphically* how small U.S. farmers profited the least on the deal, large grain corporations the most. They also showed how the Russians not only solved their own wheat shortage, but purchased at a price that was almost immediately below the very rapidly expanding world market price. They thus made a profit that U.S. farmers might have made themselves. CBS named the U.S. companies that made the largest profits, and explained how unfair inside information enabled these large corporations to make much larger profits than did small farmers.

Of course, newspapers did carry most of this material on the Russian wheat

---

[32]But the investigative reporting that uncovered the basic facts CBS reported was done by Carl Bernstein and Bob Woodward, two young, relatively inexperienced reporters for the *Washington Post* (one of whom had worked previously for I. F. Stone, one of the few successful independents in the business). Television does relatively little of its own muckraking.

deal, but they either could not or did not present the material in a way that made it sufficiently easy for the average American to understand.

The trouble is that television news coverage suffers from all the ills catalogued for newspapers, even though it is better assembled on the whole, and packaged with more effective techniques. For instance, the networks are, if anything, even more beholden to advertisers, the federal government, and public pressure groups.

Robert Collins was asked to submit an episode for a television series, *The Senator.*[33] His first proposal dealt with the question of amnesty for Vietnam draft evaders. "The producer refused the story on the grounds that advocacy of amnesty was not the consensus of the country and was therefore unacceptable."

His next proposal dealt with the question whether homosexuals, because of their homosexuality, are government security risks. But, claimed Collins, "because the treatment of the homosexual in my story was sympathetic and he was portrayed as neither nance nor psychopath, . . . the network refused the story." After all, why offend part of your audience if you don't have to.

But the major defect in television news coverage is the same as for newspapers: *most television news is given to reporters,* not discovered by them through true investigative reporting. In fact, because television channels must fill a television *screen* as well as sound track, they rely on handouts, news conferences, political speeches, and the like even more than do newspapers. It's *very* expensive to put on a network half hour evening news program and extremely hard to meet daily film deadlines. If you rely on government and big business handouts, you have a secure source of supply.

Let's look at the box score for two CBS Evening News programs (September 19 and October 1, 1974) chosen at random. (The reader may want to compare this with the box scores for the *Baltimore Sun* and *Miami Herald* given on pp. 176–177.)

There were, altogether, thirty-two separate news stories (excluding two Eric Sevareid editorials).[34] Fourteen were taken primarily from speeches, statements, handouts, or press conferences of federal government officials or candidates for federal office (for example, a Pentagon report on increased weapons costs); one from local government officials (a banker was kidnapped); one from a foreign government official (Venezuela raised the taxes of foreign oil companies operating in their country); one from a big business conference to which reporters were invited (industrialists assembled in Detroit to discuss economic problems); and nine from routinely covered sources (Dow Jones closing figures; a Senate vote to cut off economic aid to Turkey). Of the remaining five stories, three resulted

---

[33]This and the next example are taken from testimony before the Ervin Senate Subcommittee on Constitutional Rights.

[34]The Sevareid editorials illustrate another serious defect in television news reporting, that is, lack of editorial opinion and political "columnists". Most good newspapers carry at least three or four political columnists voicing their personal opinions. Eric Sevareid hardly matches, say, the array of columnists in even an average paper such as the *New York Post:* Nicholas von Hoffman, William F. Buckley, Jr., Jack Anderson, Evans and Novak, Harriet Van Horne, Mary McGrory, Joseph Kraft, and others.

from mild investigative reporting, all on inflation (a check of supermarkets in several large cities showed prices up); and two from serious investigative reporting, including one with a few informed-source statements (South Vietnam President Thieu would seek reelection with chances not as good as before, according to the CBS investigation).

So twenty-seven of the thirty-two stories resulted from the handouts, statements, or press conferences of the politically or economically powerful, a record comparable to that of most daily newspapers. And yet there are important differences. For example, a routine White House report (estimates of costs to the White House of Nixon's transition to private life) was used as a focus around which several related items were arranged, including complaints by Ford aides about the fact that Nixon men were still at the White House almost two months after Nixon's resignation.

Perhaps the best story was a true "backgrounder", informing viewers of an extremely serious and ongoing trend, namely the flow of wealth to the Arab oil countries and its reinvestment in Western industry and real estate. CBS even managed to score with the powerful by interviewing a big business giant (David Rockefeller) by the way of balancing out "expert" (that is, interested party) opinion on both sides of the issue. This was true in-depth reporting on prime time of an ongoing event of the type often overlooked or relegated to back pages by newspapers because there is no particular day on which anything spectacularly different happens (Arabs were buying into the West every day—what else is new?). Indeed it was fairly outstanding for any of the mass media.[35]

We have been trying to show that television news coverage is similar to that of newspapers, except for superior assembling of stories and better use of psychological (Madison Avenue) techniques for making the news understandable and meaningful for an average audience. Let's illustrate their similarity with two more items.

A July 1970 *Life* magazine interview with Chet Huntley, shortly before Huntley retired, quoted him as saying of President Nixon, "I've seen him under many conditions. The shallowness of the man overwhelms me; the fact that he is President frightens me." He also is quoted as saying, "Spiro Agnew is appealing to the most base elements." But if Nixon was shallow, wasn't that news? While he was a newscaster, shouldn't Huntley have given his listeners at least the evidence on which he based his opinion, if not a hint of the opinion? And if Agnew appealed to "the most base elements", shouldn't listeners have been informed of this? The answer, of course, is "no". Huntley was forbidden to do so by the theories and practices we have just discussed. (Of course, if Senator Blowhard had called a press conference and said the very same things, *then* Huntley could have quoted Blowhard on the Huntley-Brinkley Show.)

---

[35]Not that it could compare with newspaper investigative reporting of the Watergate type (extremely rare), where reporters uncover important dirty linen others suspect but cannot prove. CBS's story simply made available to a mass audience what the knowledgeable already knew.

> *I knew then we had a real con man here.* (William Shannon, *New York* magazine, October 21, 1974, after "the fall", on his opinion of Richard M. Nixon at the time of his famous 1952 "Checkers" speech.)
>
> ---
>
> Yet back *then*, when it would have been important to say so in print, Shannon failed to say so, as did all the other columnists who felt that way about Nixon.

Television news coverage is just as *provincial* as that of newspapers and mass magazines. After Nixon brought "our boys" home from Vietnam in 1973, the war in Indo-China faded from view on American television screens, just as it slid back into the pages of newspapers and magazines. Most Americans, reporters as well as their audience, simply didn't care whether hundreds of thousands of Asians continued to die in that war, or if the South Vietnamese government we defended for so long slowly sank into defeat. What Americans don't care about isn't going to get reported in the mass media, no matter how important it may be to us in the long run (and in the case of Vietnam in spite of the fact that we continued to finance and arm one side in that lengthy war).

In defense of television and radio, it should be noted that they have a problem newspapers and magazines don't have to worry about. For a given station can show only one thing at a time (and once it has been shown it is gone). A newspaper which prints a long article need not fear that the person who quits reading it after two paragraphs will turn to a competing paper; he's more likely to turn to another article. But when a television program loses the interest of a viewer, his response often as not will be to flick to a competing channel.

Consequently, serious television programs tend to be much too short for the purpose at hand, making true in-depth accounts of anything very difficult and unlikely.[36]

The television debate between Emelio Q. Daddario and Thomas J. Meskill, candidates for the governorship of Connecticut in 1970, illustrates the problem. Each candidate had ninety seconds (!) to answer questions on such complex topics as a proposed state income tax, use of the national guard on college campuses, and widespread pornography. The result was that both men had to restrict their answers to quick capsule *conclusions*, with no chance whatever to present *reasons* for their conclusions. For instance, Daddario used his ninety seconds on the question of proposed annual sessions of the state legislature to say that the present state government was a "mishmash". When asked to answer the question, he said "I am in favor of annual sessions." So was Meskill. So what?

---

[36]The great expense involved in a mass-audience television show also makes for shallow coverage, because mass audiences are less likely to prefer programs that delve into the true complexities of issues.

–

Reprinted by permission of Edward Sorel.

Theodore White Working On New Nixon Portrait

NEW YORK, Sept. 25—Atheneum in conjunction with Readers Digest Press has paid Theodore White an advance of $150,000 to write "The Nixon Story." The forthcoming book will be about "The abuse of power" and will, presumably, be quite different from his "The Making of the President 1972," in which Mr. Nixon was depicted as wise, commanding and judicious. Questioned about that book and his flattering portrait of the former President, Mr. White defended himself: "I was lied to."

Theodore White has made a fortune by writing a series of "Making of the President" books. Yet White, for all his "inside" information, was completely wrong on Nixon (a fact not likely to seriously hamper his writing career).

So here we have the two candidates for governor with the largest audience of the campaign; yet they had no chance to *explain* their positions, no chance to present any of the complexities of issues without which voters cannot vote intelligently. After all, one dull stretch of two or three minutes might well result in thousands of sets being turned to other channels.

Very few news reporters ever achieve the star status of a Chet Huntley or Walter Cronkite. But the men (and now occasionally women) who read the news to us on television do become celebrities, and more importantly, they also acquire the status of news experts. Yet it's questionable whether very many of them ever acquire true expert status on what they report.

Every four years, the three major networks pull out all stops for the presidential elections. They assign their best reporters to cover the Republican and Democratic national conventions, headed in each case by their star personality. At CBS, in 1972, that meant Walter Cronkite. He served as the focal point at the 1972 Democratic National Convention around which the other CBS reporters revolved. To the average viewer, he seemed like a fatherly expert explaining what was going on. The trouble was that on several crucial occasions Cronkite *didn't know* what was going on. His aura of authority was false, as it is for most news reporters. In effect, Cronkite had two jobs to perform: (1) explain the mechanics of convention procedure and what (openly) transpired before the convention; and (2) explain the behind-the-scenes maneuvering prior to and likely to take place at the convention itself. He performed the first job reasonably well. (CBS had a huge staff to assemble this commonly available material for him.) But he failed on the second at crucial points.

His first big failure was the most revealing. The only hope of anti-McGovern forces rested with the California delegation, and this Cronkite did understand. When the convention convened, 151 of the 271 California delegates seated on the temporary roll were anti-McGovern delegates whose right to be seated was under challenge. If the challenge succeeded, 151 pro-McGovern delegates would take their place, and McGovern would be almost unstoppable.

The complications that Cronkite did not understand centered around temporary Chairman Larry O'Brien (expected to be pro-McGovern in his rulings), and the possibility that his rulings would be overturned by the delegates themselves.

A challenge to the South Carolina delegation (on grounds it failed to adequately represent women) was the first item of business. It was known (but not by Cronkite) that just before a vote on the issue, an anti-McGovern delegate would raise the question of how many votes would be required to reapportion the South Carolina delegation. O'Brien would then rule that a majority of those eligible to vote on any issue (3016 minus those under challenge) would constitute a winning vote. On the South Carolina challenge that meant 1504 votes.

Anti-McGovern forces, of course, would then protest that ruling, and O'Brien would rule the protest not germane on grounds that it would be germane only if the difference between an absolute majority (1509 votes) and a working majority on the South Carolina challenge (1504 votes) would change the outcome.

So to make their challenge germane, anti-McGovern forces had to try to maneuver the outcome of the South Carolina challenge so that it fell between

1504 and 1509 votes. The McGovern forces, of course, would try to avoid those figures.

All of this was spelled out ahead of time by R. W. Apple, Jr., of the *New York Times,* one of the few truly expert political reporters in the business.[37] And it happened exactly as he (and other experts) expected it to. The result was a comic riot of apparently irrational vote switching (inexplicable to those not in the know) in which the McGovern forces deliberately lost the South Carolina vote rather than lose a floor fight on the question of what would constitute a winning vote. (If an absolute majority [1509] were required, McGovern might fail to carry on the California challenge. If a majority of those eligible to vote were required [1433 on the California challenge], McGovern would be assured of victory.)

Cronkite first started misinforming his viewers when the Chairman of the Ohio delegation appeared unable to complete a poll of his delegation on the South Carolina vote, and repeatedly passed when his state was called. He was trying to withhold the Ohio vote as long as possible in order to cast just the right number of votes to bring the total count between 1504 and 1509.

But Cronkite, knowing none of this, tried to make all sorts of excuses for the Chairman of the Ohio delegation. Finally, David Schoumacher, a CBS man on the convention floor, reported the truth as a rumor heard at McGovern headquarters to explain the McGovern "defeat". Cronkite pooh-poohed the rumor, and it wasn't until the next day that CBS finally explained what had happened. Most other news media were equally ill informed. (The *Hartford Courant* ran an AP story the next day beginning "A large majority of Connecticut's delegation (a majority of whom were pledged to McGovern) sided against McGovern forces late Monday night. . . . They passed twice and then voted 43 against the proposal and eight for." The AP thus didn't know that McGovern floor leaders deliberately threw votes away to make sure the vote did not come between 1504 and 1509.

Reporters rarely are expert on the topics they report about, and this goes in spades for the glamorous stars who read the news to us on television every evening. To learn about what is going on in the world, you have to turn to other sources.

Summary of Chapter Eight

The mass media do not adequately or accurately inform their audience about the news. In particular, they fail to report on the gulf between the way our society is supposed to work and the way it actually works.

1. News reporting is poor in part because most workers in the media accept an incorrect theory of news reporting, which states that (a) the usual is not news; (b) reporters should give the facts, not draw conclusions or make value judgments; (c) in-depth or background reporting should be separated from straight news reporting; (d) good citizenship sometimes requires self-censorship; and

---

[37]See R. W. Apple, Jr., *New York Times,* July 10, 1972, p. 20, for more details. In fact, the situation was a bit more complicated even than this.

(e) the opinions of authorities, or experts, are to be reported before anyone else's (the trouble being that the authorities usually turn out to be—or speak for—the powerful).

2. News reporting is also inadequate because: (a) poor procedures that save time or money tend to become standard practice; (b) workers in the media tend to be biased, just like the rest of us; and (c) media owners want to protect their investments by not offending their readers, their advertisers, or the politically or economically powerful in society.

3. The media distort the news by: (a) playing stories up or down to suit their purposes; (b) using unfair or misleading headlines; (c) slanting the first few paragraphs of a story; (d) selecting letters to the editor, columnists, editorials, photographs and even comic strips to suit their purposes; (e) failing to follow up on news stories; and (f) exuding a false aura of authority in their reporting of the news.

4. Television has become the most important of the news media because more people get their dose of daily news that way and because it provides us with an implicit world view that we bring to bear in analyzing political and social issues. But television news reporting suffers from the same general defects and problems as do newspapers and magazines. And the world view depicted in television stories is rarely allowed to seriously contradict the "official story" as to how society functions.

Exercises for Chapter Eight

1. Evaluate the coverage of a particular event or issue of national importance covered in your local newspaper with respect to: (a) objectivity; (b) original vs. second-hand reporting of the news; (c) use of headlines; (d) "establishment" viewpoint; and (e) other matters discussed in this chapter.

2. Do the same for a recent issue of *Time* or *Newsweek,* including their use (if any) of *Time*style.

3. Listen to several episodes of some television series (*not* mentioned in this chapter) and determine what world view is presented (for example, *Marcus Welby, M.D.,* presents a world in which doctors are conscientious, professional and successful in treating patients, a world in which all who need medical attention get it).

4. Evaluate the news reporting on either ABC, NBC, or CBS evening news programs with respect to the sorts of things discussed in this chapter.

5. Write a favorable *Time*style cover story on a close friend or relative. Then rewrite the story to make the friend appear in as *un*favorable a light as possible (for example, by changing adjectives, *but not the bare facts*).

Community Up In Arms Over School Textbooks

BY MANNIX PORTERFIELD

CHARLESTON, W. Va. (UPI) — "Edith is the 'saved' broad who can't marry out of her religion . . . or do anything else out of her religion for that matter, especially what I wanted her to do.

"A bogus religion, man!

"So dig, for the last couple weeks, I been quoting the Good Book and all that stuff to her, telling her I am now saved myself, you dig."

When Charleston school bells rang this month, such passages from a new series of textbooks set off a controversy that spread from this capital city to the nearby coal camps and farmlands of Appalachia.

The furor generated closed schools and mines and inspired shootings, beatings and other violence.

Hundreds of outraged parents poured into the streets, chanting "burn the books." Book advocates within the education system saw shades of fascism, not unlike the fever that swept through Nazi Germany.

The school superintendent moved his family into hiding, fearful of the anonymous death threats he received. Police forces were strained beyond their capacity, dashing from one hot spot to another to quell disturbances.

"It's mob rule," one official said at the height of the protest.

Kanawha County School Board member Alice Moore, a minister's wife, was the first to say the books, for all grades from kindergarten through senior high school in Language Arts classes, were unfit for classrooms. They quickly became the reading material most in demand. Many parents became incensed by what they found.

A poem in one text reads:

"Probably you were a bastard

"Dreaming of running men down in a Cadillac,

"And tearing blouses off women . . ."

One book compares Daniel and the lion's den from the Bible with a fable. Another likens the Genesis account of creation to a myth. Another tale is concerned with a young boy's thoughts on suicide.

Parents feel other passages instill contempt for American leaders and encourage the use of marijuana.

Parental unrest, however, runs deeper than the pages of the texts.

Beneath the protest beats another and louder drum — one that fundamentalist Christians have been sounding in the hills and hollows since their ancestors arrived on the Atlantic Coast to escape religious persecution.

Fearing a new surge of religious intolerance, the fundmentalists thus have engaged in another confrontation — another clash between Christians who believe the Bible in its entirety as the literal truth of God, and those inclined to a liberal interpretation of the scriptures.

Such forces have collided before in West Virginia. They fought in the 1950s when fundamentalist preachers successfully waged war on liquor-by-the-drink and again during the next decade over Sunday closing laws.

The textbook row began weeks before schools opened Sept. 3.

Parents organized a boycott against a store where one of the school board members who supported the texts had connections. When that failed to bring a reversal of the board's 3-2 decision to adopt the books, parents elected to keep their children home,

fearing they would be exposed to antibiblical and un-American teachings.

Fundamentalist preachers led the protest. On the first day of school, nearly one-fourth of the students stayed home.

Armed with picket signs, parents roamed the county in search of support. They found it at coal mines and some industrial plants. Public buses became targets of pickets and 11,000 daily commuters were deprived of transportation.

Thousands of miners, traditionally reluctant to step across picket lines, refused to work. When the protest crusade showed signs of sagging, the miners shored it up.

In the center of the turmoil was Indiana-born Kenneth Underwood, the county schools superintendent.

"It's like a nightmare," he told UPI. "I wonder, when people tell me to burn books, whether we live in Nazi Germany. But I have faith in the democratic process. It will work out."

But at one point, fearing a new outbreak of violence, Underwood closed all county schools for two days. He reopened them after Gov. Arch Moore agreed to use 200 more state troopers in roving patrols to guard bus garages and school property.

Supporters of the books view them as harmless, they defend the off-color language and passages from revolutionaries as chronicles of contemporary America.

Disgruntled parents view things differently.

"Anti-Christian, un-American, filthy and rotten," declared protest leaders, such as Rev. Marvin Horan.

By the end of the first week of the boycott, the protest had escalated from minor pranks to shootings incidents and beatings. Philip Cochran, 30, a United Parcel Service truck driver who was not involved in the protest, was wounded seriously at Rand, near Charleston, by a protester shooting at random. A picket received superficial wounds when shot by a janitor whose path to work was blocked by demonstrators.

Underwood and Horan then announced that they had reached a compromise in which the board agreed to a 30-day moratorium on the books. Horan's followers, however, refused to bend, and the minister backed out of the agreement. He said the board would not put its promise in writing.

Two days later, the board consented to a signed offer, and Horan relented.

Not all clergymen and not all parents sided with dissidents.

Rev. James Lewis, one of 10 Episcopal clergymen who publicly deplored the violence, chided Gov. Moore for his initial reluctance to beef up sheriff patrols with state troopers.

Lewis said he read some of the books and saw nothing objectionable, but rather found the material "conducive to the kind of freedom our country was based on."

"The material opens up all kinds of human concern and godly concern," he said. "There is a lot of potential in it."

During the third week of the controversy, nearly 1,000 parents, waving American flags, demonstrated on the Capitol lawn and shouted down the 30-day moratorium. They demanded books be stricken on a permanent basis, without benefit of a review.

Two parents decided to set wheels in motion for a legal settlement and filed suit in U. S. District Court.

Chapter Nine

Textbooks: Managing World Views

History is written by the victors.

Probably all education is but two things: first, parrying of the ignorant child's impetuous assault on the truth; and second, gentle, imperceptible initiation of the humiliated children into the lie.

Franz Kafka

Those who corrupt the public mind are just as evil as those who steal from the public purse.

Adlai Stevenson

Those who do not remember the past are condemned to relive it.

George Santayana

1. Why Textbooks Distort the Truth

Every society tries to educate its youth to be *good citizens*. Ours is no exception. Every society tries to make itself look as good as possible in the eyes of its youth. Ours is no exception. Every society tries to play up its bright spots in history, culture, and tradition and play down its dark spots. Again, our society is no exception. Nor should we expect it to be. Raw human nature is, after all, the same throughout the world, as is the survival advantage in having proud, loyal citizens.

But cultures do differ in the way in which the truth is twisted to serve cultural interests. On the average, closed societies distort truth more than open ones. During the Nikita Khrushchev regime in the Soviet Union, for instance, Joseph Stalin suddenly fell from superstar to superbum status almost overnight (he's since regained part of his lost halo). Nothing like that has ever happened in the much more politically open society of the United States, nor is it likely to.

In addition, how the truth is twisted depends on the amount of political strife occurring in a given society at a given time, and on the relative power of competing groups. The various political factions in a society naturally try to look as good as possible to the youth of that society. For instance, since World War II, blacks in the United States have become much more politically powerful, and race prejudice is an extremely explosive political issue. The result (after the usual cultural time lag) has been a radical change in the way blacks are portrayed in American public school textbooks, in particular in the late 1960s and early 1970s. The same is true, although to a smaller degree, for American Indians, and now for women.

Well, what has all this to do with a textbook on fallacies, straight thinking, and political rhetoric? Simply that we do not approach a given political argument emptyhanded or emptyheaded. The *world view* we bring to an argument in large part determines how that argument will strike us. For example, a person who sees Communism as the great political problem of our time will react much differently to an argument to restrict the Central Intelligence Agency (CIA) to information gathering than will someone who believes, let's say, that capitalism and rich capitalists are the chief villains.

As part of his class reading list, English teacher Bruce Severy selected three books: *Slaughterhouse Five* by Kurt Vonnegut, *Deliverance* by James Dickey, and *Short Story Masterpieces* edited by Robert Penn Warren. The Drake School Board didn't like the books. So they burned *Slaughterhouse Five* and recalled the other two. Severy then substituted Ray Bradbury's *Fahrenheit 451,* which is about book burning and censorship. It too was prohibited because it would be "a slap in the face of the School Board." Severy lost his job. (From an *American Civil Liberties Union* letter to prospective members)

Conservative elements in a society generally are more successful in getting their views expressed in public school textbooks than are groups in favor of serious political change, because the majority in a society usually wants to protect what it has, however little, rather than risk the great unknown of change. (The average Indian peasant, for instance, refuses to reduce the size of his family—thus setting the stage for economic progress—because he cannot be coaxed into giving up the "security" of many children to support him in his old age.)

It's common in textbooks to divide the world into "free" and "communist" camps (sometimes with an uncommitted "third world" division). *Magruder's American Government* (revised by William A. McClenaghan; Boston: Allyn and Bacon, 1969) contains a map contrasting the "free world and its allies" with the communist-controlled world (plus uncommitted nations). Of course, among the nations on the side of the "free world" were the dictatorships of South America, Spain, Haiti, and all the rest of our "free" allies.

Ideally, textbooks should teach the truth *and* good citizenship (why, after all, need the two conflict?). If everyone in a society could agree on what the truth is, it might work that way. But in large societies like ours no such agreement has ever been obtained, nor is it likely to be. So we have book burning (see news item above), censorship, distortion, and all the rest. A wise person must learn to "read between the lines", to understand which kinds of textbook information are apt to be reliable and which are not.

2. Textbook Censorship

We said that ideally textbooks would teach the truth and good citizenship. But what *is* "the truth"? How do we tell truth from falsehood, or important truth from the trivial? What is a "good citizen"? How do we teach good citizenship?

In the United States, these questions have always been answered by teachers, local school boards, and state officials, all answerable to voters. In the final analysis, then, local citizens are responsible for the content of public school classes and textbooks. Local school boards, in collaboration with other local and state officials, make the actual decisions, for instance, with respect to textbook selection. But they do so as agents of local voters, to whom they are responsible. Thus, the truth taught in American public schools is primarily what local citizens say it is, by exercising their power to vote. (Similarly, *good citizenship* is what local citizens say it is.)

And that is a large part of the problem. For voters, being human, tend to equate the truth with their own beliefs (and good citizenship with their own beliefs about good citizenship). The result often has been textbook censorship.

For instance, communities in which a majority of citizens (or a minority of *active* citizens) have certain religious beliefs often censor opposing opinions in their local schools. An example is the teaching of evolution, which has been banned or censored at one time or another in many places in the United States, and *indirectly* censored everywhere in the United States.

The censoring of texts on evolution by the state of Texas is particularly important, because Texas (along with California) exerts the most powerful censoring influence on textbooks in the United States. Texas law requires local schools to adopt only those textbooks that have been approved by the Texas State Textbook Committee.[1] Publishers thus either tailor their textbooks to satisfy this screening committee or risk loss of the enormous Texas market. The result is that textbooks used in Ohio, Oregon, or Oklahoma—in fact, anywhere in the United States—in effect have been censored by a commission of the state of Texas.

An example is the Houghton Mifflin textbook *Biological Science: Molecules to Man,* which was revised in subtle but important ways to satisfy the Texas screening committee.[2] The changes are designed to convey the impression that the theory of evolution is just a theory, an assumption which reasonable men might doubt, rather than an established scientific principle or set of laws. Students thus are protected from the challenge of an accepted scientific doctrine which may run counter to their religious beliefs.

Here are a few of the changes required by the Texas textbook committee:

Original: Evolution is not a faith, but a scientific theory. The theory has been developed to account for a body of facts.

---

[1] In certain sensitive fields, like civics and history.

[2] For details on this and many other cases of textbook censorship, see Hillel Black, *The American Schoolbook* (New York: William Morrow & Co., 1967) and Jack Nelson and Gene Roberts, Jr., *The Censors and the Schools* (Boston: Little Brown & Co., 1963).

Revision: Evolution is not a *belief,* nor an *observational fact*—it is a scientific theory.

The point of this change is to convey the false idea that the theory of evolution is a mere theory, in the weak sense of proposal or suggestion, rather than an established, well-confirmed, scientific theoretical explanation of many different observational facts.

Textbooks as Indoctrination

The House of Representatives of the State of Texas, in a 1961 Resolution desires ". . . that the American history courses in the public schools emphasize in the textbooks our glowing and throbbing history of hearts and souls inspired by wonderful American principles and traditions." (From *The Censors and the Schools,* p. 134)

Original: Like all scientific theories, the theory of evolution has been both *strengthened* and revised as research discloses more and more facts.

Revision: Like all scientific theories, the theory of evolution has been both *modified* and revised as research discloses more and more facts.

This change is important for antievolutionists, because they want students to get the idea that the basic evolutionary theory itself has been changed to take account of conflicting evidence, and thus may still prove altogether false in future. Yet the truth, conveyed accurately by the original passage, is that new evidence has continually strengthened the theory. No biological discovery has ever weakened it or led to rejections of any single major idea in it.

Original: Biologists are *convinced* that the human species evolved from non-human forms.

Revision: Many biologists *assume* that the human species evolved from non-human forms.

If there is any biological principle that biologists may be said to *know,* then surely they *know* that the human species evolved from nonhuman forms. Yet the revision intends to, and does, cast doubt on this idea *as knowledge,* relegating it to the role of an *assumption.* Further, it isn't even pictured as an assumption of all or even most biologists ("many biologists" could be less than half), yet *all* reputable biologists believe that the human species evolved from nonhuman forms.

   Finally, Houghton Mifflin was forced to *delete* the following explicit, accurate, and important statement:

To biologists there is no longer any reasonable doubt that evolution occurs.

Texas censors wanted this sentence removed above all, because it runs counter to the religious beliefs of many Texans, including in particular the almost million Texas members of the Church of Christ (who campaigned against textbooks teaching evolution). In this case, "the truth" about the origin of the human race was determined primarily by the power of a religious group acting as a political unit.

However, censorship is most common in social studies textbooks, in particular, geography, history, and civics texts. Here are a few examples from a Silver Burdett Company geography text, *The American Continents*, censored by the Texas State Textbook Committee:

Original: Today, other countries help us in protecting our country against possible attack. Radar listening posts . . .

Revision: With radar we can quickly detect the approach of enemy aircraft or missiles. But radar stations . . .

The point of the change is to play down our *need for help* from allies around the world, as the following example illustrates further:

Original: Because it *needs trade,* and because it *needs military help,* the United States *needs the friendship* of countries throughout the world. But to keep its friends, a country must help them, too.

Revision: The United States trades with countries in all parts of the world. We are also providing military help to many nations. In addition, the United States aids many countries in other ways.

The original again pictures the United States in need of friends and allies, who we then help in a mutually profitable arrangement. The revision pictures us as helping other nations for no apparent reason. Students are left to conclude that we aid other nations out of pure generosity, a view, after all, consistent with the way we are pictured in most public school textbooks.

Here is a longer passage and its revision:

Original: Getting Along with One Another. It is often hard for people of different countries to understand each other. They come from different backgrounds. They eat different foods, wear different clothes, speak different languages. The United States sometimes finds it difficult to agree with its neighbors in all things. Nor do other countries always agree with us . . . When these differences arise, we Americans often become impatient. It is often hard for us to see that other countries must first think of themselves and their own welfare, just as we do ours. *We are proud of our independence. So are they. Perhaps we should always keep in mind that only seven out of every hundred people in the world live in the United States. And these seven should not expect to tell all of the remaining ninety-three what to do.*

Revision: Different Ways of Living.   It is often hard for people of different countries to understand each other. They come from different backgrounds, wear different clothes, speak different languages. *The people of some nations have forms of government different from ours. Often they do not enjoy the same freedom and opportunity as our people.* . . . Many Americans find it necessary to understand the ways in which other people live. For example, a manufacturer who does business in India must follow business practices that are often different from those of the United States. Government officials who go to other lands must also understand the differences between those lands and our own.

One final example:

Original: This [agreement for the good of all] is one important reason why the United States takes part in the United Nations. There, almost a hundred nations meet to talk about their problems. *Only when all nations learn to work together in solving their problems can we be sure of lasting peace in the world.*

Revision: Membership in the United Nations brings the United States into contact with almost a hundred foreign nations. The representatives of all these nations meet together at the United Nations headquarters in New York City to discuss international problems. The United States government . . . has taken a leading part in the activities in the United Nations.

Clearly, the revisions are intended to remove the related ideas that we need the help of friends and allies around the world, that we help them for that reason (needs in common), that we should not expect to tell the rest of the world what to do, and that we will achieve peace only when all nations learn to work together. In their place, we find a strong, free, generous America, which trades with the world, and for unstated reasons takes a leading role in the United Nations. The whole tone of a book is changed by revisions of this kind, which are forced on authors, publishers, teachers, and students all over the country by censorship practices of the Texas State Textbook Committee.

Such censoring does serious damage to the atmosphere of the book publishing business. Publishers are in business. However altruistic or patriotic they may be, they need to make money to stay in business. The two censored texts lost sales in Texas and throughout the country simply because they were challenged by the Texas screening committee, even though their censored versions were approved by that committee. Prudent publishers from then on tailored their textbooks to avoid the notoriety of a challenge by the state of Texas.

The number of books and magazines censored out of public school classrooms and libraries runs into the thousands every year. Here are a few of the more ludicrous examples:

The Merchant of Venice (William Shakespeare)
The Sun Also Rises (Ernest Hemingway)
The Catcher in the Rye (J. D. Salinger)
The Grapes of Wrath (John Steinbeck)
Andersonville (McKinley Kantor)
Look Homeward Angel (Thomas Wolfe)
1984 (George Orwell)
Brave New World (Aldous Huxley)
The Invisible Man (Ralph Ellison)
Native Son (Richard Wright)
Slaughterhouse Five (Kurt Vonnegut, Jr.)
Marjorie Morningstar (Herman Wouk)
MS magazine

If you were wondering why you read books like, say, Sir Walter Scott's *Ivanhoe* in high school, maybe the answer is that they were the only ones left.

3. Distortion in History Texts

a. *"Whatever happened to the American Indians?"* We said before that every society tries to make itself look as good as possible in the eyes of its youth. If that is true, it should be reflected in the textbooks of a culture. We should expect history and civics textbooks in the United States to portray our country as having and living up to very high ideals, as always right in its dealings with other nations (with trivial exceptions), and in general as the greatest nation on earth. We should expect the omission or distortion of as much as possible that is sordid in our past, and the exaggeration of all that is good. We should expect the skeletons in our national closet that cannot be ignored (for instance, slavery and racial segregation) to be discussed primarily at the point in our national history when they have somehow been corrected or atoned for, or else on a note of optimism, as problems in process of solution.

And that is just what we find when we examine the textbooks used in the United States in the past,[3] as well as those used today. To illustrate this, let's

---

[3]For instance, see Ruth Miller Elson, *Guardians of Tradition: American Schoolbooks of the Nineteenth Century* (Lincoln, Neb.: University of Nebraska Press, 1964).

examine current textbook coverage of one of the more sordid chapters in our past—the theft of half a continent from its previous owners, the American Indians.

When Europeans first came to what is now the United States, the land was inhabited by hundreds of American Indian tribes. They owned the land in every sense of that term, except perhaps that they did not have legal deeds filed in local courthouses. Today, the descendants of those Indians own an insignificantly small and relatively undesirable portion of the nation's real estate.[4] And yet, only a tiny amount of land was ever purchased from the Indians by the white man or given to him without severe arm twisting.

The problem for public school textbook writers (not to mention most others writing on U.S. history) is to get around the obvious fact that if we didn't buy the land from the Indians, and they didn't give it to us, then we must have obtained it by grand theft rivaling any other case in history.

In general, the problem posed by this skeleton in our closet is solved by textbook writers in four ways:

(1) Much is made of famous but rare cases in which land actually may have been bought from the Indians. The "purchase" of Manhattan Island for $24 worth of trinkets is a favorite example.

(2) Much is made of treaties between whites and Indians which ceded land to whites. The wars, slaughter, and threats of further slaughter which preceded these "treaties" are occasionally mentioned, usually omitted. The later breaking of these treaties is very rarely discussed.

(3) The "objective" style in which most texts are written is used to mask the horror of the slaughter and the immensity of the theft of land. When adjectives are used, they tend to be emotively positive when discussing white settlers, and emotively negative when discussing Indians.[5]

(4) And finally, when there is no explanation compatible with our sense of morality that can be made plausible even to children, the question of land transfer is simply ignored. Only a few instances of theft or atrocity can be included in any given textbook, for more might make it apparent even to average students that we did in fact take the land from its previous owners, and did so by force and violence—all of which is contrary to the image of national goodness and virtue all textbooks must convey if they are to avoid textbook censors and succeed in being adopted in American public schools.

Let's now look at a typical grade school history textbook, *The American Adventure*,[6] and see how it deals with the problem of land transfer from Indians to whites.

The first reference to the problem is one of the few which attempts to justify Indian ferocity (p. 45):

---

[4]Excluding the far north of Alaska, where the Eskimos (not really Indians, anyway) are fighting a last-ditch battle for a share of the oil wealth in that area.

[5]See American Indian Historical Society, *Textbooks and the American* (San Francisco: Indian Historial Press, 1970).

[6]By Emmett A. Betts and Carolyn Betts (New York: American Book Co., 1965).

White settlers often seized Iroquois land, and then the Indians would fight back, sometimes killing whole populations of settlers. Warfare was justified by Iroquois law. They had to protect their land.

But even in this rare passage it is the Indians who do the killing; white slaughter of Indians is passed over.

The next reference is to the Delaware Indians (p. 48):

The Delaware began selling their land to the Dutch in 1616, to the Swedes in 1638, and to the English in 1682. . . . The Delaware feared the warlike Iroquois as well as the whites who were settling in their area. Their history includes several moves to escape from these two groups.

The whites thus are pictured as just another group, like the Iroquois, harassing the Delaware, rather than the prime threat to Delaware existence they actually were. And the fact that the Delaware "sold" their land because they were, in effect, forced to is not explicitly stated.

Now we are treated to the Manhattan Island story:

In 1625, Peter Minuit, the governor of New Netherlands, purchased Manhattan Island from the Indians for about $24 worth of colorful trinkets and ornaments. . . . when the Indians later attacked the settlement, the Dutch built a wall around it. . . . the Dutch set up patroonships, a system by which wealthy men sent families to America to settle. These settlers received a piece of land in New Netherlands.

So we're treated to a dubious story about the "purchase" of Manhattan Island, a tiny portion of the Dutch domain in America, while the question of land title for the much larger remainder of their territory is passed over.

Succeeding pages deal with discussions of the Jamestown colony, the settling of Plymouth, Boston, Rhode Island, and Maryland, all without reference to the question of how the land changed hands. Then the question is raised with respect to Pennsylvania:

The king [of England] owed Penn's father a larger sum of money. To rid the country of Penn and pay off the debt, he offered the Quaker land in America. Penn accepted the offer and sailed. The Indians of the Pennsylvania region . . . were friendly to Penn. *No land was taken from the Indians without fair payment.*

No question is raised about an English king's *right* to give away land he didn't own—this question is rarely asked in textbooks. And the key sentence (in italics) is simply false, first because most of the land in Pennsylvania was taken from the Indians without payment even in Penn's day, and second because the few cases in which land was paid for were never fair. (Notice the giveaway expression *"taken* from the Indians".)

> Publishers must try to avoid statements that might prove offensive to eco-
> nomic, religious, racial or social groups, or any civic, fraternal, patriotic
> or philanthropic societies in the whole United States. *(Textbooks Are Indis-
> pensable,* published by the American Textbook Publishers' Institute)

After Pennsylvania, the settling of New Jersey, the Carolinas, and Georgia,
are discussed without mention of the important question of land title transfer.

From the 1750s to 1811 neither the Indians nor land ownership is significantly
mentioned. This period included our purchase from France of the vast Louisiana
territory, which today comprises about one-third of the contiguous continental
United States. This was a land filled with many Indian groups, yet Indians are
mentioned only once, in an account of the Lewis and Clark expedition:

> Their journals were filled with descriptions of plants, animals, Indians, and
> rivers.

Our purchase of this land from the French is recorded, but not the fact that
the land was taken from its true owners, the Plains Indians, by force.

Finally, the story reaches Texas and the far west—Oregon, Utah, and California.
Land transfer from Indians to whites is never mentioned. In *The American Adventure,*
the American Indian has faded into the sunset.

b.   The Soviet Union's role in World War II   Estimating the number of deaths
caused by World War II is difficult. Common estimates place the total dead
at between 30 and 40 million, and the Soviet Union's dead at 15 to 20 million,
roughly half of the total.

The United States lost 322,000 soldiers (almost no civilians), about 88 percent
of them in the European theater of war. The Germans were defeated by a combina-
tion of British, American, and Soviet military action, but the Russian effort was
incomparably greater than that of Britain and America combined. From the period
June 1941, when Germany invaded Russia, to the end of the war in Europe,
the largest and most powerful element of the German Army fought in Russia
against the Soviet Army. The overwhelming majority of German military losses,
in equipment and men, were inflicted on them by Russian forces on the Eastern
front, not by British and American forces in Africa or Western Europe. (There
were a great many more Russian *civilian* deaths than all the American deaths
in all the wars in our history.)

But *no* textbook used in American public schools plays it that way. Every
text emphasizes our role in Europe in World War II and plays down the Soviet
role. One reason for this is to make our own country look better than everyone
else's. Another is to prejudice readers against communism, communist governments
and countries, and in particular the Soviet Union. The cold war had to be fought
in textbooks as well as elsewhere, and it was. It still is.

Let's see how World War II is portrayed in one of the better junior high school texts, *The Free and the Brave.*[7] This text has a total of eighteen pages on World War II (plus six on the causes of and the prelude to the war). This translates into approximately 1300 lines of type and twenty-seven photos, drawings, and maps. One map is of Europe in 1940, showing German expansion up to that time. Another shows Japanese and American troop movements in the Pacific, and a third shows Allied and German invasion routes in Europe and North Africa, including German and Soviet movements in Eastern Europe. Four of the photos and pictures show Axis military forces (including one photo of Hitler and Mussolini), twelve show American military forces or leaders (including two of Roosevelt—one with Churchill—and two of Eisenhower), four show the American home front, and four show miscellaneous items. *Not one photo or drawing concerns the Soviet Union or the communist effort in World War II.*

Of the approximately 1300 lines of printed matter telling the story of World War II, only twenty-nine could conceivably be construed as relating to the Soviet Union.[8] Here they are, in order of appearance:

> Within a short time after the start of the war, Germany and the Soviet Union had succeeded in smashing Poland and dividing it between them. (p. 653) . . . in June, 1941, [Hitler] turned his powerful army against his recent ally, the Soviet Union. Sure that his troops could conquer that country in a short time, he had decided to wait before finishing off Britain. . . . *Help for the Soviets.* The United States immediately agreed to send landlease supplies to the Soviet Union. Americans and Soviets were now strangely tied together by a common enemy, the Germans. (p. 655) . . . [By concentrating on Europe first, the United States] could take advantage of the fact that Britain and the Soviet Union still remained unconquered. (p. 658) . . . The German submarines [tried] to prevent [U.S.] supplies from reaching the British and the Soviets. . . . Both the British and the Soviets felt hardpressed by the Nazis in 1942. (p. 660) . . . As the Allies tore into Germany [the time is now summer 1944]—and as the Soviet Union's troops, having fought back the German invasion, pushed westward into the eastern part of Germany[9]—. . . . (p. 664) . . . The Soviets by now [spring 1945] were deep inside Germany too. The Americans might have taken Berlin ahead of them, but Eisenhower ordered the troops of his command to meet them in central Germany. This action angered some people, who foresaw that the Soviet Union, one of our allies in the war, would be troublesome in the postwar days.

Only two of these sentences bring out details of Russia's role in grinding down and defeating the major part of the German war machine: ". . . the Soviet Union's troops, having fought back the German invasion, pushed westward into the eastern

---

[7]Henry F. Graff, *The Free and the Brave,* rev. ed. (Chicago: Rand McNally, 1970).

[8]In addition, there are a few flashback references in the chapter on the Cold War, for instance, to the Yalta agreements and to the last-second entry of the Soviet Union into the war against Japan.

[9]This was a revealing slip by the textbook's author, since the Soviets were our allies in World War II, and thus Soviet (as well as British and American) troops were Allied troops.

part of Germany," and "The Soviets by now were deep inside Germany too." Russian dead and wounded—military or civilian—are never mentioned, either individually or in total. (Our dead, of course, are listed.) No Russian military leader and no Eastern Front battle (not even Stalingrad) is mentioned by name.

The student is led to believe that the United States, although it entered the European war rather late (December 1941), did the major fighting against the Germans and deserves the major credit for their defeat. Students are likely to feel that the most important events of the European theater of World War II were our D-Day invasion of France and the Battle of the Bulge. Something clearly was happening on the Russian front, but it must have been of minor importance, since it is hardly ever mentioned.

And yet no student left with this impression of what happened in World War II could possibly understand the postwar period, in particular our relations with the Soviet Union.

High school texts tend to be longer and more detailed than junior high texts. So their coverage of the Russian effort in World War II tends to be more detailed, and hence better. Yet the percentage of space given to the Russians is not much greater than in junior high school texts, and students are still left with the impression that we did most of the *successful* fighting and were the chief victors over Nazi Germany.

The high school history text *The American Experience* devotes thirty-five pages to World War II, but only about one page of printed matter and a couple of photos concern the Soviet Union.[10] (The major portion of the printed matter consists of an unusual three-fourths page continuous account of fighting on the Russian front from late 1941 to early 1943, although even here the size of the various battles is reduced in one's mind by the single (erroneously low) statistic given, that is, 100,000 German prisoners taken at Stalingrad.

In other words, even in high school, students are given a false impression of the relative war efforts and suffering of the United States and the Soviet Union —our efforts are emphasized, and theirs almost ignored. Could it be otherwise, given the postwar political situation and the ordinary workings of human nature?

c.   The U.S. role in the war in Vietnam   Perhaps the most delicate topics a history text must deal with are those of the very recent past, so recent that they actively intrude on current politics. The Vietnam war posed an extremely serious problem for textbook writers of the late sixties and early seventies because that war was still in progress, and remained an extremely important political issue to the end, and beyond. (Unlike most of our previous wars, this one divided the nation.)

And yet, textbooks had to present a favorable picture of our effort in Vietnam. Hence, as usual, the conservative view of history is the one they presented.

We should expect, then, that public school textbooks will play down, distort, or ignore those facts about the Vietnam war pressed on us by opponents of

---

[10]Robert Madgic, Stanley S. Seaberg, Fred H. Stopsky, and Robin W. Winks, *The American Experience* (Menlo Park, Calif.: Addison-Wesley, 1971).

U.S. policy which picture the United States in a bad light. Here are a few of these generally accepted *facts:*[11]

(1) At the end of World War II, the Communist Viet Minh, led by Ho Chi Minh, took control of most of Vietnam from the Japanese who had taken over during the war from the French.

(2) The French fought to regain control of their former colony, finally being defeated by the Viet Minh in 1954. The United States paid most (approximately 80 percent) of the French Vietnam military expenses during that period.

(3) At a Geneva peace conference in 1954, it was agreed that the Viet Minh forces would be removed from the South, permitting temporary French rule there, and French forces would be removed from the North, permitting temporary Viet Minh rule there. In return for this it was agreed that a Vietnam-wide election would be held in 1956 to determine the government of the reunited nation. The United States did not sign the agreement but informally agreed to abide by it.

(4) Very soon after the agreement was signed, an anti-Communist government was set up in the South, led by Ngo Dinh Diem, in violation of the Geneva agreement. The United States heavily supported that Saigon government from its inception.

(5) In 1956, President Diem of the Saigon government announced that there would be no nationwide elections, thus violating the Geneva agreement again. (It was generally believed that Ho Chi Minh would be the inevitable victor in a nationwide election.) The United States supported Diem in his action.

(6) The United States provided the bulk of South Vietnam's military arms in the civil war that ensued between the Viet Cong (chiefly Communist) anti-government forces and the Diem forces.

(7) In early 1965, when it looked as though the Diem forces would be defeated, we introduced fighting troops (eventually totalling 500,000 men) and started bombing North Vietnam. At about the same time, North Vietnam introduced regular Communist troops from the North into South Vietnam.

(8) The United States' fighting methods (for example, free fire zones), weaponry (napalm and fragmentation bombs) and bombing procedures (defoliation bombing, bombing of Northern dikes and cities) led to several hundred thousand civilian deaths, many more refugees, and millions of acres of destroyed towns and countryside. In addition, at least one major atrocity occurred—the murder of approximately 150 civilians by U.S. forces at My Lai.

(9) Many people in the United States protested against the war, at first only college students and intellectuals, but later liberals and left-wingers generally, until finally a majority of Americans opposed the war.

Of course, we cannot expect a junior high or even high school text to mention every one of these points. But if they skip most of them, while emphasizing facts

---

[11]Commonly accepted by most nongovernmental authorities, including major encyclopedias such as the *Encyclopaedia Britannica* and *Encyclopedia Americana.*

that cast us in a favorable light, then this is evidence that conservatism has, as usual, triumphed in its attempt to turn history to the purposes of good citizenship.

Let's examine eight junior high and high school U.S. history texts, and see how they dealt with the United States involvement in Vietnam.

(1) Only one of the eight, *The Record of Mankind,* mentioned most of the nine points mentioned above, or would be recognized as even close to accurate by opponents of the war.[12] It was the only one that attempted to provide a *balanced* account of the war, taking both sides of the argument seriously. The other seven in effect defended the U.S. effort in Vietnam by including standard pro-U.S. arguments as though they were fact, or at least best judgments of fact, while omitting or distorting most of the anti-U.S. arguments. Here is an example from the junior high school textbook *One Nation Indivisible:*[13]

> *Armistice in Southeast Asia.* At a nineteen-nation conference in Geneva in July, 1954, an armistice was arranged. . . . Vietnam was divided near the 17th parallel, much as Korea had been divided at the 38th; the Communists occupied the north, the other side the south.

No reference is made to an election scheduled for 1956, to the temporary nature of the division into north and south, or to the designation of the French as temporary rulers of the south (notice the concealing phrase ". . . **the other side the south**"). Nor is there mention here or later of the installation of the Diem government contrary to the 1954 agreement, or to our support of that unpopular government.

Here is how another text, *History U.S.A.,* dealt with some of the issues centered around the crucial 1954 agreements.[14]

> In the face of this decision [the U.S. decision, following French military defeat, not to apply its new policy of massive retaliation in Vietnam] the French moved to end the war. Northern Indochina was turned over to a Communist government, and the southern part was divided into three small weak countries: South Vietnam, Laos, and Cambodia, all looking to the United States for protection.

The distortion in this passage is so extreme that coupled with selective omissions it amounts to simple falsification. Northern Indochina was *not* "turned over" to a Communist government—the Viet Minh had just won a great military victory, and with it control of most of the south as well as almost all of the north. No

---

[12]Hutton Webster and Edgar B. Wesley, *The Record of Mankind,* 4th ed. (Lexington, Mass.: D. C. Heath & Co., 1970).

[13]Landis R. Heller, Jr., and Norris W. Potter, *One Nation Indivisible,* 3rd ed. (Columbus, Ohio: Charles Merrill, 1971).

[14]Jack Allen and John J. Betts, *History U.S.A.,* rev. ed. (New York: American Book Co., 1971).

Drawing by David Levine. Copyright © 1969 NYREV, Inc. Reprinted by permission from
The New York Review of Books.

Hamburger Hill: David Levine is considered to be one of the best political caricaturists
in recent years. But many of his best works, such as the above, would not be permitted
to appear in public school textbooks, because they picture American presidents too severely.
This cartoon would be censored because it portrays two American presidents as mass
murderers.

mention is made of the 1954 Geneva agreement, the elections scheduled for 1956
and then cancelled, or even Communist agreement to the *temporary* division of
Vietnam.

If the *temporary* nature of the division had been pointed out, students might
well have observed a parallel between our involvement in Vietnam and the Soviet
involvement in Germany after World War II. In the one case, the Soviets took
advantage of the agreed-on temporary division of the defeated Germany to set
up and support a Communist state in East Germany. In the other case, the United
States took advantage of the temporary division of Vietnam following the Communist defeat of the French to set up and support an anti-Communist government

in South Vietnam. But that makes us look as evil as the Russian Communists, and hence has to be distorted in some way so as to avoid that undesirable impression.

Let's look at one final textbook excerpt illustrating how Vietnam coverage was distorted to keep us from looking like the bad guys. Most of the war criticism coming from the left had to do with the illegitimacy of our involvement (which is why the Geneva agreements had to be distorted or omitted in textbook coverage) or with the way in which we fought the war. Protestors argued against our use of free fire zones, napalm, and fragmentation bombs on civilian populations that "might" harbor disguised Viet Cong, and against our general insensitivity to Vietnamese life, which resulted in major atrocities like My Lai (not mentioned in any of the examined texts) and many minor incidents. They also objected strongly to our massive air bombing of North and South alike (as well as of Laos and Cambodia), which dropped on this relatively small area more explosives than were dropped on Germany and Japan in all of World War II. They argued that this activity resulted in several hundred thousand unnecessary civilian deaths in this futile cause, and many more serious injuries including vast numbers of women and children. Here is how this was pictured in a typical textbook, *Building the American Nation*:[15]

> Many Americans were becoming discouraged [by 1968] by the war in Viet Nam. Neither side seemed able to win. . . . President Johnson knew that many Americans did not like the Viet Nam War and that many blamed him for it. . . .
> As the Viet Nam War continued, many Americans felt that a change in the draft law was necessary. . . . why were Americans divided [on Viet Nam]? . . . By the summer of 1969, the fighting in South Viet Nam was slowing down sharply. Yet the war dragged on. Some Americans now argued that the United States must get out of Viet Nam no matter what North Viet Nam might do. Some of these Americans held peace marches and protests.
> . . . By April of 1970, nearly 110,000 American troops were withdrawn. Many Americans still disliked the war, but most seemed to support President Nixon's plan for peace.

The authors of this excerpt are trying to protect the image of the United States. Protestors are pictured as having turned against the war because they became discouraged and felt neither side could win, not because they objected to the brutal way we fought the war or to the fact that we were there in the first place.

---

[15]Jerome R. Reich and Edward L. Biller, *Building the American Nation*, rev. ed., (New York: Harcourt Brace Jovanovich, 1971).

Would the Americans who ". . . held peace marches and protests" in 1969 have recognized their motives in reading this text?

4. *Distortion in Civics Texts*

Civics texts are less common than they used to be; some schools have gone over to broader social science texts.[16] Still, civics texts remain in common use, and may well be the most propagandistic of all public school textbooks.

> Most American heroes of the Revolutionary period are by now two men, the actual man and the romantic image. Some are even three men—the actual man, the image, and the debunked remains. (Esther Forbes, *Paul Revere*, 1942).

a.   Civics texts distort actual practice   Civics textbooks concentrate on the *theoretical machinery* of government; what they say about actual practice is generally false or distorted, as it would be if civics texts were designed to confirm the false thesis that our system works just about as it is supposed to.

Here is an example from a typical civics textbook, *American Civics*.[17] To illustrate how our court systems work, a fictionalized version of a real case is presented in which a "Hilda Gray" is accused and convicted of kidnapping. The case is appealed all the way to the Supreme Court, and the proper rules and procedures are followed in every instance.

The text then states (p. 105):

> From the case you have just studied, you can see how fully "equal justice under the law" is enjoyed by citizens of the United States. At each step of the way, Hilda Gray was given her full legal rights. All of us can be thankful we live in a country where anyone accused of a crime has a right to receive a fair, public trial in a court of law.

The Hilda Gray case concerns federal courts. But it is clear that the quoted paragraph, which ends discussion of the case, is meant to apply to all courts. Later in the text, similar cases from state and local courts are described in which both the letter and the spirit of the law are scrupulously observed.

---

[16]These new texts are generally superior to most civics texts, but they still try to protect America's rosy image.

[17]William H. Hartley and William S. Vincent, *American Civics* (New York: Harcourt Brace Jovanovich, 1970).

Inconsistency in Textbooks

The textbook *American Civics* has a section on "The American Way Versus the Communist Way" (pp. 269–273). It compares economic systems, labeling ours a "free economy" and theirs a "command economy". The comparison, of course, is very flattering to us, and unflattering to the Communists' command economy. The reader is given to understand that our free system is far superior, both in theory and practice.

But the section ends with three paragraphs, intended perhaps to make better "cold warriors" of American students, but nevertheless inconsistent with what has gone before. These paragraphs cite "rapid gains" in Soviet industry, and "advances" in science and education, citing Sputnik I as an instance. In the last paragraph, we read: "The Soviet leaders have proved that a command economy may be a threat to our American way of life. If the United States is to continue to be the greatest nation in the world, we cannot sit back and relax our efforts." The reader is left to wonder why so much effort will be needed to stay ahead of the Communists if our system is so superior to theirs.

The trouble, of course, is that courts in the United States rarely work that way. Hilda Gray appealed her case all the way to the Supreme Court; most people can't even afford a good lawyer for their original trial.

In fact, a great many Americans convicted of crimes (indeed probably most) don't even have a trial. They are never *proven* guilty: they *plead* guilty. And their plea of guilt has little or nothing to do with actual guilt or innocence, or even with possible evidence against them.[18] They plead guilty as a way of bargaining with the court. In return for the guilty plea, the court charges and convicts them of a lesser crime than they were originally charged with, a crime for which the penalty is much lower.

This is the procedure in criminal courts in many, perhaps most, large cities in the United States. The typical accused person has insufficient time to confer with his lawyer. (Frequently, his lawyer is court-appointed, and is seen for the first time on the trial date.) The defendant has little or no money for an investigation which might reveal evidence in his favor. On the day he is to be tried, he is confronted with an offer (usually bargained for between the prosecutor and his court-appointed lawyer); he will be charged with a lesser crime in return for pleading guilty. He must decide whether to risk a long sentence in jail in the hope of being declared innocent or accept a shorter sentence in return for pleading guilty. If he is innocent, this means he must decide whether to gamble on receiving justice or accept a lesser penalty. The vast majority decide not to gamble on justice.

---

[18]Since most never have a trial, statistics on the percentage of those who really are guilty are not much better than mere guesses.

Here is a description of the process that you will *not* find in any current civics textbooks:[19]

> Plea bargaining is what the lawyers call it. No trial. No jury of peers. No exhaustive search for truth. No exacting legal rules. . . .
>
> A lawyer who knows next to nothing about his client or the facts of the crime with which he is charged barters away a man's right to a trial. . . .
>
> A prosecutor who knows little more about the case than what a policeman tells him hurriedly trades off . . . the responsibility for providing for those charged . . . a full hearing. . . . The judge, who has abdicated his authority to bartering lawyers, acquiesces in all this and sanctifies it for "the record."

This system has developed because of crowded courtrooms, a shortage of judges, and the inability of the poor either to hire good lawyers or to spend the amount of time away from their jobs that snail-paced courtroom procedures require. But they don't tell you about such things in civics textbooks.

Let's look at one more example of distortion from the same text. Unit Four concerns the American economy and how it works. It accurately describes the formal machinery of American business (in simplified form, of course). It explains about preferred and common stocks, bonds, legal monopolies, antitrust laws, etc. And it gives a simple account of an Adam Smith-type theory of the free market, which it says our economy operates under (excluding certain public utilities).

Neglecting for the moment the controversial nature of the free market theory, we can question the *accuracy* of the account. It simply isn't true that our system involves a free market in which the government is a referee. Think of labor unions and collective bargaining, or the way in which the federal government attempts to manage the economy by means of its fiscal and monetary policies.

In addition, the impression is given that there is genuine *price* competition among producers of a given product, as is required in a true *laissez-faire* economy. But only a cursory examination of the prices of gasoline, automobiles, or steel reveals that sometimes there is price competition, often there is not. How often, for instance, do standard brand cigarettes of the same type differ in price by even one penny? How is it that when R. J. Reynolds or American Tobacco raise prices, the others always do also?

Needless to say, no mention is made of a single instance of outright collusion on the part of businessmen, such as the famous electrical conspiracy of the early 1960s, nor of the feebleness of antitrust laws in actual practice (for instance, the continued submission of identical bids on contracts for heavy electrical equipment construction even after the electrical conspiracy trial).[20]

---

[19]"Crime in the Courts: Assembly Line Justice", *The Washington Monthly*, May 1970, pp. 28–29. The article is well worth the attention of anyone who wants to understand how criminal courts work in America.

[20]See for instance, Fred J. Cook, *The Corrupted Land* (New York: The Macmillan Co., 1966), or "The Incredible Electrical Conspiracy", *Fortune*, April–May 1961, or the *Wall Street Journal*, January 9, 10, 12, and 13, 1961.

Under our free enterprise system, any citizen can start any lawful business he wants to. He can seek work in any field that interests him. He can go into partnership with others. He can live in any part of the country. The government does not tell him how to run his life. It does not tell him what he can own or what he must do for a living. Except to the extent that regulation is needed in the public interest, the American government leaves business "on its own". A government that lets business alone is said to be a *laissez-faire* government. Adam Smith . . . (Richard E. Gross and Vanza Devereaux, *Civics in Action.* Chicago: Field Publications, 1971)

Textbook ambiguity: This passage is true if construed to state the ideals of our society, but false if construed to state how our system actually works. How do you suppose most students will take it? (Public school textbooks commonly *ask a question* when they should provide an evaluation—one way to remain "objective". Did the writer of this text just engage in such shenanigans?

b.   Controversial theories are stated as facts.   Civics textbooks describe all of the controversial theories of government and economics which have gained assent as our "official myths", or "official ideals", as though all sane, loyal Americans accept them, and, worse, as though they are *true.*

Yet, save perhaps religion and sex, nothing is more controversial than the topics these texts deal with. A perfect example is the *laissez-faire* free-economy theory, which almost every civics text presents as though no informed American would doubt its correctness. One need only read the tiniest fragments from the writings of, say, Milton Friedman or Leon Keyserling to realize that the topic is drenched in controversy.

None of this comes through in civics texts. Instead, we generally read that Americans disagree with the peoples of other nations, chiefly Communists, on these matters, and no room is left for doubt about where the truth lies. But little or nothing is said about disagreements among Americans.

c.   Objectivity is used to hide distortion.   Civics texts, like history texts, indoctrinate by using the appearance of objectivity and evenhandedness to conceal the differences between our principles and our practices. And yet they need ways to avoid or at least negate those painful facts that cannot be totally ignored.

An example is racially segregated schools: A textbook may want to mention the 1954 Supreme Court decision, but this decision carries with it the implication that before 1954 there were segregated schools that were separate but *not* equal. The text *American Civics* solves the problem this poses by the device of the unrebutted "second party" opinion (p. 390):

This Supreme Court decision immediately led to a bitter controversy. Many school systems, particularly those in the Southern states, claimed that their separate schools for Negroes were equal to the schools attended by white students.

The text thus does not actually *say* that the segregated Negro schools of the South were equal. Hence, it can't be accused of falsehood, since Southerners did claim they were equal. But it gets the thought across that perhaps many Negro schools in the South were equal to white schools, thus tending to uphold the "official truth" of freedom and *equality* for all Americans. The beauty of the ploy, of course, is that it preserves the "objectivity" of the textbook.

d.   Minority groups are poorly dealt with.   As might be expected, minority groups tend to be invisible in civics texts (as they are in history texts), and when they are mentioned, their treatment is distorted.

For example, many, perhaps most, civics texts (history texts, too, for that matter) don't even mention the migrant laborer, although they do say a great deal about farmers and farming. However, *American Civics* does deal with migrant laborers—in exactly two sentences (pp. 324–325):

> Others [*other sharecroppers*] move their families from farm to farm, making only a bare living. These day-to-day farm workers are called migrant farm laborers.

The implication that only sharecroppers become migrant laborers is, of course, false. But the important error in this passage (which comes in the middle of a long section on farming) is the quick way in which migrants are passed over in two short, dry sentences. The reader is not told of the virtual peonage of the migrant, nor is he told how they are denied their legal rights.[21]

By now it is generally recognized that women have been discriminated against in ways other than just the denial of the vote.[22] In particular, it is generally agreed that even today women frequently receive less pay than men do for the same job; often are not seriously considered for "higher" positions in industry or government (witness the paucity of female cabinet members throughout our history, and the fact that in a recent year there was no tenured female faculty member at Harvard University); and are all-too-often counseled into the typing-shorthand track in high school (how many men do you see in shorthand classes?), so that they are trained for jobs that permit relatively little advancement.

A civics text which pointed out these facts, and perhaps urged bright women students to avoid the typing-steno route, would perform a useful service. But

---

[21]See, for instance, Robert Coles, "Peonage in Florida", *The New Republic,* January 11, 1969, and the *New York Times* article "Court Abuse of Migrants Charged in South Jersey", August 16, 1970, p. 1.

[22]Women constitute a curious "minority" group, since there are more women than men in the United States. In treating them as a minority group, we may appear to be committing the fallacy of *questionable classification,* since the category under discussion really is "oppressed group", not "minority group". The explanation is simply that the term "minority group" frequently gets interchanged with "oppressed group" in everyday life, because in the United States these days the most visible recipients of oppressive discrimination are minority groups.

to do so it would have to admit that there is discrimination by sex, and very few texts seem willing to make that admission.

> Women, in general, have aptitudes and qualities that make them more suited to certain types of work than men, such as secretarial work, nursing, and teaching young children. . . . many think that the enlarged opportunity for women's work outside the home has had an undesirable effect on their interest in the home and on the home itself. . . . Should there be any difference in pay between men and women for the same kind and quality of work? Should married women whose husbands are able to work hold jobs that other girls and women would like? [End of section]. (C. H. W. Pullen and James F. Reed, *Todays Problems.* Boston: Allyn & Bacon, 1967)
>
> ---
>
> Sex stereotypes are rapidly disappearing from American textbooks, or at least becoming more subtle. In this example, the controversial "old-fashioned" view of working woman is touted first through the anonymous "many think" phrase and then by asking loaded questions, left unanswered.

American Civics mentions women *qua* women many times. It mentions them as housewives, in the armed forces, and on farms. It mentions their attaining the right to vote. But only twice does it hint at current discrimination against women.

The first appears in a section on the Department of Labor (p. 80):

> Working women get special help through the Department's Women's Bureau, which strives to promote good working conditions, wages, and hours for all women workers.

Perhaps the average adult Russian, long trained in reading between the lines of Communist newspapers, would be able to conclude from this that working conditions, wages, and hours for women must not be as good as for men, otherwise there would be no need to strive to promote them. But the average American student is unlikely to be as perceptive.

The other reference to discrimination against women is more extended. But in essence it says that women once were discriminated against in employment, in particular in highly trained and professional jobs, but now all that is rapidly changing. The emphasis is on rapid change toward the official line, not on the past evil. Here are some excerpts (pp. 348–349):

> Even in the 1920s and 1930s, . . . many Americans believed that a woman's place was in the home. Few careers, except teaching and nursing, were open to women. *Now all this is changed.*
>
> . . . what was said [about career opportunities] *is equally true for both young men and young women.* Even in the armed forces. . . .

America's business firms are urging young women to train and study for many scientific and technical jobs that were *once* open only to men.

Nothing is said about how junior high school and high school counselors (to say nothing of parents) urge young women to train for low-level office jobs, nor about the reality of the personnel man's almost automatic classification of women as typists, clerks, and secretaries.

Finally, here is a passage from the same section that may well reveal more about our ingrained deep-down discrimination against women than most males will care to admit to:

The profession of nursing is a field in which young *women* are urgently needed. The shortage of nurses is great at the present time.

And what about easing that shortage with young *men?* (Men do serve successfully as nurses.) What of the even greater shortage of M.D.s? Why not urge young women to become M.D.s?

Nowhere in the text are statistics given comparing the percentage of female doctors with that of female nurses. The reason is obvious. The overwhelming number of doctors (and dentists) are men; the overwhelming number of nurses are women. The same sexual correlation is true for persons *training* to be physicians or nurses. But these facts tend to cast doubt on the official line that all of us, men and women, have equal opportunity in the United States.[23]

. . . in a series of basic readers used in many private and public schools, a second-grade reader starts out with a description of how our country might look to an astronaut. The country he surveys has men taking most of the active, achieving roles, and women generally portrayed as homemakers, nurses or teachers. In a book that focuses on historical figures, youngsters learn about George Washington Carver, King Alfred, Robert Bruce, William Tell, Alexander the Great, Copernicus, Galileo, Johannes Kepler, Henry Ford and the Wright brothers. Searching for feminine greats (Queen Elizabeth, perhaps, or Joan of Arc?), a diligent reader will finally come upon two: Nurse Florence Nightingale (not pioneer doctor Elizabeth Blackwell) and the Negro educator Mary McLeod Bethune. Mrs. Bethune and Negro contralto Marian Anderson are often among the few women who appear in books about important people in American life; rather a one-token-buys-two-rides approach. (From *The Family Circle,* 1971)

Sexism in textbooks starts early.

---

[23]An interesting sidelight on this topic is the fact that civics texts, in comparing our system to a communist one, do not mention that a far greater proportion of doctors in the Soviet Union are women than is true in the United States.

We have now provided some information about the way in which migrants and women are dealt with in civics texts. Were we to do the same for Mexican-Americans, Puerto Ricans, Indians, and, in particular, homosexuals, the results would be similar; if anything, the discrimination against these groups receives even less attention.

e.   Civics texts lag behind.   If migrants, women and homosexuals tend to be invisible in civics texts, and their unfair treatment swept under the rug, so also do Negroes—but not to the extent that they used to be.

The difference is that starting soon after World War II American public opinion on Negroes began to change, and the Negroes' fight for their rights began to pay off, even if very slowly. Negroes became a political power, and their cause became much more popular.

The result has been a change in the way blacks are dealt with by all textbooks, including civics texts.[24] Negroes get mentioned more often; greater effort is made to point out how particular kinds of discrimination (previously neglected in civics texts) have been or are being corrected; and Negroes now even appear in photographs.

Let's examine two editions (1961 and 1966) of another textbook, *Building Citizenship,* and see what we find.[25] (There was also a 1965 edition, which is of interest only for the minor differences between it and the 1966 edition.) These editions were published only five years apart; yet there are interesting and important differences in their treatment of the American Negro (although in general there are very few other significant differences between the two).

The major change between the two editions is in photographs. There are fifty-three such changes, out of hundreds of pictures (at least one photograph, often more, appears on nearly every page). Of these, thirty-eight show one or more persons recognizably Negro. Typical is the photo (p. 251) of a smiling Negro boy holding up a large fish he's just caught, which replaces a picture of a smiling white boy doing exactly the same thing (the caption remains the same).

Of the fifteen changes in which Negroes are not pictured, most are required by changing events (the new Supreme Court instead of the old; a more current replacement for *Senator* Lyndon Johnson). Even so, over two-thirds of the photo changes replace all-white scenes with ones that are racially mixed (in one case, all black). In almost all of these changes, the caption remains the same, because the picture's topic remains the same (students in a classroom, a business conference, a nurse in action, policemen on duty). It should be mentioned that not one definitely recognizable black face is pictured in the earlier (1961) edition. (There are two or three borderline cases.)

---

[24]One of the more interesting changes is in the names used to refer to blacks. The word "Negro" was introduced to replace "colored" (and other terms, like "darkie") when they became offensive. Now, "Negro" is being replaced by "black", which long ago was considered offensive and replaced by "colored".

[25]This text has been in use for a long time. The original author was Ray Osgood Hughes (Boston: Allyn and Bacon, 1921); it has been revised by C. H. W. Pullen and by James H. McCrocklin, the latter being responsible for both of the versions considered here.

Negroes are mentioned significantly about six or seven times in the 1961 edition, but over twenty times in the edition of 1966. It is true, however, that most of these changes are one-liners. (We don't want to give the impression that the changes in the 1966 edition are more substantial than they are.)

Still, they are interesting, even if only token gestures. Let's illustrate by a bit of comparison shopping.

In the 1961 edition (p. 286), we read:

> Some people found fault with Theodore Roosevelt because they said he acted as if he had discovered the Ten Commandments. Quite likely, however, many more people become interested in applying the Ten Commandments to present day life because they admired something in "T.R."

This is changed in the 1966 edition (same page, same exact spot on the page)[26] to read:

> Some people find fault with [brace yourself] Martin Luther King because he acts as if he had discovered the Ten Commandments. Quite likely, however, many more people have become interested in applying the Ten Commandments to present day life because they admire Dr. King's fight against racial discrimination.

If there is any other reason for downgrading poor old "T.R." than the authors' desire to say something about Negroes (without getting too specific), it's hard to imagine what it is.

Masons and miners get eliminated à la Teddy Roosevelt in a discussion of causes of unemployment (p. 477). In 1961, we read: "The work of masons and miners, for example, is 'seasonal.' " This is changed in the 1966 edition to: "Racial discrimination sometimes illegally prevents individuals from getting jobs."

Several of the 1961 references to Negroes have been changed in the later edition. After mentioning good old Booker T. Washington and Tuskegee Institute, the 1961 version states (p. 204): "Poets, musicians, lawyers, doctors, and skilled trades-men *of whom we are all proud* have arisen among the Negro people." Those too young to have seen former heavyweight champion Joe Louis in action aren't likely to appreciate the import of the phrase "of whom we are all proud". Mr. Louis (who, of course, was not then referred to in public as "Mr." Louis) almost always was introduced as "a credit to his race", or some such locution. The 1966 edition changes this passage to read: "Since their emancipation, outstanding Negroes have achieved in each major field of human endeavor." An odd locution, but it had to fit the space vacated by the sentence it replaced.

Material on the poll tax contains perhaps the most significant textual changes, at least for the theory that edition changes in general were just tacked-on token gestures, and not an attempt to portray life as it really is in America. The major

---

[26]Most pages in this text read word for word the same in both editions and are in the very same type. The photos represent the only change that would justify a new edition. This should be noted in assessing the changes concerning Negroes.

change on the poll tax (p. 149) is simply deletion of the key paragraph (the one in which the term appears in italics and is explained), replaced by a paragraph on the sales tax. This seems innocent enough, and hardly connected to Negroes, since they aren't mentioned in either the deleted paragraph or its replacement. But this change begins to look peculiar when the reader follows a reference to Section 78 and discovers (p. 155) another paragraph on the sales tax, which also seems to be the *key* paragraph on that tax. (For instance, it italicizes the term "sales tax", and uses that term in a sentence which makes its meaning clear.) The new paragraph on the sales tax, on p. 149, begins to look suspiciously like filler material.

But why did the paragraph on the poll tax have to be deleted or at least changed? The answer may be its last sentence (it contains only three others, all short):

> Since people's wealth differs so much, this kind of tax does not agree with the principle of ability to pay; *but taxes of this kind are seldom high enough to be a very great burden on anybody.*

The emphasized clause had to be changed, and not just because it is false. (It was just as false in 1961.) For it also contradicts two changes made elsewhere in the 1966 edition. The first is inserted into p. 18:

> Our government is removing the last barriers which have kept many eligible Negroes from voting, *such as poll taxes* and literacy tests.

The second is mention of the Twenty-fourth Amendment to the Constitution which abolished poll taxes (p. 135):[27]

> A few states required the payment of a poll tax before a person could vote. The Twenty-fourth Amendment, which was submitted to the states in 1962 and ratified in 1964, outlawed the poll tax as a voting requirement in federal elections. In many states a person may have to show that he can read, write, or understand the state constitution. New federal voting rights are designed to eliminate these provisions *when they are used to prevent Negroes from voting.*

What we have shown so far is that this textbook gives greater and fairer treatment to Negroes in later editions than in earlier ones. But two questions remain. First, why use the term "tokenism" even in reference to the 1966 text with all its pictures of Negroes and twenty-odd textual references? And second, why assume that the improved treatment of this minority group is due to the pressure of changed public opinion?

---

[27] Obviously, we can't score the 1961 text for failing to mention a Constitutional amendment that did not yet exist. But we can score it for failing to indicate the true intent of the poll tax, and for writing falsely about its effect.

The first question is best answered by reference to what is omitted, as well as to the one-line nature of the text changes. The 1966 text does not mention the 1954 Supreme Court decision outlawing segregated schools (omitted perhaps because segregated schools are not discussed), the KKK or White Citizen Councils, lynchings, segregated public facilities, or big-city ghettos. Of the few references to discrimination, most are made, as usual, in the process of explaining how they have been or are being eradicated. Finally, this text has room to discuss dozens of relatively unimportant governmental agencies, such as the National Youth Administration and Mothers' Pension Fund. It has room for the Knights of Labor, 4-H Clubs, The National Safety Council, Future Farmers of America, A.F. of L., C.I.O., C.C.C., National Grange, Universal Postal Union, American Farm Bureau Federation, R.O.T.C., and the good old P.T.A. But it discusses no Negro organizations in the text, and only one institution (Tuskegee Institute). A picture caption does describe Roy Wilkins (pictured with President Johnson at the 1964 Civil Rights signing) as "executive secretary of the National Association for the Advancement of Colored People".[28] But neither the N.A.A.C.P. nor any other group whose aim is the advancement of Negro rights is discussed in the text. Their existence or function is never explained.

Now let's deal with the second question: Why is it a fair assumption that better textbook treatment of blacks follows and results from the pressure of public opinion (rather than the reverse, as it should be if the function of schools is to teach the truth, not indoctrinate with the official story)?

In the first place, the nature of the textual and photo changes seems better explained by outside pressure than by any heartfelt need on the part of the authors (as we have gone to some pains to illustrate—think of the replacement of Teddy Roosevelt by Martin Luther King in the very same story). Even the existence of a 1966 edition seems to have no other explanation.

But equally important is the fact that after 1954 textbook treatment of the Negro improved much more rapidly than that of any other minority group, thus mirroring (with a small time-lag) the state of affairs in the United States in the last twenty years.

There are many groups discriminated against in the United States. But until a few years after this 1966 text was published, only one was a large center of controversy, and only one was the recipient of a publicly acknowledged and widespread "official" change in attitude. Americans in large numbers owned up to at least part of the evil of our treatment of blacks, and admitted it was wrong. In addition, Negroes have more political power than they did, an important fact, because they constitute over 10 percent of the population.

However, the situation did not change in this way for the other minority groups. There was publicity from time to time about them, but it never made a sufficient dent. The migrant laborer is a good example. And until recently, so was that strange "minority" group, *women.*

---

[28]The photo caption continues, "Looking on are some of the people who helped to steer the bill through Congress." And they are all white. The reader is left to wonder what Roy Wilkins or the N.A.A.C.P. have to do with passage of a Civil Rights bill.

We showed how discrimination against migrants and women was glossed over in one text *(American Civics);* it could be demonstrated for most others as well. More importantly, it could be shown that no significant improvement occurred in the textual treatment of these or other minority groups from earlier to later editions.[29]

Of course, this does not prove the thesis at issue. But it does provide significant evidence. When public opinion and political pressure began to turn in favor of the Negro after remaining the same for many years, blacks then received fairer coverage in civics texts (in history texts too, although we have not provided evidence of that). But during the period in question, public opinion and political pressure did not change nearly as much with respect to other minority groups. And textbook coverage of these groups in turn did not change as much as did that of the Negro.

The test of true education is *understanding,* and the best test of understanding is the ability to foresee events, or at least not be unduly surprised at their occurrence. If American public school textbooks helped students to true understanding, say of their own system and how it really works, would the Watergate scandal have been such a shock to them? Would they have accepted without concrete proof the Watergate cover-up story provided by President Nixon and his aides in the crucial four-month period before Nixon's reelection in 1972? Would they have accepted our government's denial that we had interfered in the internal affairs of Chile and then later accepted the clearly untrue explanation of *why* we had in fact interfered? Or would they have accepted President Johnson's Gulf of Tonkin excuse for waging a devastating war in Vietnam?

The answer to all of these questions is *no.* An electorate with a true understanding of our history and of how our system works in practice would have accepted none of these without evidence. Of course, indoctrinating textbooks are only one reason so many Americans were taken in by their leaders on these issues. It is, however, an important reason, and one about which something could be done, since citizens at a local level do exercise primary control over public schools.

But textbooks are only a part of the public school educational setting. The larger problem is one of tone. Students are presented with *opinions* as if they were *fact.* They thus are not taught how to think *critically.* On the contrary, they are taught to accept what "authorities" tell them, even in areas in which experts disagree.

This text was written in a completely different spirit. A student who accepts its contents *uncritically* has missed its main point, which is that in controversial social and political matters free men must be their own experts, or at least must be able to judge for themselves the opinions of those who call themselves experts. A free society does, after all, depend on a *correctly informed* electorate, not an indoctrinated one.

---

[29]An exception is the treatment of American Indians in some textbooks.

Summary of Chapter Nine

Every individual confronts political and social issues with a particular *world view* that determines his perception of those problems and the answers he will accept.

Textbooks are supposed to teach "the truth". But what the truth consists in is decided primarily by local school boards responsible in the last analysis to local citizens. One result of this is textbook censorship, which usually works to distort the truth so as to portray America, or some group in America, in a favorable light, whether deserved or not.

(Example: Censorship of a biology text in order to present the theory of evolution as a theory or conjecture, rather than an overwhelmingly supported scientific doctrine.)

Textbooks also distort by omitting or glossing over the negative aspects of our society. (Example: The embarrassing question of land transfer from Indians to whites usually is glossed over by emphasizing the $24 in trinkets paid to purchase Manhattan Island.)

In particular civics texts usually portray the ideals of American society as if they were actual practice. (Example: The civics text that portrays a fictionalized court case in which the defendant's rights are scrupulously respected. This scrupulous respect for rights is presented as a norm in our society when in fact it is an unusual exception.)

Exercise for Chapter Nine

In college, the subject matter dealt with in high school civics classes becomes the province of political science and (to some extent) other social science courses. Along with this change in title, there is a broadening of subject matter and a change in motive. Indoctrination with the "American way" surely is not attempted in the typical social science course or text. But some social science texts still display a few of the defects we have been discussing, including an "objectivism" that hides a controversial point of view, distortion of the difference between theory and practice (often by ignoring practice that doesn't conform to theory) and an unconscious bias against certain groups (for example, women). College history texts also often display these defects.

Examine one of your history, political science, or other relevant social science texts (or get one from the library) for evidence of bias, distortion, suppressed evidence, or "textbook objectivity", and write a brief paper on your findings. Be sure to *argue* (present evidence) for your conclusions, trying, of course, to avoid fallacious argument.

Exercise for the entire text

In the last chapter of this text, we tried to show that primary and secondary school textbooks are not models of correct inquiry. College texts (in the opinion of this author) are far superior. But college textbook writers are human, too, the present writer unfortunately not excepted. This text, as all others, has presuppositions (only some of them made explicit), and no doubt contains fallacious reasoning in spite of the author's best efforts to reason cogently. So, as a final exercise, write a brief critique of this textbook with respect to: (1) its major presuppositions and (2) possible fallacious arguments. (Be sure to *argue* for your findings.) And then, as part three of your paper, evaluate the presuppositions you discovered, and if you find them faulty, explain what (if anything) you would put in their place.

Answers to
Starred Exercises

Chapter One, Exercise I

2. *Appeal to authority.*

7. *Popularity.*

10. *Irrelevant reason.* It's not guts but being right that should engender support.

17. *Provincialism.* Eisenring obviously was looking at the matter with the bias of a life insurance man. Who else would say that the discovery of wonder drugs which would vastly increase human longevity is *"fortunately* rather unlikely"?

19. *Ambiguity.* Freud was talking about psychological repression, Roche (supposedly) political repression.

24. *Slippery slope.*

Chapter Two, Exercise I

1. *Common practice.*

4. *Tokenism* (or *hasty conclusion*).

7. *Questionable analogy.*

14. *Ad hominem* argument. Spock's political views and activities are irrelevant to the quality of his baby care book.

16. *Two wrongs make a right.*

22. *Two wrongs make a right.*

24. *Questionable analogy.*

Chapter Three, Exercise I

1. *Begging the question.* Bachelors *are* never married men.

4. *Inconsistency.* In stating ". . . that was *music* you just heard", Buckley implies it was good music, which contradicts what he said before.

5. *False charge of fallacy.* Liberals were not inconsistent, as the passage implies (in spite of *saying* just the opposite). The situation had changed.

10. *Suppressed evidence.* Deposits in practically every bank and savings and loan association are insured by an agency of the federal government.

18. *Questionable premise (unknown fact).* How do Evans and Novak know these things?

27. *False dilemma.* The choice isn't necessarily between the autos we now have or no autos at all. There are all sorts of reasonable possibilities in between (e.g., more and cheaper public transport to reduce the number of private autos).

32. *Straw man* and *ad hominem* argument. Meany started out to discuss the idea that we should *listen* to the younger generation, but then he switched to the straw idea that we *entrust the government* to them. His argument against young people was *ad hominem* because it attacked their habits (pot-smoking and Woodstock get-togethers), not their views, and it is their views that "these people constantly" suggest we listen to. (What would Meany have thought about the argument that we shouldn't listen to the older generation, on the grounds that they drink more alcohol than the younger?)

33. *Inconsistency* and *questionable premise.* A sound argument has all true premises. An argument with inconsistent premises has at least one false premise. John's statement that some sound arguments have inconsistent premises is questionable.

39. *Inconsistency* (between words and actions).

44. *Suppressed evidence.* The U.S. also exports goods, in fact a great deal. But then we have to import too, otherwise, we're in effect giving our goods away free. So to get the benefits of export trade, we also have to import.

Chapter Four, Exercise I

1. *Suppressed evidence.* A lot more cars drive a lot more miles now than in the 1930s.

4. *Questionable cause* and *unrepresentative sample.* (1) What about the possibility that the psychological or social forces that lead to heroin addiction also make smoking marijuana more likely; (2) we'd also need to know the incidence of marijuana smoking among non-heroin addicts in the same social or economic classes as the heroin addicts; (3) addicts who seek treatment may be different from addicts in general.

6. *Suppressed evidence. All* consumption of certain drugs (pot, heroin, LSD) is illegal, but only a tiny fraction of alcohol consumption is illegal.

10. *Questionable statistics.* Who can know, now, whether happiness is on the rise?

14. *Unrepresentative sample* and *small sample.*

19. *Faulty comparison.* Britain is wealthier than it ever was. It is, however, poorer relative to other Northern European countries. But the *relevant* comparison,

to see whether Britain can still afford to be preoccupied with distribution, is between the wealth she had then (when she could afford to be) and now, not between what she has now and what other nations have, since the latter is irrelevant to the consumption of goods in Britain.

Chapter Five, Exercise 5

2. *Pro:* "brilliance", "genius".
   Con: "cunning".

7. *Neutral:* "interest".

11. *Pro:* "adorn", "ornament".
    Con: "encumber", "weight down".

Chapter Six

2. Here is a summary of the arguments given by Jeffrey St. John in his column (margin notes have been omitted) in support of his conclusion that the Equal Rights Amendment (ERA) to the Constitution should not be passed:
   a. Legal scholars believe that the legal position of women cannot be stated in a simple formula. The reason Justice Frankfurter gives—that a woman's life cannot be expressed in a simple relation—comes close to just saying the same thing *(appeal to authority*—because their reasons are not provided, and other experts disagree).
   b. Senator Sam Ervin and legal scholars argue that the amendment will have no effect on discrimination *(appeal to authority)*.
   c. And would nullify all existing (possible or future) laws that make distinctions between men and women *(appeal to authority)*.
   d. Passage of the ERA would create a great court backlog of cases leading to legal and social anarchy *(questionable premise)*.
   e. Which is the aim of a minority of women's liberationists, who intend to exploit this result to achieve political power (very *questionable premise*. Also a bit of a *straw,* uh . . . *person,* because not true of the great majority of those favoring ERA).
   f. The effect of ERA, desired by Women's Liberationists, would be to do away with marriage contracts, the home, and children, and push us into a lifestyle like that in hippie communes (extremely *questionable premise*. St. John apparently believes marriage contracts would be illegal because entered into between *men* and *women!)*[1]
   g. Women's liberationists desire this in order to bring down the whole of society (another extremely *questionable premise)*.

---

[1]However, it is *possible* that courts would hold marriages between homosexuals legal. Why he thinks this would be a threat to heterosexual unions only St. John can say.

h. The women's liberationist campaign is false, misleading, and dangerous *(questionable evaluation)*.

i. The discrimination it is against is based not in law but in custom and in social attitudes, especially concerning careers and employment. [see below]

j. Women's lib wants to use the power of the state to forbid individual discrimination (as opposed to discrimination forced by law). [see below]

k. A distinction not made by those who favor ERA *(questionable premise—*in fact just plain false).

l. The same chaos will follow passage of the ERA that followed the 1964 Civil Rights Act. *(begged question:* Did chaos result from the 1964 Civil Rights Act? *Questionable analogy:* Even if it did, why compare that to the ERA?).

m. Legal scholars argue that the "due process" and "equal protection of the law" clauses of the Fifth and Fourteenth amendments are sufficient for the reforms demanded by Women's Libbers (i.e., ERA is not necessary). *(appeal to authority—*other experts have challenged this—and *irrelevant reason—*If true it shows ERA to be superfluous, not wrong.)

(Most of the persuasive emotively charged words—*"militant* minority of women"; a *legal avalanche* would be *unleashed"*—have been omitted from this summary along with the low blow analogy comparing political feminists with Lenin.)

Item (c) is the crux of St. John's argument against ERA. Is it true that passage of ERA would make laws that distinguish between men and women illegal? Since many believe it would, we should not say dogmatically that it would not. Yet, there are simple arguments (none mentioned by St. John—*suppressed evidence?)* indicating it would not, which must be refuted or at least examined, before (c) can be accepted. For ERA only provides women what one would have supposed they, as do men, already have, namely equal protection, or equal rights, before the law.

Rational discrimination always has been thought to be legal. Lenders and borrowers, for instance, have equal rights under the law, as do adults and children. This means that they cannot be discriminated against (or for!) *without a relevant reason.* A child cannot be treated differently from others except for good reason; for instance, lack of experience or developed intelligence may lead to laws instructing courts to provide legal guardians to protect the economic or legal rights of children (exactly as it does for senile adults). But no one would suppose this automatically violates a child's right to equal protection of the law. Similarly, it would seem plausible to suppose that laws distinguishing between the child-raising duties of a husband and wife based on the wife's special ability to provide mother's milk, or laws providing separate rest rooms for men and women on grounds of social custom, or laws forbidding women the right to engage in professional boxing on grounds of anatomical differences, would *not* violate women's rights to equality before the law. In short, it seems plausible to hold that equality before the law does not rule out *relevant* or *reasonable* discrimination, whether towards women, children, bankers, or thieves, but only irrelevant or irrational discrimination, again whether directed against women, children, bankers, or thieves.

The interesting aspect of (i) and (j) is that they muddle the issue, (i) because most but not all of the relevant discrimination is individual as opposed to forced by law, and (j) because women's liberationists want ERA to help fight against both kinds of discrimination. Moreover, it is curious to be against rectifying individual discrimination by law since that is the way most harms done by individuals are rectified. Rape, for instance, is not a harm required by law—it is an unfair harm done by one individual against another—which is the main reason why there are laws against it. Of course, it does not follow that we should try to rectify all unfair harms by law. For one thing, a danger of greater harms may result; for another, it depends on one's overall political and moral theories. But surely the reverse does not hold either, and that is what Jeffrey St. John has to claim.

3. Here is a summary of the Jenkin Lloyd Jones political column (the margin notes have been omitted):

   1. Hubert Humphrey said it is time liberals got on the side of law and order.
   2. Four days later, as if to illustrate the point (provide evidence for it?), the federal office building in Minneapolis was bombed.
   3. This building contains a military induction center, and has been a target of antiwar demonstrators.
   4. Humphrey said that describing all who espouse violence and disruption as "well-meaning" makes the liberal cause less credible.
   5. Some people mean by "police brutality" any attempt to resist snipers and rioters.
   6. Talk of police brutality becomes irrelevant (relatively unimportant?) when we discover the size of the Black Panther arsenals and the number of policemen killed (by Panthers?).
   7. Libertarians who protested the firing by the State of California of the Communist professor, Angela Davis, as a violation of academic freedom have not publicly recanted.
   8. Since the alleged use of her guns in the murder of four persons at the Marin County Courthouse, these libertarians have been quiet.
   9. The presidential commission appointed by President Johnson spent $2 million and concluded that completely free pornography has no relation to sex crimes.
   10. This report ignores FBI statistics showing that rape increased 17 percent from 1968 to 1969, the largest increase for any major crime except larceny.
   11. Dr. Victor B. Cline, professor of clinical psychology, claims the report of the president's commission greatly distorts the evidence.
   12. Humphrey is right that anarchy inevitably brings on repression.

13. (Humphrey is right that?) you can't have freedom or social progress without law and order.

Notice that when stripped of unwanted emotive terms, and put into plain English, the column loses a good deal of its initial appearance of plausibility.

Now we have to evaluate these claims. Assertion (11) clearly is intended to refute the conclusion of the pornography commission stated in (9). It appeals to an expert to support the implicit claim that pornography does cause sex crimes, contrary to the commission report. But this *appeal to authority* is fallacious. First, many other psychologists, perhaps most, as well as most ministers, criminologists, etc., would tend to agree with the commission and disagree with Mr. Jones' psychologist. Where experts disagree violently, it generally is fallacious for the layman to consider any particular expert's *opinion* as good evidence. (His reason and arguments are another matter.) And second, there are some matters, such as religion, politics, and morals, in which, if the issue is important enough, each man must become his own expert, even if those said to be experts are in general agreement. (Just think of yourself living in some fifteenth-century European monarchy where all the "experts"—so far as the layman could tell—took for granted the doctrine of the divine right of kings.)

Assertion (10) also is intended to refute the conclusion stated in (9). FBI statistics on the increase in rape from 1968 to 1969 are presented as good evidence against the commission's conclusion rejecting pornography as a cause of sex crimes. They *are* evidence, given the increase in the availability of what was taken to be pornography at the time. But they are not *sufficient* evidence to warrant acceptance of the theory that pornography *causes* sex crimes. We need to know much more before the quoted statistic becomes more than marginally significant: how the FBI statistics were gathered; the incidence of sex crimes for other years in the sixties during which pornographic material was on the increase; whether the increase in sex crimes was greater in those areas of the country where the increase in pornography was greatest; whether sex crimes increased in other nations (for example, Denmark) which adopted an "anything goes" attitude toward pornography. Some of this information was in the commission's report, but Mr. Jones failed to furnish it for us (because it tends to confirm the commission's findings?).

Assertion (2) (that the federal office building was bombed "as if to illustrate his point"), may *illustrate* the first point, but it doesn't provide good evidence for it. It implies the frequently heard charge that liberal "coddling" of militants is responsible for much recent violence. But it isn't good evidence for this implication because it doesn't show a *causal* connection between liberal attitudes toward militants, in particular, liberal attitudes on the law and order issue, and militant violence.

Similarly, assertion (3) (that the bombed building—containing an induction center—had been a target of antiwar demonstrators) seems designed to support the idea that left-wing radicals committed the bombing, and thus to support the view that liberal attitudes on the law and order issue were responsible for much violence. It does support the idea that left-wing radicals committed the bombing. But it does nothing for the view that left-wing militant violence was caused by liberal softness on law and order.

What we are left with, then, is a series of unsupported assertions. The question now is whether some of them are acceptable on their face or after reflection on the matter, given legitimate beliefs and background knowledge which we bring to bear on Mr. Jones' political column.

In assertion (1), to get his fellow liberals on the right side of the *political issues* of the day, Humphrey made use of a *false dilemma:* you're either for or against law and order, and liberals had better be for. Thus, he masked the real issue between liberals and their opponents, which was not law and order (taken literally—see below). All but the radical fringes were for law and order. The real issues were how best to get law and order, which laws, and whose order. Liberals pointed to police violence and to unequal enforcement of laws in favor of powerful groups and against minorities. They argued against increasing police power as a way to curb violence. Most other groups joined President Nixon in stressing the violence of left-wing radicals and the need for stronger laws to aid police in curbing that violence.

Assertions (4) and (5), though true, are irrelevant to the main issue. But (6) (police brutality becomes irrelevant) is another matter. Lurking behind it is the fallacy *two wrongs make a right,* the idea that police brutality is justified because it is a response to evils such as the killing of policemen.

Statements (7) (libertarians haven't recanted on their protest of the Angela Davis firing) and (8) (they've been quiet since the alleged use of her guns to murder) both seem to have been true, on independent evidence. But the question whether libertarians *ought* to have recanted was begged. (Many libertarians argued that her firing violated principles of academic freedom, whatever she may later have done.) Statements (7) and (8) both attacked libertarians themselves rather than their positions. Their failure to recant, their silence, tells us nothing of the merits of any positions they may have espoused. To argue otherwise (as Jenkin Lloyd Jones seems to have done) is to use the fallacy of *ad hominem* argument.

That leaves assertions (12) (anarchy leads to repression) and (13) (freedom and social progress require law and order), both of which the reader is likely to accept, and for whose truth there exists almost limitless evidence. But did Mr. Jones mean "law and order" literally? (In its nonliteral use, "law and order" meant harsh measures to obtain literal law and order. It also sometimes was a euphemism for repression of blacks.) He used that expression at the beginning of his article when quoting Humphrey and also at the end. Did he mean it literally in one use and not the other? Whatever the answer to that question, the *reader* should make sure in dealing with the first and last statements in the article that both uses of the phrase "law and order" are given the same interpretation. Otherwise, he should use different expressions in restating the assertions made in the paper. If he fails to do this, he runs the risk of guilt for the fallacy of *ambiguity*.

The point is an important one. When catch phrases like "law and order" are used, the writer (or speaker) often wants one meaning to be used in convincing us that it is good (or bad), and another when talking about his opponent's position. He wants "law and order" taken literally when the reader decides whether to be for or against it, but figuratively when the reader evaluates claims that liberals are against it and thus are criminal coddlers. So he wants to have his cake and eat it, too; anyone who lets him have it both ways commits the fallacy of *ambiguity*.

That gets us to what is probably the point of the political column. In all likelihood, Mr. Jones wanted liberals to be thought of as against law and order in the *literal* sense of that expression. There were two things to be gained from such an identification. First, liberal candidates would be more easily defeated by that label at election time, and second, it would make it much more difficult to sell the liberal position on how to *achieve* law and order, thus leaving the field clear for the more popular idea that harsher police tactics and more stringent laws were called for. His job was made easier by the fact that the liberals were against law and order in the nonliteral sense. He thus played on the usual confusion surrounding ambiguous expressions. Those who want to think straight have to learn not to be taken in by such devices.

Chapter Seven

(1) *Humor.*

(3) *Questionable premise.*

(9) *Jargon.*

(24) No fallacy. Maybe they do. This is a *legitimate* appeal to authority.

Exercise for Entire Text:

(I'll never tell.)

Bibliography

1. Fallacies (Chapters 1–4 and 6)

Barker, Steven F. *The Elements of Logic* (New York: McGraw-Hill, 1965).

Beardsley, Monroe. *Thinking Straight* (Englewood Cliffs, N.J.: Prentice-Hall, 1970).

Chase, Stuart. *Guide to Straight Thinking* (New York: Harper & Row, 1962).

Chase, Stuart. *The Tyranny of Words* (New York: Harcourt Brace Jovanovich, 1938).

Copi, Irving M. *Introduction to Logic* (3rd ed.) (New York: Macmillan, 1968).

*Effros, William G. *Quotations Vietnam: 1945–1970* (New York: Random House, 1970).

Fearnside, W. Ward, and William B. Holter. *Fallacy, the Counterfeit of Argument* (Englewood Cliffs, N.J.: Prentice-Hall, 1959).

Gardner, Martin. *Fads and Fallacies in the Name of Science* (New York: Dover, 1957).

Gordon, Donald R. *Language, Logic, and the Mass Media* (Toronto and Montreal: Holt, Rinehart and Winston of Canada, Ltd., 1966).

Hamblin, C. L. *Fallacies* (London: Methuen & Co., 1970).

*Hinds, Lynn, and Carolyn Smith. "Nixspeak: Rhetoric of Opposites," *The Nation,* February 16, 1970.

Huff, Darrell. *How to Lie with Statistics* (New York: W. W. Norton, 1954).

*Kahane, Howard. *Logic and Philosophy* (2nd ed.) (Belmont, Calif.: Wadsworth, 1973).

Kamiat, A. H. *Critique of Poor Reason* (New York: privately printed, 1936).

Kytle, Ray. *Clear Thinking for Composition* (New York: Random House, 1969).

Michalos, Alex C. *Improving Your Reasoning* (Englewood Cliffs, N.J.: Prentice-Hall, 1970).

*Morgenstern, Oskar. "Qui Numerare Incipit Errare Incipit," *Fortune,* October 1963.

Moulds, George Henry. *Thinking Straighter* (Dubuque, Iowa: Kendall/Hunt, 1966).

Pitt, Jack, and Russell E. Leavenworth. *Logic for Argument* (New York: Random House, 1966).

Thouless, Robert H. *Straight and Crooked Thinking* (New York: Simon & Schuster, 1932).

* Asterisks indicate items referred to in the text.

2.   Language (Chapter 5)

*Burrows, William E. "A Guide to Fielding's Guide," *(MORE)*, June 1974, p. 12.

Cazden, Courtney. *Child Language and Education* (New York: Holt, Rinehart and Winston, 1972).

Gambino, Richard. "Watergate Lingo: A Language of Non-Responsibility," *Freedom at Issue,* no. 22 (November/December 1973), pp. 7–9, 15–17.

Orwell, George. "Politics and the English Language," in *The Collected Works of George Orwell.*

Postman, Neil, Charles Weingarten, and Terrence Moran, eds. *Language in America* (New York: Pegasus, 1969).

Rank, Hugh, ed. *Language and Public Policy* (Urbana, Ill.: National Council of Teachers of English, 1974).

Safire, William. "White House-ese," *New York Times Magazine*, August 3, 1975, p. 47.

3.   Advertising: Selling the Product (Chapter 7)

*Baker, Samm Sinclair. *The Permissible Lie* (Cleveland and New York: World Publishing Co., 1968).

Gibson, Walker. *Sweet Talk: The Rhetoric of Advertising* (Bloomington: Indiana University Press, 1966).

*Glatzer, Robert. *The New Advertising: The Great Campaigns from Avis to Volkswagen* (New York: Citadel Press, 1970).

*Hopkins, Claude. *Scientific Advertising* (New York: Crown Publishing, 1966).

*McGinniss, Joe. *The Selling of the President 1968* (New York: Trident Press, 1969).

Napolitan, Joseph. *The Election Game and How to Win It* (New York: Doubleday, 1972).

*Ogilvie, David. *Confessions of an Advertising Man* (New York: Atheneum, 1963).

*Rowsome, Frank, Jr. *They Laughed When I Sat Down* (New York: Bonanza Books, 1959).

Whiteside, Thomas. *Selling Death: Cigarette Advertising and Public Health* (New York: Liveright, 1971).

4. *Managing the News (Chapter 8)*

Cirino, Robert. *Don't Blame the People* (Los Angeles: Diversity Press, 1971).

*Corry, John. "The Los Angeles Times," *Harpers,* December 1969.

Dinsmore, Herman H. *All the News That Fits* (New Rochelle, N.Y.: Arlington House, 1969).

Hentoff, Nat. Column in the *Village Voice,* October 22 and 29, 1970 (on *New York Times* treatment of a particular type of news).

Hentoff, Nat. "Fair Play on the Printed Page," [*MORE*], January 1972, p. 9.

*Hersh, Seymour M. *My Lai 4: A Report on the Massacre and Its Aftermath* (New York: Random House, 1970).

Kempton, Murray. "The Right People and the Wrong Times," *New York Review of Books,* April 8, 1971.

McGaffin, William, and Erwin Kroll. *Anything But the Truth: The Credibility Gap—How the News Is Managed in Washington* (New York: G. P. Putnam, 1968).

*McIntyre, Mark. "Muting Megaphone Mark," [*MORE*], July 1974, p. 5.

*Marks, John D. "The Story That Never Was," [*MORE*], June 1974, p. 20.

Nelson, Madeline, "Money Makes the Press Go 'Round," [*MORE*], March 1974, p. 1.

Perry, James B. *Us and Them: How the Press Covered the 1972 Election* (New York: Potter, 1973).

Rowse, A. E. *Slanted News, A Case Study of the Nixon and Stevenson Fund Stories* (Boston: Beacon Press, 1957).

Smith, Robert M. "Why So Few Investigative Reporters?" [*MORE*], November 1973, p. 7.

*von Hoffman, Nicholas. "Where Not to Find Your New Car," [*MORE*], November 1973, p. 7.

*Wilson, George. "The Fourth Estate," *Village Voice,* January 1, 1970.

5. *Textbooks: Managing World Views (Chapter 9)*

*American Indian Historical Society. *Textbooks and the American Indian* (San Francisco: Indian Historian Press, 1970).

*Black, Hillel. *The American Schoolbook* (New York: William Morrow, 1967).

*Elson, Ruth M. *Guardians of Tradition: American Schoolbooks of the 19th Century* (Lincoln: University of Nebraska Press, 1964).

Harrison, Barbara G. *Unlearning the Lie: Sexism in School* (New York: William Morrow, 1974).

*Nelson, Jack, and Gene Roberts. *The Censors and the Schools* (Boston: Little, Brown, 1963).

Popovitch, Luke. "Realerpolitic: The Texts Are Getting Better," *Washington Monthly,* March 1973.

Indexes

Index of Persons

Index of Publications

Index of Topics